PT405 GER

GERMAN WOMEN WRITERS
1900 - 1933

Twelve Essays

GERMAN WOMEN WRITERS
1900 - 1933

Twelve Essays

Edited by

Brian Keith-Smith

The Edwin Mellen Press
Lewiston/Queenston/Lampeter

Library of Congress Cataloging-in-Publication Data

German women writers, 1900-1933 : twelve essays / edited by Brian
Keith-Smith.
     p.   cm. -- (Bristol German publications ; v. 3)
    Includes bibliographical references.
    ISBN 0-7734-1340-5
    1. German literature--Women authors--History and criticism.
2. German literature--20th century--History and criticism. 3. Women
and literature--Germany--History--20th century. I. Keith-Smith,
Brian, 1934- II. Series.
PT405.G457 1993
830.9'9287'09041--dc20
                                         93-11957
                                         CIP

This is volume 3 in the continuing series
Bristol German Publications
Volume 3 ISBN 0-7734-1340-5
BGP Series ISBN 0-7734-1360-X

A CIP catalog record for this book
is available from the British Library.

Copyright © 1993 The Edwin Mellen Press

All rights reserved. For information contact

The Edwin Mellen Press
Box 450
Lewiston, New York
USA 14092

The Edwin Mellen Press
Box 67
Queenston, Ontario
CANADA L0S 1L0

Edwin Mellen Press, Ltd.
Lampeter, Dyfed, Wales
UNITED KINGDOM SA48 7DY

Printed in the United States of America

Contents

Editor's Introduction

German Women Writers 1900-1933 started life as a volume of essays to be written by friends of the editor who hoped to learn much about some of the writers to be included in his forthcoming anthology. Some essays, for various reasons, were never written, but their would-be authors remain friends! The faithful contributors have had their patience tried sorely, and the editor hereby dedicates the volume to each of them as a form of peace-offering and thanks!

The essays were at first intended to present some individual works by women writers of the period forgotten by literary historians and by the reading public and to introduce some lesser-known German women writers to British and American readers. What began as an attempt to find out more about the apparent dearth of German women Expressionists developed into a quite different volume. The contributors were given a free hand to explore and comment on their chosen writer, and some have concentrated on single works or on collections of works. Eda Sagarra's introduction was always intended as a background survey, and the other essays gradually formed themselves into an approximately chronological order. Their varied styles and scope correspond happily with the editor's hopes and reveal, in his opinion, the need to apply different styles and approaches to different writers and works.

There were of course many other important women writers who published in German during the first thirty-three years of this century, some better known than those included here. It was, however, never the aim to produce a collection on the most prominent women writers, nor to pretend that those included have more claim to be highlighted than any others. If any justification is needed for the choice, then it must be that each essay partly fulfils its author's need to come to terms with the particular work or author in question. It has become clear through correspondence, conversations and work towards an anthology that there is a vast field of literature by German women writers of this period as yet little read and sparsely taught in colleges in Britain, America and in German-speaking countries. The various works of reference that are now appearing offer an enticing insight into much of value that has been forgotten, but − as anyone working in the field will know − they tend to borrow from each other, and several writers disappear without trace for lack of biographical detail, or because they published only in periodicals, or because their books are practically impossible to find. If this volume encourages readers to find out more about these and other writers, it will have more than achieved its primary object.

German Women Writers 1900-1933 is the third volume in the Bristol German Publications series and the first to be published by the Edwin Mellen Press. Special thanks are due to Mrs Brigitte Morton of the Edwin Mellen Press whose patience as typesetter surpassed that of all the contributors put together. They are also due to Celia and Peter Skrine for their revisions and proofreading. The illustrations appear by permission of the Deutsches Literaturarchiv in Marbach (Deutsche Schillergesellschaft), except for that of Lou Andreas-Salomé, the holders of whose right we have tried in vain to contact. We are grateful for permission to reproduce the photograph of Berta Lask from the Allgemeiner Deutscher Nachrichtendienst GmbH, and that of Jo Mihaly from Herder Verlag.

Brian Keith-Smith
Department of German
University of Bristol
February 1993

List of Illustrations

Lou Andreas-Salomé. Reproduced from Linde Salber, *Lou Andreas-Salomé* (Berlin: Rowohlt Monographie), p. 99. Lou Andreas-Salomé Archiv, Göttingen.

Elsa Bernstein. Reproduced from Ernst Brausewetter, *Meisternovellen deutscher Dichterinnen* (Berlin, Vol. 1, 1897).

Hedwig Landauer-Lachmann. Oil painting by Julie Wolf-Thorn. DLA, Marbach.

Lily Braun im Jahre 1910. Reproduced from Lily Braun, *Gesammelte Werke*, Bd. 1 (Berlin: Klemm, 1923).

Jo Mihaly. Reproduced from Jo Mihaly, *...da gibt's ein Wiedersehn!* (Freiburg: Kerle, 1982), opposite p. 193.

Adrienne Thomas. DLA, Marbach.

Emmy Ball-Hennings. Photograph by Holdt. DLA, Marbach.

Berta Lask. Reproduced from *Meyers Neues Lexikon*, Bd. 8 (Leipzig, 1974, 2. Aufl.), p. 377. Allgemeiner Deutscher Nachrichtendienst.

Frida Bettingen. DLA, Marbach.

Bess Brenck-Kalischer. Woodcut by Otto Felixmüller. Reproduced from *Menschen* 2 (1919) Heft X (68/69), p. 7.

Anna Seghers. Photograph by Lotte Jacobi. DLA, Marbach.

Gertrud von le Fort. DLA, Marbach.

1

The German Woman Writer 1900-1933: Socio-Political Context and Literary Market

Eda Sagarra

The Socio-Political Context

The symbolic significance of the year 1900 as marking the beginning of a new age for women was widely registered by politically self-conscious women in Germany. The feminist Hedwig Dohm described the century in millenary terms as a 'Weltwende', while at the opposite end of the political spectrum, the *Bismarck-Frauen-Kalender* for 1901 apostrophized it in verses addressed 'Zum neuen Jahrhundert!' as follows:

> Die Frau gehorcht mit frohem Streben
> dem Weckruf einer neuen Zeit.
> Frei sind die Bahnen ihr gegeben
> und Mut und Kraft sind ihr Geleit.[1]

Though the actual yield in terms of giving women greater access to civic and political rights may have been meagre, the previous decade had witnessed in many areas of social and political life a degree of popular mobilization hitherto unknown, in the broad context of which the women's question established itself in the public mind.[2] The first decade of the new century was to see the struggle for women's rights firmly placed on the political agenda. Political parties, however little some might sympathize with the aims of what was now widely accepted as *die Frauenfrage*, felt nonetheless under constraint to respond or at least to be seen to respond to it. National newspapers began to employ correspondents on a regular basis, generally women, to report on women's issues. Women's history, literature and literary biography began to seem the appropriate concern of scholars in German studies, among them Adalbert Hanstein, Hugo Lachmanski, Heinrich Spiero and Ludwig Geiger.[3] Similarly, the journal of the Goethe-Gesellschaft began to record its awareness of contemporary developments by devoting a substantial number of its articles in the 1890s and 1900s (their authors included Lily Braun (1865-1916)) to women in the age of Goethe. The pioneering work of documenting women's literary history (which almost a century later is only just beginning to be put on a secure foundation[4]) had been initiated almost two generations before the beginning of the period under discussion by the documentary work of some of Germany's leading historians.[5] The Insel and Kiepenheuer editions of Caroline Schlegel's letters by the Berlin Germanist Erich Schmidt (*Caroline. Briefe aus der Frühromantik, nach Waitz vermehrt*, Leipzig: Insel, 1913) and Ernst Wieneke (*Caroline und Dorothea Schlegel in ihren Briefen*, Weimar: Kiepenheuer, 1914) were conceived, like those of their predecessors, in terms of women as the object rather than as the subject of their history. However, the changed public consciousness regarding women in the new century, not least among women themselves, was demonstrably registered in the immense success of Schmidt's edition, which did much to focus attention on the role of women in German Romanticism, and on Caroline in particular.

Undoubtedly the most lively forum for discussion of *die Frauenfrage* at the turn of the century was afforded by the periodicals, many of them with party political allegiance. It is difficult today, in the absence of a major study of the subject, to capture the sense of vigour, enquiry and raised expectations which was reflected in the sheer mass of contemporary political journalism about, and increasingly by, women. A number of such journals were expressly founded to place women's concerns on the political agenda. This was, for example, the case with *Die Gleichheit. Zeitschrift für die Interessen der Arbeiterinnen* (1891-1919), edited by Clara Zetkin (1865-1933), in response to the policy decision of the 1891 Erfurt Socialist Party conference to make *die*

Frauenfrage part of the offical party programme. Two years later, in 1893, Helene Lange (1848-1930) founded *Die Frau. Monatsschrift für das gesamte Frauenleben unserer Zeit*, the first number of which appeared dated 1893-4. It was followed in 1895 by the fortnightly review *Die Frauenbewegung. Revue für die Interessen der Frau* under the editorship of Minna Cauer (1842-1922), which had a monthly supplement on legal issues under the editorship of Dr. jur. Anita Augspurg (1857-1943) entitled *Zeitschrift für Frauenstimmrecht*. In most cases, women's issues came to occupy a prominent role in established periodicals too, such as the *Sozialistische Monatshefte*, or the organ of the liberal Left under Friedrich Naumann, *Die Hilfe*.[6] But equally women's issues began to be represented increasingly – though without the political dimension of the previously mentioned periodicals – in Christian publications such as the Catholic *Caritas. Zeitschrift für die Werke der Nächstenliebe im katholischen Deutschland*, which first appeared in 1896; Karin Bruns has shown in the case of the *Bismarck-Frauen-Kalender* (from 1908 *Bismarck-Jahrbuch für Deutsche Frauen*) how, from the late nineteenth century on, extreme conservative and nationalist periodicals adopted and adapted emancipatory vocabulary and aspirations from the Women's Movement.[7] The changing nature of the mass market in the 1890s and early 1900s and the impact of this on women in their everyday lives is documented in the case of individual periodicals such as *Die Gleichheit* which, against the wishes of its editor, was developed as a magazine and as a result raised its circulation from 9,500 copies per issue in 1900 to some 112,000 in 1913. It was also reflected in the sheer plethora of new enterprises, targeting women's real or supposed interests in virtually every facet of contemporary life, from the Colonial and Navy leagues to *Die gesunde Frau. Zeitschrift zur Verbreitung gesundheitlicher Anschauungen der Frauenwelt* (1897), edited by Margaret Pochhammer, who had founded the *Verein zur Besserung der Frauenkleidung* in 1896.

The period 1900-1933 began and ended with events hardly favourable to women, who in 1900 constituted more than half the German population of some 61 million. The century opened with the promulgation of the Civil Code, the *Bürgerliches Gesetzbuch* (1900), which, despite the vigorous discussion which had accompanied it over two decades in and outside the Reichstag, was retrogressive rather than progressive in a number of areas, such as married women's property, divorce law and the treatment of unmarried mothers.[8] Moreover, the actual practice of justice in subsequent years and up to the end of the Second Empire proved, particularly with regard to family law, notoriously less liberal than the Civil Code might seem to imply.[9] The period here under discussion closed with Hitler's seizure of power on 30 January 1933. A little over three months later, on 10 May 1933, the works of a number of women authors, including some of the writers discussed in the present volume, such as Berta Lask (1878-1967), were publicly burnt.

Even prior to the Nazi seizure of power, discriminatory measures against women in employment, anticipated in 1926 by the mobilization of public opinion by the Ministry for Public Employment against the so-called "Doppelverdiener", had found legislative expression in Chancellor Brüning's treatment of women in the public service in 1932. The lack of organized protest elicited by the Brüning government's policy was both a reflection of dominant thinking in German society in the face of mass unemployment, the second cataclysm within a decade, and an encouragement to the National Socialists after 1933 to proceed to implement their policies of systematic exclusion of women from positions of power or influence in the party machine and therefore from public life. Women were to retain only the characteristically segregated activity permitted in organizations such as the *Deutsches Frauenwerk*, the *Bund deutscher Mädel* and the *National-sozialistische Volkswohlfahrt*.[10] The voluntary dissolution of the historic *Bund deutscher Frauenverbände* in May 1933 was at once milestone and symbol. With its 60 constituent associations and 500,000 members, the organization's growth and development from the first decade of the new century onwards had been a prominent feature of women's political history.

Yet the period 1900-1933 also saw immense changes in the constitutional, political and socio-economic spheres which had a profound and positive effect on women's lives. Some, such as the extension to women of the right of assembly (*Reichsvereinsgesetz* 1908),[11] the improvement in teacher training and the piecemeal lifting of the prohibition on women reading for degrees at German universities, were the result of government policy decisions; others, including the franchise, were an indirect effect of the First

World War. Well before the war, commercial developments in the literary market, the growth of mass literacy and the general rise in disposable income, coinciding with the massive upsurge in the economy after 1895, had tangible and in general beneficial consequences for the woman writer, as for her male counterpart. For her, there was the additional social benefit of an increased degree of personal independence, thanks to the easier access to publication provided by developments in the mass media.

The First World War and the 1918-19 German Revolution together provide the period 1900-1933 with an ambivalent symmetry: they allot equal fourteen-year periods to the pre-war years and to the lifespan of the Weimar Republic. The war, which polarized women writers as it did their male colleagues, was undoubtedly a major accelerator of change.[12] But it was not always or even generally the initiator it has been claimed to be.[13] Thus in the area of women's employment, although the war economy sent many thousands of women into hitherto traditionally male jobs in munitions, factories and heavy industry, including even the mines, substantial inroads had already been made into the notion of sex-specific work by long-term structural changes in the pre-war German industrial economy, which by the period 1896-1913 was already in the late phase of its development.[14] Though the overall percentage of women in paid employment did not, surprisingly, increase much in the years 1900-1913, rising from 34.9% in 1907 to 35.6% in 1925,[15] what was significant were the new areas of employment which became open to them. In particular, women joined the ranks of the *neuer Mittelstand* in ever larger numbers: the number of women employed as office workers and shop assistants increased by a factor of 300% from about half a million in 1907 to 1.5 million in 1925.[16] However, low pay and subordinate status within industrial, commercial or public organizations minimized the socio-political impact as regards women's emancipation, despite popular literature's fondness for casting the 'secretary' in the role of upwardly mobile heroine.[17]

The impact of improved access to education for women in the late nineteenth and early twentieth centuries was, in common with the history of the Women's Movement in Germany itself, one of the central areas of concern to politically conscious women of liberal and socialist views, just as the defence of the church schools polarized Catholic opinion in Germany as it did in France. Girls' schools had been almost exclusively in private hands before the turn of the century, which however saw the beginning of the integration of girls' secondary education into the state system. This was the focus of vigorous debate and agitation in favour of raising the standards in female teacher training. It was this concept of parity in quality, if not necessarily in subject spread, with boys' schooling which gave such urgency to women's determination to win the right to read for a university degree in their own country. In the first year of the century Baden initiated the process by opening the doors of its universities to women; Prussia was the last to follow, with evident reluctance, in 1908. However, Prussian as well as Reich civil servants proved supportive of the idea of greater access to medical training for women in the years that followed, on the grounds that women were needed to treat and undertake research in women's diseases. By contrast, women's progress in gaining access to the legal profession before the end of the monarchy was minimal, eliciting the comment from a modern historian that 'the history of women in the legal profession in Imperial Germany is thus almost no history at all'.[18]

The early women students, in Germany as elsewhere, tended to be drawn from well-to-do backgrounds, not least for financial reasons,[19] and accordingly the growing numbers of women teachers in the early decades of the new century tended to be of a higher social class than their male colleagues. Far fewer men were attracted to elementary school teaching, which in the early twentieth century, in contrast to earlier times, was characterized by low status and poor conditions. The readiness of women to accept such conditions, and thus help solve the state's difficulties in recruitment to the profession, proved a fertile source of tension between themselves and their male colleagues. Less commented upon in current feminist historiography, but of particular importance as regards women's access to the literary market, is the overall impact of improved primary and secondary education at national level. This point is made by Renate von Heydebrand with reference to a representative sample of Westphalian women writers in the broad area of *Heimatliteratur*: many came from rural backgrounds, and there were some from the lowest social classes, such as Josefa Berens-Totenohl (1891-1961), the daughter of a smith, who grew up in a home without books and came through school and the Lehrerinnenseminar to authorship of a number of works, including two of the best-known novels of the Third Reich: *Der Femhof* (1934) and *Frau Magdlene* (1935).[20]

A major agent of change, both in terms of impact on public consciousness and of government policy with regard to women, derived from German women's self-organization. Though women's associations in Germany reach back well into the nineteenth century, the years between 1900 and the outbreak of war saw changes in scale appropriate to the age of mass democracy. Thus where in 1901 some 137 women's associations grouped in the BDF (*Bund deutscher Frauenvereine*) comprised some 70,000 members, in 1914 the numbers had reached half a million, making the German Women's Movement the third largest (after those in the United States and Great Britain) in the world.[21]

This increase reflected the impact of the 1908 legislation on women's participation in political life, but the period was also characterized by major ideological splits. Thus the progressive Marie Stritt (1856-1928), whose programme had included votes for women, equal education and paternal responsibility for illegitimate children, was ousted from the presidency of the BDF in 1910 by the conservative Gertrud Bäumer (1873-1954), while other radical figures, such as Helene Stöcker (1869-1943), were marginalized or removed. Where hitherto the strength (not least of logical argument) had rested in the *human* quality of the democratic aspirations of the Women's Movement, increasingly the newly mobilized German women's organizations directed their energies towards areas of exclusive concern to women. To some degree, in paradoxical anticipation of National Socialist ideology, the notion of 'equality' came under attack by bourgeois women in the immediate pre-war period, who favoured 'difference' and the notion of women as 'healers and bonders' of the 'national community'. Contentious political issues, notably the vote for women, remained to divide bourgeois and socialist women and radical and conservative feminists, but the substantive point is that the Women's Movement was integrated into the national life on the eve of the First World War to such a degree that the government charged the BDF in 1914 with the organization of welfare services.[22] As a matter of policy, the authorities began to employ women in an advisory capacity to assist German housewives in coping with the demands of the wartime economy. The signal success of the voluntary organization known as the NFD (*Nationalfrauendienst*) raised women's self-consciousness and the public awareness of their societal role. Although undoubtedly and even stridently nationalistic during the war — and in this little different from women's organizations in other combatant nations — the BDF's enhanced self-awareness lent great urgency to its demands for full democratic rights, in addition to voting rights, including equal access to employment in the public and municipal service. Moreover, there occurred a new if still relative degree of rapprochement and mutual understanding between bourgeois and socialist women through their communal work on the home front. The socialist movement had shown itself ambivalent on the subject of pacifism, distancing itself from the radical line taken by Clara Zetkin as editor of the socialist women's journal *Die Gleichheit* in 1914. She was actually dismissed by the Party from both her editorial post and her seat on the national executive in 1917. But with increasing hardship on the home front from 1916 onwards, many women socialists rallied to her views and women were involved to a very significant degree in the munitions workers' strikes in April 1917 and January 1918.[23]

Historians interested in the Women's Movement have hitherto tended to concentrate on bourgeois and socialist organizations because of their alleged monopoly of emancipatory potential. Yet in a survey of women's history in Germany between 1900 and 1933 it should be recalled that in terms of both size and endurance, Christian women's organizations possessed a homogeneity that the *Bund deutscher Frauenvereine* lacked and a membership which, combined, easily doubled that of the Federation.[24] An important precondition of the rapid development of the Christian women's associations, both from the perspective of the church authorities and in the minds of the women themselves, was the decline in belief and church-going practice of German males, more particularly at a time when the secularization of life began to register itself on the general consciousness of Christians. A politically self-conscious Protestant women's organization, the *Deutscher Evangelischer Frauenbund*, was founded by Paula Mueller to provide a Christian alternative to the secular BDF at the beginning of the new century. It reached 10,000 members in 1910, but never offered a serious challenge to the *Protestantische Frauenhilfe*.   This exclusively Prussian organization possessed the supreme psychological advantage of having been founded by the Empress (in 1899). Within one year it had 13,000 members, a decade later the number had risen to 200,000 and by the end of the war it was the largest women's organization in Germany.

Less spectacular, but in some senses more consciously and socially feminist in its refusal to become a clerically controlled organization, was the *Katholischer Deutscher Frauenbund* or Catholic German Women's League.[25] Founded at the turn of the century in Cologne, erstwhile capital of liberal German Catholicism, its constitution actually subordinated the only male branch's spiritual directors to the autority of the (female) president.[26]   Its membership reached an estimated 50,000 in 1914 and doubled during the war. More importantly the KDF, with its organ *Frauenbund*, whose name-change on the eve of the war to *Frauenland* marked the League's transition from regional to national movement, aimed through communal religious worship and social activity at mass membership;[27] here the working classes were no longer, as so often in Christian organizations, the object of middle-class charity, but an integral part of the movement. The reluctance of the Catholic Bishops' Conference to permit the League's affiliation to the *Katholikentag* after 1908, unless represented by men, delayed official recognition of the organization until 1915. It was only admitted to the central organization of the Catholic Church in Germany, the *Katholikentag*, in 1921. The League's leaders refusal to accept these conditions and the fact that they continued to operate for so long outside the recognized parameters of Catholic public life, suggests a not inconsiderable degree of feminist consciousness during this period. During the Weimar period, partly to counter the Prussian Socialist administration's accelerated attempts to bring the educational system under full state control, specifically during Carl Heinrich Becker's period of office as education minister (1925-30), the Catholic Church in that state, both clergy and laity, developed a variety of initiatives in which women had their share. Women were well represented in the Catholic Youth Movement and in the liturgical reform movements – this last especially vigorous in the Republic of Austria, as was *Pax Christi*, a form of pacifist revival. As in the case of the

German Youth Movement generally, all of these groupings, it should not be forgotten, had an attractive social dimension for the participants.

Women's suffrage was vigorously resisted, even as late as the Reichstag debate on the afternoon of 8 November 1918, one day before the abdication of the Kaiser, and despite the immense contribution of women to sustaining the home front during the war years. It was finally granted by the *Rat der Volksbeauftragten* in December as one of its first measures. This must clearly rank as one of the major achievements of the period. Scarcely a month later, when women were given the opportunity in the elections of 19 January 1919 to demonstrate their commitment to their new democratic right, they responded with a participation rate of some 90%. Forty-one women deputies, i.e. 9.6% of the total, were elected to parliament in 1919, of which more than half represented the Majority Social Democratic Party.[28] The Central Party and German Democratic Party each had six women deputies, with smaller numbers in the German People's Party, the German Nationals and the Independent Socialist Party. The ballot papers – grey for men, white for women – made it possible for later historians to analyse female voting behaviour. Participation rates by women voters declined somewhat in subsequent elections, but remained high throughout the Weimar Republic, the female franchise benefiting the parties of the centre and the right more than those of the left.

For many women, notably in the middle and upper ranks of society, the beneficial changes wrought in their lives between 1900 and 1933 through technology and fashion were uppermost in their perceptions of the times in which they lived. These changes included the mobility afforded by the massive development of the national and local transport systems since the founding of the Reich, accessibility of domestic electricity and labour-saving devices in the home, and also such matters as the 'Reformkleid' movement of the early years of the century, copied from American and English counterparts.[29] Beginning in the late nineteenth century, a vogue for popular histories of women's dress, 'scientific' articles in family magazines, with detailed physiological drawings of the affected organs, and medical treatises couched in readable prose, had given an edge to the medical profession's denouncement of tight lacing of women's bodies[30] as the source of women's ailments and the deformation of their inner organs – with consequent negative effects 'on the health of the nation'.

Not just the physical harm inflicted by 'unnatural' underclothes, but also the bulk and sheer weight of the outer clothes (for day clothes generally serge, in the interests of durability) became at the turn of the century the object of widespread and rational criticism. Speaking to the German Tailors' Conference at Krefeld in 1900, Ellen Key (1849-1926), who in the same year published her famous *Das Jahrhundert des Kindes*, attributed epoch-making significance to the new style of women's dresses, which hung from the shoulder. Yet the loose or waistless dress retained ideological overtones throughout the period (similar to the 'Bubikopf' hairstyle in the 1920s), an issue which is captured with subtle social comment by Thomas Mann in his use of the motif in *Unordnung und frühes Leid*.[31] Clearly, too, the development of sport in early twentieth-century life, and of women's participation in certain forms of outdoor exercise, notably walking, cycling and climbing, had an impact on, and was stimulated by, changes in women's clothes; the same was true for women's involvement in the various strands of the Youth Movement.[32]

The popularity of sport and the almost obsessive interest in the hygienic aspects of women's clothing are related to early twentieth-century Germany's increasing preoccupation with the nation's health. The years just before and after the turn of the century had seen genuine progress in the reduction of infant and child mortality among those living above the poverty line, and advances in medicine (and hygiene) relating to the treatment of women brought about a substantial decline in infant mortality between 1914 and 1929. Not unrelated to this was the decline in the birthrate, which was associated with an increasing and no longer class-bound use of contraception, as well as a massive increase in abortion, which was related to the economic crises of the Weimar period. The annual congress of German medical doctors in 1925 reported an estimated 800,000 abortions in that year, with a 2.5% mortality rate among the women concerned.[33] The statistical evidence of the falling birthrate is indeed striking, with 4.5 children per union in the years 1871-1914 falling to 2.2 in the early Weimar years, to 1.98 in 1925-9 and to 1.33 in 1933. Placed in the context of national preoccupation with biological arguments in political thinking throughout this period, it gave focus to the popular obsession even in circles not committed to National Socialist policies with the 'threat to the German race'; this found characteristic expression in the publications of the Weimar academic, Friedrich Burgdörfer, with his dictum: 'Ein gesundes Volk kann geknechtet, unterdrückt, zerrissen, aber nicht ausgetilgt werden [...]   Kein Volk stirbt eigentlich aus, es wird ausgeboren.'[34] It is hardly surprising that public opinion in the late Weimar years linked the 'biological' crisis to the issue of women's emancipation or that the portrayal of emancipated womanhood in contemporary literature, as well as the modern woman author and journalist, became popular soft targets for propaganda even before the Nazi seizure of power in 1933, and of discriminatory policies thereafter.[35]

The Literary Market

It has been estimated that 25% of literature published in the Wilhelmine Empire was written by women, although this is hardly reflected in any of the major histories of German literature available.[36] Developments in the literary market in the period under discussion, notably the commercialization of publishing and the industrialization of the press, had brought with them a quantitative and qualitative extension in publishing opportunities for women writers, as for their male colleagues. Most notable were the developments in the periodical press, and, particularly from the 1880s onward, in the growing readiness of the literary journals to publish work by women authors.   Julius Rodenberg, as Marie von Ebner-Eschenbach constantly reiterated in her extensive correspondence with him, was directly responsible for establishing her reputation as a major writer of prose fiction, through his publication of her work in the *Deutsche Rundschau*. She in her turn acted as a kind of mediator for younger, less established women.[37] In 1893 Rodenberg published a commissioned article on German women writers by Hermann Grimm.[38] By the turn of the century, and indeed up to the time of the proscriptions of the Third Reich, women authors were publishing widely in the major and minor literary journals of the day. Among the most prominent whose works appeared in a wide variety of periodicals were Else

Lasker-Schüler (1876-1946) and Ricarda Huch (1864-1947).[39] The sheer variety and vibrancy of women's writing is well illustrated by the careers of three authors who were regarded by their contemporaries as among the major women writers of the day: Isolde Kurz (1853-1944), Annette Kolb (1870-1967) and Anna Croissant-Rust (1860-1943).[40] Carl Muth's periodical *Hochland*, founded in 1903, also deserves mention in this context because it offered Catholic women authors access to a national readership much larger than the regional one which had hitherto been available to them.

Women writers representing a variety of literary genres and ideological positions thus published a substantial portion of their work in journals and magazines. They ranged from the naturalist writer Helene Böhlau (1859-1940), the impressionist poet Irene Forbes-Mosse (1864-1946) and radical feminists such as Hedwig Dohm (1833-1919) or Helene Stöcker, to authors of conservative outlook, such as Lulu von Strauß und Torney (1873-1956), author of the much-admired 'Nordic' ballads, and the East Prussian Agnes Miegel (1879-1964), who became a member of the Prussian Academy of Writers after its purge by Goebbels, and the successful Austrian Catholic writer and novelist, Enrica Handel-Mazzetti (1871-1955), who resigned from the Austrian PEN Club when that body protested against the 1933 book-burning and who proved so ready to give allegiance to National Socialism after the Anschluß. Kristina Zerges has shown in her study of the socialist press how substantial a proportion of the literature published in periodicals and aimed at a mass readership, such as *Die Neue Welt: Illustriertes Unterhaltungsblatt für das Volk* (1876-1919) (from 1892: *Illustrierte Beilage für Wissenschaft, Belehrung und Unterhaltung*) or *In Freien Stunden: Romane und Erzählungen für das arbeitende Volk* (1897-1918/19), was actually written by 'bourgeois' (and aristocratic!) women writers. Among these were Gertrud Franke-Schievelbein (1851-1914), Ilse Frapan-Akunian (1848-1908), Irmgard Keun (1910-1982), Isolde Kurz, Irma von Troll-Borostyáni (1847-1912), Hermynia Zur Mühlen (1883-1951) and, above all, no doubt on account of the proletarian subject matter of much of her early work, Clara Viebig (1860-1952).[41]

Women benefited both as individuals and collectively from self-help organizations which were a feature of the German literary market from the late nineteenth century onwards. Among these were the *Schutzverband deutscher Schriftsteller* (1900), the *Verein deutscher Bühnenschriftsteller*, founded eight years later to combat the threat posed by the growth in power of theatre agencies and, most notably, the organization known as the Lyric Cartel, set up in 1902 to counteract the financial might of commercial interests in publishing.[42] In the last years of the Weimar Republic, women, among them Berta Lask both as member of the board and as secretary, were represented in the necessarily short-lived but highly innovative *Bund proletarisch-revolutionärer Schriftsteller* (1928-33), which set itself the task of countering the commercially-determined dominant culture of the time. Over the period as a whole, local associations set up to promote access to imaginative literature may arguably be said to have benefited women writers even more than their male counterparts, given their underrepresentation in the public sphere and their relative lack of the contacts enjoyed by those in paid employment.[43]

The commercialization of the literary market, increasingly located in the metropolitan centres of Berlin, Vienna and, to a lesser extent, Munich, thus brought greatly enhanced opportunities for writers in the form of a massive increase in the demand for fiction for serialization in the newspapers. Collections of stories ceded pride of place to the novel, as the Leipzig publisher Wilhelm Friedrich informed a crestfallen Detlev von Liliencron: 'buchhändlerisch ist ein schlechter Roman besser als der schönste Band schönster Novellen'.[44] Yet a perusal of the publication lists of individual women authors in the columns of *Hinrichs Fünfjahrs-Katalog* and *Deutsches Bücherverzeichnis* for the years 1895-1925 gives ample evidence of the continuing success on the book market of this genre, while the demand of newspaper editors for *Novellen* for serialization is well known.

The actual number of copies of works of prose fiction printed per edition increased by a factor of ten or more between the 1870s and 1900s, coinciding with the decline of the lending libraries, the fall in the price of books, and the increasing numbers of books published, trends which owed much to the growing ability of Germans to buy their own books. Moreover, by the turn of the century the proliferation of new publishing ventures, aimed at maximizing their profits, ensured that a single novel or *Novelle* would first appear in pre-published form as a serial and would be reprinted after publication in book form in one of the 'Romanreihen', such as Engelhorn's, or in an inexpensive 'Bibliothek schönster Romane', or even as the text of a shorthand primer for the new generation of office workers. The family magazines, including from the beginning of the century those of socialist persuasion, drew on the services of a large number of women both as authors and as members of the editorial staff. Women were also well represented as authors of the so-called *Hintertreppenromane*, which exploited the success of Eugenie Marlitt (1825-1887), Wilhelmine Heimburg (1850-1912) and Hedwig Courths-Mahler (1867-1950). During the Weimar era an attempt was made by the socialist press to combine political education with the public appetite for popular novels when it launched the 'Rote-Eine-Mark-Romane' series.[45]

The link between gender and genre in this period of German literary history is only beginning to be charted; indeed the present volume can be said to constitute a contribution to this area. For the period 1900-1933 as a whole it would no doubt be true to say that the majority of women writers continued to favour the traditional 'female' genres of novel, *Novelle*, and lyric poetry, and that they did not in general challenge tendencies dominant in the nineteenth century and reaching back to the late eighteenth century to think in terms of sex-specific literary genres.[46] They did, however, extend their range into areas hitherto associated with male authors, as for example the historical novel with a pronounced 'local' flavour, the most distinguished practitioner of which was surely Ricarda Huch, who had studied philosophy and history in Zurich and learnt much from the work of Louise von François (1817-1893). Similarly, women began to figure prominently in the early years of the century (as well as in the late 1920s and 1930s) as authors of peasant and *Heimat* literature, among them Martha Renate Fischer (1851-1925) and Luise Westkirch (1853-1941), whose novels were set in North Germany, or the Catholic authors, Enrica Handel-Mazzetti and Hermine Villinger (1849-1917), who wrote about their native Upper Austria and the Black Forest respectively. And in the early years of the century, a decade later than their male colleagues, and a generation or more later than their bourgeois sisters, working-class women began to record their personal and collective memories in autobiography. For all of these, and many others, it was the development of the commercial literary market that gave them access to a nationally based readership. But it is arguably also the vibrancy and diversity of that literary market that helped prompt other women, such as Berta Lask, to break so openly with the convention of sex-specific genres, or, as in the case of Else Lasker-Schüler, Marieluise Fleißer (1901-74), Anna Seghers (1900-83) and Hermynia Zur Mühlen, to be 'unconventional' in their exploitation of a particular 'traditional' genre. As the careers of Lou Andreas-Salomé (1861-1937), Lily Braun or the law court reporter and novelist Gabriele Tergit (1894-1982) demonstrate, the diversity of women's participation and achievement in various forms of literature, as well as in the theatre, film, cabaret and journalism, demonstrates their ability to dissolve inherited distinctions between creative writing and *Gebrauchstexte*. All this reinforces the underlying thesis of the present volume that, whatever the discontinuities and *Ungleichzeitigkeiten* characteristic of this period in German literature, the years 1900-1933 can indeed be said to constitute an important phase in the history of women's writing in Germany.

NOTES

[1]*Erinnerungen und weitere Schriften von und über Hedwig Dohm*, compiled and ed. by Berta Rahm (Zurich: Ala, 1980), p. 149. 'Zum neuen Jahrhundert!' is quoted by Karin Bruns in 'Das moderne Kriegsweib. Mythos und nationales Stereotyp heroischer Weiblichkeit 1890-1914' in *Literatur im historischen Prozeß*, ed. by Annegret Pelz, Marianne Schuller, Inge Stephan, Sigrid Weigel, Kerstin Wilhelms. Frauen-Literatur-Politik, N.F. 21/22 (Hamburg: Argument, 1988), p. 136.

[2]Geoff Eley, 'Notable Politics, the Crisis of German Liberalism and the Electoral Transition of the 1890s' in *In Search of a Liberal Germany. Studies in the History of German Liberalism from 1789 to the Present*, ed. by Konrad H. Jarausch and Larry Eugene Jones (New York, Oxford and Munich: Berg, 1990), pp. 187-215, (p. 213).

[3]See Adalbert von Hanstein, *Die Frauen in der Geschichte des deutschen Geisteslebens des 18. und 19. Jahrhunderts*, 2 vols (Leipzig: Freund & Wittig, 1899-1900), Heinrich Spiero, *Geschichte der deutschen Frauendichtung seit 1800* (Leipzig: Teubner, 1913), Hugo Lachmanski, *Die deutschen Frauenzeitschriften des 18. Jahrhunderts* (Berlin: B. Paul, 1900), Ludwig Geiger, *Bettina von Arnim und Friedrich Wilhelm IV. Ungedruckte Briefe und Aktenstücke* (Frankfurt/M.: Literaturanstalt, 1900) and *Therese Huber. Leben und Briefe einer deutschen Frau* (Stuttgart: Cotta, 1901).

[4]A major achievement of feminist scholarship in German studies since the late 1980s has been in the editorial field, notably in the publication of the edited letters of women writers such as Rahel Varnhagen (1771-1833). See *Rahel Levin Varnhagen. Die Wiederentdeckung einer Schriftstellerin*, ed. by Barbara Hahn and Ursula Isselstein (special number 14 of *Lili. Zeitschrift für Literatur und Linguistik*, Göttingen: Vandenhoeck & Ruprecht, 1987) and above all the current Deutsche Forschungsgemeinschaft-sponsored editions of the correspondence of Rachel Varnhagen and Pauline Wiesel, ed. by Marianne Schuller *et al.*, and of Therese Huber, ed. by Magdalena Heuser and Barbara Leuschner.

[5]E.g. Heinrich Düntzer, *Briefe von Schillers Gattin an einen vertrauten Freund* (Leipzig: Brockhaus, 1858), Ludwig Urlichs, *Charlotte von Schiller und ihre Freunde* (Stuttgart, 1860-65) and Georg Waitz, *Caroline von Schelling, Briefe an ihre Geschwister* (Leipzig: Hirzel, 1871).

[6]See Ute Gerhard and Ulla Wischermann, 'Liberalismus-Sozialismus-Feminismus. Zeitschriften der Frauenbewegung um die Jahrhundertwende' in *Deutsche Literatur von Frauen*, ed. by Gisela Brinker-Gabler, 2 vols (Munich: Beck, 1988), II, pp. 268-84, 525f., 561f. Their useful survey does not include the still almost wholly uncharted area of conservative and Christian periodicals.

[7]Rahm, pp. 132-44.

[8]The number of unmarried mothers in Germany in this period was the highest in Europe. See John E. Knodel, *The Decline of Fertility in Germany 1871-1939* (Princeton: P.U.P., 1974).

[9]Marianne Weber, *Ehefrau und Mutter in der Rechtsentwicklung. Eine Einführung* (Tübingen: J.C.B. Mohr, 1907; reprint Aalen: Scientia, 1971), pp. 407-573 and C. Damm, 'Die Stellung der Ehefrau und Mutter nach Urteilen des Reichsgerichts von 1879 bis 1914. Eine Untersuchung zum Spannungsverhältnis zwischen dem Ideal der Gleichberechtigung und der

von Recht und Ideologie legitimierten sozialen Wirklichkeit' (unpublished dissertation, University of Marburg, 1983). Quoting from Damm, Ute Gerhard suggests in her discussion of the relationship between legislative reform and social reality on the basis of preliminary findings that 'die Rechtspraxis in der Regel gegenüber den gesetzlichen Errungenschaften eine traditionelle, retardierende, und damit für Frauen nachteilige Rolle gespielt hat und der Sieg der juristischen Denkweise emanzipatorischen Tendenzen wenig förderlich war'. See 'Die Rechtsstellung der Frau in der bürgerlichen Gesellschaft des 19. Jahrhunderts. Frankreich und Deutschland im Vergleich' in *Bürgertum im 19. Jahrhundert. Deutschland im europäischen Vergleich*, ed. by Jürgen Kocka with the assistance of Ute Frevert (Munich: dtv, 1988) I, p. 442.

[10]Claudia Koonz, *Mothers in the Fatherland. Women, the Family and Nazi Politics* (London: Jonathan Cape, 1987), pp. 145f. and 175-219. See also Dorte Winkler, *Frauenarbeit im Dritten Reich* (Hamburg: Hoffmann & Campe, 1977).

[11]Systematic legislative discrimination against women's right of assembly goes back to the era immediately following the 1848 revolution where, notably in Prussia, the *Vereins- und Pressegesetze* of 1850 and after had expressly prohibited women from attending public meetings or from joining or founding political organizations. This clearly was to prove a serious handicap for the development of women's organizations in the decades following the founding by Louise Otto-Peters (1819-95) of the *Allgemeine Frauenverein* in 1865. The Socialist Party, after its acceptance of women's rights as part of official party policy in 1891, hit on the effective strategy of appointing (necessarily male!) *Vertrauenspersonen* to liaise with women.

[12]While Else Lasker-Schüler, Ricarda Huch or Annette Kolb expressed (unpopular) scepticism, the enthusiastic lyrical outpouring of war poetry in *Schwert aus der Scheide* (1916) earned the self-styled apolitical Isolde Kurz the title of 'Deutsche Mutter'. Patriotic lyrics on the subject by Ina Seidel (1885-1974) (*Neben der Trommel her*, 1915) were included in almost every anthology of war poetry.

[13]See for example Ursula von Gersdorff, *Frauen im Kriegsdienst 1914-1945* (Stuttgart: Deutsche Verlagsanstalt, 1969).

[14]Ute Frevert, summarizing Stefan Bajohr, *Die Hälfte der Fabrik. Geschichte der Frauenarbeit in Deutschland 1914-1945*, 2nd edn (Marburg: Verlag Arbeiterbewegung und Gesellschaftswissenschaften, 1984). See *Frauen-Geschichte. Zwischen Bürgerlicher Verbesserung und Neuer Weiblichkeit*, N.F., vol. 284 (Frankfurt/M.: Suhrkamp, 1986), p. 151f.

[15]Frevert, p. 171.

[16]Ute Frevert, 'Traditionelle Weiblichkeit und moderne Interessenorganisation: Frauen im Angestelltenberuf 1918-1933' in *Geschichte und Gesellschaft*, 7 (1981), No. 3/4, pp. 507-33 (p. 511).

[17]It is Irmgard Keun's ability to combine satirization of this trend in *Das kunstseidene Mädchen* (1933), with the pathos recognised by her contemporary, the psychologist Alice Rühle-Gerstel, which constituted the novel's special appeal at the time of its original appearance and explains its popularity today since its recent re-issue in paperback. Rühle-Gerstel described Doris and her world as: 'Ein halbseidener Beruf, halbseiden wie die Strümpfe und Hemdchen der Ladenfräulein, halbseiden wie ihr Gemüt und ihre Gedankenwelt... Ihrer wirtschaftlichen Situation gemäß Proletarierin, ihrer Ideologie nach bürgerlich, ihrer Arbeitswelt zufolge männlich, ihrer Arbeitsgesinnung nach weiblich.

Schillernde Gestalten, von schillerndem Reiz oft, ebenso von schillernder Fragwürdigkeit, auf alle Fälle von schillernder Sicherheit ihres sozialen und seelischen Daseins'. Quoted in Frevert, *Frauen-Geschichte*, p. 170.

[18]See James C. Albisetti, 'Women and the Professions in Imperial Germany' in *German Women in the Eighteenth and Nineteenth Century. A Social and Literary History*, ed. by Ruth-Ellen Böttcher-Joeres and Mary Jo Maynes (Bloomington: Indiana U.P., 1986), pp. 94-109 (p. 96).

[19]Konrad H. Jarausch, *Students, Society and Politics in Imperial Germany* (Princeton: P.U.P., 1982), p. 109.

[20]'Ermöglicht wird die schriftstellerische Arbeit auch gerade von Frauen bäuerlichen, ja ärmlichen Herkommens zunächst einmal durch die verbesserte Schulbildung auch für Mädchen', in Renate von Heydebrand, *Literatur in der Provinz Westfalen 1815-1945. Ein literarhistorischer Modell-Entwurf* (Münster: Regensberg, 1983), p. 201. On Berens-Totenohl, see pp. 206ff.

[21]See Barbara Greven-Aschhoff, *Die bürgerliche Frauenbewegung in Deutschland 1894-1933* (Kritische Studien zur Geschichtswissenschaft 46, Göttingen: Vandenhoeck & Ruprecht, 1981).

[22]Ute Frevert, *Frauen-Geschichte. Zwischen bürgerlicher Verfassung und Neuer Weiblichkeit* (Frankfurt/M.: Suhrkamp, 1986), p. 156f. Also cf. Richard J. Evans, 'Liberalism and Society: The Feminist Movement and Social Change' in *Society and Politics in Imperial Germany*, ed by Richard J. Evans (London: Croom Helm, 1978), pp. 186-214.

[23]Frevert (1986), p. 163.

[24]Michael Phayer, 'Protestant and Catholic Women confront Social Change' in: *Another Germany. A Reconsideration of the Imperial Era*, ed. by Jack R. Dukes and Joachim Remak (Boulder and London: Westview, 1988), pp. 95-113 (p. 97).

[25]Catholic women's self-organization in 1848-9, associated with the *Piusverein* as forerunner of the *Katholikentag*, deserves mention here, not least because the subject has as yet made so little impact on research.

[26]By contrast the Protestant women were controlled by the parent organization, the *Evangelischer Kirchlicher Hilfsverein*, whose board was exclusively male.

[27]Phayer, p. 102f.

[28]Frevert (1986), pp. 165ff.

[29]See Sigrun Bohle, 'Mode, Schönheit oder Gesundheit?' in *Die Frau im Korsett. Wiener Alltag zwischen Klischee und Wirklichkeit 1848-1920* (Exhibition Catalogue of the 88th Special Exhibition of the Historisches Museum der Stadt Wien, Vienna: Museen der Stadt Wien, 1984), pp. 107-110.

[30]See C.H. Stratz, *Die Frauenkleidung und ihre natürliche Entwicklung* (Stuttgart: Enke, 1900, 4th edn 1920) and Justus Thiersch, *Die Schädigung des weiblichen Körpers durch*

fehlerhafte Kleidung nebst Bemerkungen über die Verbesserung der Frauenkleidung (Berlin: Hermann Walther, 1901).

[31]The same clothes worn by both sexes (the adolescent twins) and also by the insolent male servant link them in their differentiated provocation of their parents'/master's world. The decline in numbers of servants after 1918 was a general phenomenon associated with the development of a capitalist economy as well as the economic crises affecting the middle classes. In the case of women servants it was attributed widely by their employers to the impact of women's emancipation on the 'lower orders'.

[32]See Romano Guardini's comment, reflecting the suspicion felt by official Catholic circles towards the emancipatory implications of the Youth Movement, particularly with regard to women: 'Jugendbewegung. Heute macht man sich nicht leicht klar, was das damals bedeutete. Wer zu ihr gehörte, war charakterisiert: für die einen in besonderer Weise nahestehend und vertrauenswürdig, für die anderen Gegenstand der Ablehnung' in *Berichte über mein Leben. Autobiographische Aufzeichnungen*, ed. by Franz Heinrich, Schriften der Katholischen Akademie in Bayern, vol. 116 (Düsseldorf: Patmos, 1984), p. 34.

[33]See *Sozialgeschichte der deutschen Literatur von 1918 bis zur Gegenwart*, ed. by Jan Berg *et al.* (Frankfurt/M.: Fischer, 1981), p. 195, and for the impact of the abortion issue on contemporary literature, p. 155.

[34]Quoted in Renny Harrigan, 'Die Sexualität der Frau in der deutschen Unterhaltungsliteratur 1919-1933' in *Geschichte und Gesellschaft* 7 (1981), No. 3/4, pp. 412-37 (p. 418).

[35]See Marielouise Janssen-Jurreit, 'Nationalbiologie, Sexualreform und Geburtenrückgang, über die Zusammenhänge zwischen Bevölkerungspolitik und Frauenbewegung um die Jahrhundertwende' in *Die Überwindung der Sprachlosigkeit. Texte aus der neuen Frauenbewegung*, ed. by Gabriele Dietze (Neuwied: Luchterhand, 1979), pp. 139-75.

[36]Wolfgang Langenbucher, *Der aktuelle Unterhaltungsroman. Beiträge zur Geschichte und Theorie der massenhaft verbreiteten Literatur* (Bonn: Bouvier, 1964. *Bonner Beiträge zur Bibliotheks- und Bücherkunde* 9), p. 67. Paradoxical as it might seem, the reader would in fact get more information on the contribution of women authors to the literary market in the nineteenth century from reading the volumes of Heinrich Spiero or R.M. Meyer (note 3 above) than from histories of German literature published up to the end of the 1980s. That this is changing is already evident, for example, in Bertelsmann's new *Literatur-Lexikon*, ed. by Walter Killy (Munich: Bertelsmann, 1988-), 15 volumes. Peter Skrine and Eda Sagarra, *Blackwell's History of German Literature 1500 to the Present*, currently in preparation, will include a systematic treatment of German women writers.

[37]See her letter of 22 November 1896 in Helmut Brandt, 'Marie von Ebner-Eschenbach und die "Deutsche Rundschau"', in: *Die österreichische Literatur. Ihr Profil von der Jahrhundertwende bis zur Gegenwart 1880-1980* (Graz: Akademische Druck- und Verlagsanstalt, 1989), p. 1008, requesting Rodenberg to accept a piece by Hermine Villinger. To publish in so influential an organ as the *Rundschau* 'wäre für sie von höchster Wichtigkeit'. There are some 242 letters from her to Rodenberg in the archives of the Weimar National Research Centre (Brandt, p. 1002). Besides some letters from the friend of her old age, Enrica Handel-Mazzetti, which discuss the literary market (the body of the correspondence is in the Stifter archive in Linz) and from Lou Andreas-Salomé, the Vienna

City Library also contains letters to her from aspiring writers such as Martha Renate Fischer and Anselma Heine.

[38]*Deutsche Rundschau*, 74, January-March number.   Hermann Grimm, son of Wilhelm and nephew of Jakob Grimm, was the husband, son-in-law, brother-in-law and uncle by marriage of noted women writers. He had recently lost his wife Gisela, youngest daughter of Bettina von Arnim. His two nieces by marriage, daughters of Bettina's second daughter, Armgart, were Elisabeth von Heyking (1861-1925), née Flemming, author of the autobiographical *Briefe, die ihn nicht erreichten* (Berlin: Gebr. Paetel, 1902, 85th edn, 1918) and the lyric poet and storywriter, Irene Forbes-Mosse, who was banned from writing by the Nazis.

[39]The list for Lasker-Schüler includes Michael Conrad's *Die Gesellschaft* and the *Magazin für die Litteratur des In- und Auslands*, the major expressionist journals *Der Sturm* and *Die weißen Blätter*, also *Revolution, Neue Jugend*, as well as *Der Brenner, Die Fackel* and *Die Schau(Welt)bühne*. Huch published in *Die Gegenwart, Die Neue Rundschau*, as well as such diverse organs as the Viennese art magazine *Ver Sacrum, Jugend, Süddeutsche Monatshefte* and *Die Schaubühne*.

[40]Kurz's work appeared in journals as diverse as the *Magazin für die Litteratur des In- und Auslands*, Franzos's *Deutsche Dichtungen* and the prestigious *Jugend*. Kolb published i.a. in *Die Neue Rundschau, Die weißen Blätter, Das Forum, Hyperion, Morgen, Der neue Merkur*. The poetry and prose tales of Croissant-Rust, who had been one of the editors of the Munich journal *Modernes Leben* (1891) favoured *Kleine moderne Blätter, Jugend*, Naumann's patriotic liberal organ, *Die Hilfe*, which changed its name in 1910 to *Wochenschrift für Politik, Literatur und Kunst*, increasing the coverage of literature in the process, and the regionally self-conscious *Die Rheinlande* and *Deutsche Monatshefte*. Information here and in note 39 is taken from Fritz Schlawe, *Literarische Zeitschriften. Teil I. 1885-1910*, 2nd revised edn, and from *Teil II. 1910-1933* (Stuttgart: Metzler, 1965 and 1972).

[41]Kristina Zerges, *Sozialdemokratische Presse und Literatur. Empirische Untersuchungen zur Literaturvermittlung in der Sozialdemokratischen Presse 1876 bis 1933* (Stuttgart: Metzler, 1982), p. 34ff. and p. 72ff. In this context Heide Soltau makes the important point that a substantial number of formerly progressive women writers, instancing in particular Clara Viebig, Gabriele Reuter (1859-1941) and Helene Böhlau, distanced themselves demonstrably in their work of the Weimar years from liberal positions. Heide Soltau, 'Die Anstrengungen des Aufbruchs. Romanautorinnen und ihre Heldinnen in der Weimarer Zeit' in *Deutsche Literatur von Frauen* ed. by Gisela Brinker-Gabler, II, pp. 220-235 (p. 224).

[42]See Wolfgang Martens, *Lyrik Kommerziell. Das Kartell lyrischer Autoren 1902 bis 1933* (Munich: Beck, 1975).

[43]Heydebrand indicates that in the Sauerland this was the case for Josefa Berens-Totenohl, the "Sauerland nightingale" Christine Koch (1896-1951) and the *völkisch* poet Maria Kahle (1891-1975). See Heydebrand, p. 207ff.

[44]Martens, p. 21.

[45]See Wilhelm Rohrwasser, *Saubere Mädel: starke Genossen — proletarische Massenliteratur?* Untersuchungen und Materialien (Frankfurt/M.: Stroemfeld/Roter Stern, 1975).

[46]See the discussion on the relation between gender, genre and literary market in Lydia Schieth, *Die Entwicklung des deutschen Frauenromans im ausgehenden 18. Jahrhundert*, *Helicon: Beiträge zur deutschen Literatur*, 5 (Frankfurt/M., Berne, New York and Paris: Peter Lang, 1987), pp. 2ff.

Lou Andreas-Salomé

2

Lou Andreas-Salomé and Female Sexuality at the Turn of the Century

Carol Diethe

The epithet 'Victorian', which conveys prudery in sexual matters, is just as aptly used to describe the Wilhelmine Germans as it is the British of the same period. What was markedly different in Germany was the fact that paternalistic values were much more strongly enforced than in Britain, which after all had a strong queen on the throne rather than the chauvinistic Kaiser Wilhelm (who ruled from 1888-1918). The writing of the female German writers of the Wilhelmine period almost invariably demonstrates that women were constantly willing to accept a male evaluation of their role, and amongst them Lou Andreas-Salomé is no exception.[1] Although Lou consistently sets forth a passionate belief that biology has been kind to women, allowing them a richer, more unified life than men, her acceptance of a different nature for woman is fundamentally a 'Männerurteil' in line with the conventional view that women were weaker and more emotional at best, silly and childish at worst.[2]

In spite of the vigorous debate on sexual matters which flourished in Europe around the turn of the century, surprisingly little new thinking emerged with regard to female sexuality. Doctors seemed to find it a near-impossibility to separate the two very distinct fields of female sexuality and female reproduction. Furthermore, with prosperity increasing for the middle classes as the century wore on and as the German industrial revolution belatedly gathered pace, the bourgeois male's vested interest in ensuring that his children actually *were* his grew accordingly. Foucault argues that the bourgeoisie deployed sexuality for class purposes, and that 'l'apparition des technologies medicales du sexe' is proof, not that the bourgeoisie was repressing its sexuality, but that it was obsessed with it.[3] He cites the way the rich woman was marginalized and falsely idolized as the first step in the process:

> Le personnage qui a été d'abord investi par le dispositif de sexualité, un des premiers à avoir été 'sexualisé', [...] ce fut la femme 'oisive', aux limites du 'monde' ou elle devait toujours figurer comme valeur, et de la famille où on lui assignait un lot nouveau d'obligations conjugales et parentales: ainsi est apparue la femme 'nerveuse', la femme atteinte de 'vapeurs'; là l'hystérisation de la femme a trouvé son point d'ancrage.
>
> (p. 160)

Although Foucault points out that those subjugated often connive at their subjugation, it must be remembered that the (middle-class) doctors were swift to cash in on the new rash of maladies to which the leisured woman was prone, such as 'neurasthenia'; a wealthy woman had to be strong indeed to break away from medical convention. Even Charlotte Perkins Gilman and Virginia Woolf were unable to escape the dreaded 'rest cure'. Very little consideration was given to the possibility that the respectable lady might harbour a high libido. Krafft-Ebing even stated categorically that this could not be the case, otherwise 'müßte die ganze Welt ein Bordell und Ehe und Familie undenkbar sein'.[4] This constituted the received opinion of the time, which meant that sexual counselling never went much further than advising men to be as chaste as their wives. There were notable exceptions, however: Wilhelm Bölsche, whom Lou had met in Berlin in 1899, wrote in *Das Liebesleben in der Natur* (1900-1903) that, in view of the fact that in nature the female is stronger than the male, the Women's Movement for emancipation would have to make people change their opinions and view women as 'gleich stark'.[5] He insisted that women were intellectually equal to men; but in this, Lou's opinions differed, as we shall see.

There was another school of thought whereby women were viewed as sexual predators on men, and their sexuality was then construed in the worst possible light. This misogynist strand of opinion began with Schopenhauer and was continued, though significantly modified, by Nietzsche and people who admired his ideas, such as Leo Berg, the German critic, and Otto Weininger, the notorious Viennese philosopher who in *Geschlecht und Charakter* (1903) sought to prove, by spurious biological argument, that women were genetically inferior to men.[6] Of course, there were humane and intelligent men – often to the left politically – who insisted that the sexes were equal. Thus August Bebel:

> Man darf sagen, daß in dem Maße, wie die Triebe und Lebensäußerungen bei den Geschlechtern sich ausprägen..., um so vollkommener ist der Mensch, sei er Mann oder Frau.[7]

Friedrich Engels and, to a lesser extent, Karl Marx, supported the principle of sexual equality; but they were not medical men, and sexuality was rapidly spreading through every corridor of the medical world. It was not until Iwan Bloch announced, in *Das Sexualleben unserer Zeit* (1907), that in his view woman's 'geschlechtliche Sensibilität' was at least as great as that of the man, that what we now regard as medically self-evident fact came to be represented as a viewpoint.[8] Even then, Bloch hedged his argument with so many provisos as to woman's 'organisch bedingte leichtere Suggestibilität' (p. 79) and her greater 'Emotivität', leading to a 'leichtere Ermüdbarkeit' (p. 81), that much of the force of his argument was lost.

There is yet another strand of opinion which embraced female sexuality in the Wilhelmine era. This did not seek to make woman's sexuality into a nervous sickness or worse, but aimed at neutralizing woman through praise of her mystique. As Peter Gay writes:

> Men's defensiveness in the bourgeois century was so acute because the advance of women all round them was an attempt to recover ground they had lost... One favourite instrument of men's self-defence was the tired yet indefatigable cliché about women being the mysterious sex.[9]

Gay goes on to point out that Freud, who did so much to open up the debate on sexuality, was nevertheless 'not...wholly immune to this pervasive old theme' (p. 171), and indeed, even as late as 1933, Freud confessed himself still somewhat baffled by the female psyche:

> Wollen Sie mehr über die Weiblichkeit wissen, so
> befragen Sie Ihre eigenen Lebenserfahrungen, oder Sie
> wenden sich an die Dichter, oder Sie warten, bis die
> Wissenschaft Ihnen tiefere und besser zusammen-
> hängende Auskünfte geben kann.[10]

If men were confused, so were women. Left-wing campaigners for women's rights largely ignored the question of female sexuality, but their sisters on the right gravitated towards the standpoint of upholding what were seen as feminine virtues such as patience, loyalty, motherliness, etc.; in other words, mystique. There were women in the movement for women's rights who campaigned for more liberal attitudes to female sexuality, such as Helene Stöcker.[11] But the views of her opponent, Helene Lange, were more widely accepted, especially after 1908, when 'moderate' feminists swamped the Women's Movement as soon as the repeal of the *Reichsvereinigungsgesetz* made it legal for them to do so: in effect, these feminists were what we would now term right-wing. When Lange outlined the task of a wife as that of her husband's helpmeet, she was voicing the view of the majority of bourgeois women and nearly all men in Germany at that time: 'Sie (die Frau) ist eine Macht im Heim, als Mutter, als.Gefährtin des Mannes.'[12]

Lou Andreas-Salomé did not regard herself in any way as a campaigner for women's rights, but her views align with those of the right wing of the movement in that she believed that a woman's psyche was different from a man's, and that a woman's role was best fulfilled in the domestic sphere. Where she differs is that she does view woman as suffused with sexuality, an idea she may have borrowed from Nietzsche.[13] But whereas Nietzsche made fun of the mystique of 'das Ewig-Weibliche', Lou takes it seriously and allows it to weave into her discussion of the physiology of sex.[14] Rejecting the tendency to make women with a high libido sound like nymphomaniacs, which even well-informed doctors such as Schrenck-Notzing were wont to do,[15] she finds much to be praised in woman's erotic enjoyment, but has many illogical quirks to her argument as well. Put briefly, because these points will emerge more fully later, Lou believed that eroticism ends when marriage begins; the sexuality suffused through woman's being then converts into a sort of comfortable radiance.

It must be mentioned here that Lou remained a virgin for the first ten years of her marriage to the oriental scholar, Fred Charles Andreas, until the twenty-one-year-old Rilke became her lover in 1897. She then had several other lovers with whom she had an (apparently) enjoyable sex life, whilst remaining married to Andreas. Cordula Koepcke relates that Lou kept the true nature of her relationship with Rilke (and subsequent lovers) secret from Andreas.[16] Speculation is rife as to why Lou would not allow her marriage to be consummated. Livingstone writes of 'the strange compulsion of her marriage', as though she were drawn to Andreas by inner necessity, and speculates that Lou, a strong woman, felt she might be submerged if she consummated her marriage.[17] However, Mackey points out that some casual comments made by Lou in her *Lebensrückblick* (in the afterword – she omits Andreas in the main body of the book!) indicate that the marriage was by no means serene, and that her many trips abroad were an attempt to escape from a 'solitude à deux'.[18] Lou speaks of feelings of 'Schrecken' which she had to master, not at the idea of intercourse as such, but at having to confront Andreas's emotional demands. When he was (understandably!) jealous of her friendship with Rilke Lou recalls:

> ... Und hieraus wiederum ergaben sich für mich unwillkürlich andersartige Gefühlseinstellungen als verliebte zu Jenem: nämlich Zufluchtsverlangen vor Schrecken, vor denen ich machtlos war und die unsere Tage und Nächte zu qualvoll durchlittenen werden ließen.[19]

Although, as Koepcke points out, Lou tried to erase written evidence of her sexual relationship with Rilke, it is clear that they had a passionate love affair and remained good friends, though there was more emotional dependence on Rilke's side than on Lou's. Indeed, Mackey actually states that Lou took up her study of psychoanalysis 'dans un grand effort pour lui aider et soulager ses crises'.[20] Lou subsequently wrote a good deal on psychoanalysis, which has been collated into the recently published volume *Das 'zweideutige' Lächeln der Erotik; Texte zur Psychoanalyse* ed. by I. Weber and B. Rempp (Freiburg: Kore, 1990). Lou was on close terms with Freud and his daughter Anna, and was a well-regarded practitioner of psychoanalysis in her own right.

What are we to make of a childless woman who writes of maternity as woman's destiny, of a woman who speaks approvingly of marriage but denies her husband sexual intercourse, who writes disapprovingly of women who

make writing their main pastime, when she herself does just that? Should
Lou's ideas on female sexuality be accepted in good faith? I shall argue that
the main inconsistencies are in line with social circumstances, as outlined in
the introduction; in addition, Lou's privileged status as a member of the upper
class gave her a certain insensitivity to others, especially to working-class
women.[21]   And we must not forget her wilful nature, singled out by
Nietzsche's sister as her dominant characteristic. Nor must we forget Lou's
deeply religious attitude to life, although she turned away from conventional
religion: an experience which left her deeply shocked.

The two essays on sexuality which Lou wrote at the turn of the century
– 'Der Mensch als Weib' (1899) and 'Gedanken über das Liebesproblem'
(1900) – contain many, if not all, of the paradoxes in Lou's life and thought
which have been mentioned above.[22] The later essay 'Die Erotik' (1910), the
title of which promises so much, actually adds very little to the earlier essays
and I shall incorporate my comments on it when I discuss the two turn-of-the-
century pieces. 'Der Mensch als Weib' begins as a factual, biological account,
but rapidly becomes clouded by Lou's tendency to shroud her ideas in
elevated language, in keeping with the mystique about which we have spoken.
Firing a salvo at the feminists, Lou asserts that the female is less highly
developed than the male, but then declares this to be her strength. Indeed her
belief that men lose through being more highly developed [differentiated] is a
building block in all her writing on women. Woman has her 'Heimat' around
her like a snail, as though she were still part of the larger universe: 'als sei sie
mit dem allerhaltenden unendlichen Ganzen noch unmittelbarer verbunden,
daher an ihren Ur- und Grundboden noch träger gebunden' (p. 9). This
enables her to act with condescension towards the upstart male to whom she
is, if anything, superior: to speak of equality is irrelevant.

Lou correctly describes the human egg cell as enormous in relation to
the tiny sperm cell, citing C. Claus (*Grundzüge der Zoologie*) and J. Rank
(*Grundzüge der Physiologie des Menschen*). She challenges the idea that man is
the more active partner in human reproduction, but admits that the mistake is
easy to make:

> Auch der rein lokale Umstand, daß bei der Umarmung
> der männliche Samen in das Weib eindringt, und dieses
> ihn empfängt, begünstigt die Verwechslung, während der

Leib des Weibes doch nur den Zusammenkunftsort für
beide Teile abgibt.

('Der Mensch als Weib', p. 11)

The differentiated man is needed for one small act only, whereas all the
woman's physical and mental qualities are needed for the development of the
child. (Incidentally, this is the nearest Lou comes to speaking of sexual
intercourse.) In 'Die Erotik' Lou returns to this theme, referring to maternity
as a 'lebenslänglicher Akt' (p. 121), and to the unfortunate onward march of
development which severs people from 'des Lebens Lebendigstem', a fact
which, to Lou, is tragic.

Although Lou says somewhat grudgingly that the male 'hat seinen Wert
in dem, was er so leistet und entwickelt' ('Der Mensch als Weib', p. 15), she
goes on to describe his sexual pleasure as rough and momentary in
comparison to the 'tiefere Schönheit' of female sexual enjoyment. As so
often, we have Lou, the radical, speaking candidly of female eroticism while
Lou, the arch-conservative, simultaneously clothes it all in a mist of
generalities which are intended to highlight the female mystique.

Das Weib lebt das Geschlechtliche fort und fort in der
Struktur ihres gesamten Wesens aus...sie lebt ein
geschlechtlich gesteigertes Leben nicht nur im eng
spezialisierten, sondern schon im weiten und allge-
meinsten Sinn, auch außerhalb der besonderen
Ausübung ihrer engern weiblichen und mütterlichen
Funktionen.

(ibid., p. 18)

By being in tune with the 'Rhythmen des All-lebens' ('Die Erotik', p. 129),
women lay claim to the existential possibility of motherhood even if they do
not actually give birth. And by the same token, Lou argues, the capacity to
give birth, to bring forth a new existence in miniature, ensures that every
woman retains a virginal propensity even when sexually mature, radiating
'dieses besondere Glück des ewig Jungfräulichen und ewig Mütterlichen'
('Der Mensch als Weib', p. 18).

So crucial is the creative aspect of maternity to Lou that she draws a
parallel between woman and the artist. The artist has something of woman's
sensitivity; ultimately, though, he is ruled by his intellect, whereas a woman
excels in 'ihrer Art, praktisch da zu sein, − ihrer Art zu leben...' (p. 22). Lou
gives no consideration to the possibility of women being taken seriously as

creative artists in their own right, since this is a field mapped out for goal-orientated men.   She pours scorn on women who reject domesticity to follow 'mit wunderlicher Stupidität dem Lockruf aus ihrem eigenen Hause heraus, hinaus auf die Landstraße' (p. 28).   Women who seek to challenge men, intellectually or practically, enter upon 'ein wahres Teufelswerk' in which they will have to exhibit an ambition alien to their nature:

> Eben die Abwesenheit dieses Ehrgeizes macht ihre natürliche Größe aus: die sichere Gewißheit, daß es eines solchen Beweis-Erbringens nicht bedarf, um als Weib die höchste Selbstberechtigung in sich zu fühlen, daß sie nur ihre schattenspendenden Zweige von sich zu strecken, dem Müden zur Ruhe, dem Dürstenden zur Labe da zu sein braucht, ohne Sorge darum, wieviele Früchte man draußen auf dem Markt zusammenzählen könnte.
>
> (p. 24)

Lou gives an elaborate extension of the tree analogy which is not altogether happy, since she is slightly uncertain as to how to interpret the windfall fruits!   One is also reminded of a very different and misogynist application of the tree analogy in James Stephens's poem, 'A Woman is a Branchy Tree'.[23]   Lou sees woman's role as static: ripening, blossoming, sending forth shoots, offering shade: to depart from this role forces women to elbow their way through life 'wie der Mann' (p. 28).   In an untypical aside (because she seldom has any regard for social factors) Lou mentions that some women are unfortunately compelled to work; this is a 'soziales Übel' of which the only redeeming feature would be the hope that such women might be able to bring the feminine virtues of 'Weibesseele, Heimat und Harmonie' to the male world of work.

To realize her connection 'zum Ganzen' (p. 37) is the task of woman, her journey of self-discovery, until she is finally swallowed up by eternity, as a droplet is swallowed up by the ocean.   Man, on the contrary, puts up a muscular fight to the death.   Here Lou, having taken us to the nether reaches of transcendentalism, suddenly reaches out again for the physiological foundation of her argument, and concludes that woman, with the soft curves of her neck and shoulders, is physically constituted for a 'gentler death', sinking down gracefully 'damit Schönheit zu Schönheit sich finde' (p. 38).

The essay 'Der Mensch als Weib' certainly degenerates towards the end, as the above remarks on death demonstrate; some good points are made, such as woman's need to accept the rhythm of her menstrual cycle, and not to try to work against it; but the essential argument of women's different nature becomes more and more tendentious. The denial of woman's natural capacity for reasoning has been converted into the argument that for a woman, to feel is to think. 'Was nicht in unser Gefühl eintritt, das beschäftigt unser Denken nicht lange' (p. 26). With some dismay, the reader follows the essay in a downward spiral to the end, where woman kneels – not to the man, a point strenuously made by Lou – but to the Almighty, on behalf of them both. And yet...

And yet we can never dismiss Lou entirely. She can appear outrageous to the radical feminist, but it can sometimes be fruitful to disagree with her. Even the final image of woman in this essay, as guiding man to his inner bliss, repays examination as it echoes much of what Jung was to say two decades later, and still reverberates today in the works of thinkers such as Joseph Campbell, who died in 1990:

> I have frequently thought that mythology is a sublimation of the mother image... The sexual mystery in India, and in most of the world, is a holy mystery... The act of generating a child is a cosmic act and is to be understood as holy.[24]

This line of argument would place Lou in a central position in the history of myths and ideas, though it would not, of course, make what she said about female sexuality correct.

In 'Gedanken über das Liebesproblem', Lou uses less physiological data as a basis for her argument, although she does repeatedly refer to the physical attraction involved, usually with regret at the way it causes relationships to operate on a superficial level. The thrust of her essay, spelt out at the beginning and implicit throughout, is that one has to love oneself sufficiently in order to love one's partner. Lou explains that there are two dominant character traits: the 'egoist' and the 'Samaritan', both deeply unsatisfactory. But there is also a median type, which contains elements of the other two 'in einer wunderlichen und widerspruchsvollen Weise darin gemischt', where the person feels he is making a journey 'in sich selbst

zugleich über sich selbst hinaus ins Ganze des Lebens' (p. 49). This type of
personality is the one to which all erotic connections attach. It is interesting
that Lou seems to suggest something of Rousseau's *amour de soi-même* here:
the self-regard which we all possess as survival instinct. As Mackey points out,
'rien de plus saloméen que cette défense de l'individu dont elle s'est toute la
vie fait le champion'.[25]

The person in love behaves more like the egoist than the Samaritan: he
or she is demanding and selfish. It is indeed a sobering thought that we care
comparatively little about who our loved one actually is; it is the attendant
feeling of being in love that matters. The state of being in love is thus intermediary:

> Die erotische Beziehung ist also eine Mittelform
> zwischen dem Einzelwesen als solchem, dem Egoisten,
> und dem sozial empfindenden Wesen, dem Herden- und
> Brudertier.
>
> ('Gedanken über das Liebesproblem', p. 53)

(The mention of the Nietzschean herd animal in this context is an idea to
which we shall return.) When we are in love, we are forced to pay attention to
the body's physical demands, but the mental dimension is overlooked at our
peril. Again Lou launches into a quasi-mystical explanation of something
which might be better stated in plainer terms:

> ...mit jedem offenen Blick auf das Wesen der Erotik
> assistieren wir gleichsam einem uralten, uranfänglichen
> Schauspiel, − einem Geburtsvorgange des Psychischen
> in seiner ganzen Pracht aus dem großen, allumfassenden
> Mutterleibe des Physischen.
>
> (p. 54)

Put simply, Lou means that a mental *and* physical heightening arises out of
erotic experiences to enrich the individual; the mention of birth and the womb
are not directly relevant to the argument as such, but support an
interpretation in line with the comments of Joseph Campbell quoted in note
24. From the clinical point of view, one could equally well argue that Lou, like
the doctors of the time, and like nearly everyone else, mistakenly and
inextricably linked sexuality with procreation, whereas modern birth control
methods have allowed us to stop doing this. Lou goes on to make the point
that 'alle Liebe beglücke, selbst die unglückliche' (p. 58), a view which she
repeats almost verbatim in 'Die Erotik' (p. 99). In the midst of the often

awkward and rigid prose, the central point – that sex is *good* for you – shines like a beacon.

Lou points out that sexual intercourse unites the body and soul and heightens the individual's awareness and capacity for action. Newcomers to sex often have a confused expectation of love, and are embarrassed at having to actually *do* something with their sexual parts; their alienation from their own bodies is so great that it is almost as if a third person were there as spectator ('Gedanken über das Liebesproblem', p. 56, 'Die Erotik', p. 98). But just as married couples can quarrel and still be deeply in love, the body and soul can overcome such difficulties through erotic fulfilment:

> Solch ein Fest, solch eine Feier ist die wahre
> Erscheinung des erotischen Rausches, in dem der
> Liebende Körper und Seele in inniger Umschlingung in
> sich eins fühlt und daher jenes Gesunden, jene kraftvolle
> Erneuerung verspürt wie nach einem göttlichen
> Wunderbad.
> ('Gedanken über das Liebesproblem', pp. 57-58)

In spite of the words *Fest*, *Feier*, and *göttlich*, none of which Lou uses lightly, it must be stressed that we are not yet discussing love here. The sexual pleasure enjoyed in such a conjunction of body and soul merely opens the door to love, which needs an intellectual dimension – *Geist* – before Lou can actually speak of it. Her comments on the creative aspect of sexuality again lead her to make comparisons with the artist; this time she points out the inspirational power of the erotic and compares it to the artist's bouts of inspiration:

> ...alle Liebe [ist] eigenmächtige Schaffenstat, Schaffens-
> lust, veranlaßt durch den geliebten Menschen, aber nicht
> um seinetwillen, sondern um ihrer selbst willen. Deshalb
> muß das Erotische auch ohne allen Zweifel, seinem
> Wesen nach, – gerade wie das Geistesschöpferische
> auch – als ein intermittierender Zustand aufgefaßt
> werden, der kommt und der aussetzt, und dessen
> Intensität oder Glücksfülle durchaus nichts Bestimmtes
> über seine mutmaßliche Dauer im besonderen Fall
> aussagen kann.
> (p. 64)

The prime function of the erotic, then, is to lead us to ourselves, it is 'ein Nachhause-Kommen zu uns selbst im geheimnisvollen Einklang aller Kräfte' (p. 65). Lou now describes how common it is for people to ignore this aspect of the erotic; they idealize their partners, yet live in a fog of ignorance about their own true selves and, hence, about external reality. An even worse mistake is for the lover to model him- or herself on the beloved; the more intelligent the person, the worse will be the damage. The horizons of both partners will be limited: Lou cites as proof the paradox one often finds of widows who during their marriage seemed to be devoted and timid wives, but who suddenly become strongly independent on the death of their husbands (p. 70).

Lou is perhaps unnecessarily scathing about ordinary, humdrum married couples who substitute habit for deeper knowledge (one thinks here of Nietzsche's loathing of the *Herdenmensch*). In old age they still keep up the illusion of having been in love: but in reality, by fusing their personalities, they have ended up as non-entities:

> So sitzen sie da und reden in lauter Übertreibungen von der Liebe. Denn sie übertreiben noch heute: das müssen sie tun, weil sie es sich nicht anders erklären können, – und im Erklären waren sie nie stark, – wie es denn eigentlich ist, daß man immer selbstischer wird, je lieber man einander hat, und daß zwei nur dann Eins sind, wenn sie Zwei bleiben.
>
> (p. 73)

Lou laments that it is rare indeed for couples to remain separate in the way she recommends, for it is only then that true love can occur. This is one of her firm convictions: Pfeiffer tells us that she wanted to give the essay 'Der Mensch als Weib' the title 'Die Zwei als Eins'.[26] In view of this, we must remain largely strangers to those whom we love, something which constitutes 'eine heimliche Tragödie' (p. 81), but is a small price to pay in exchange for the rich reward of self-knowledge.

It is significant that Lou stresses the dangers of stemming erotic love, or of denying it a spiritual dimension (p. 77). Erotic attraction is, however, fundamentally physical and should not be confused with anything else. Lou points out that we can be erotically attracted to a person who is damaged physically only if we were attracted to that person *before* the damage occurred (a viewpoint many would challenge). In 'Die Erotik' she goes further, pointing out that erotic appetite needs to be satisfied like any other physical appetite, and is at its most natural when there is a turnover of partners, an astoundingly bold view for the time:

> Man kann sagen: das natürliche Liebesleben in allen seinen Entwicklungen, und in den individualisiertesten vielleicht am allermeisten, ist aufgebaut auf dem Prinzip der Untreue.
>
> (p. 93)

Ideas such as this, and further pronouncements as to the dangers of stemming sexual desire (p. 89), point forward to the later debate on sexology which occupied doctors such as Hirschfeld, Freud and Jung in the first three decades of the century, and lie beyond the scope of this survey. From the essays discussed we have seen that Lou is sufficiently avant-garde to make a telling point on occasion, but too hidebound in her own particular kind of mysticism to shed significant light on female sexuality. One can understand how comfortable she must have felt with the mystical aspects of psycho-analysis. In addition, she felt constantly constrained to keep in favour with the male intellectuals with whom she worked, as Biddy Martin has recently stressed.[27]

We are left to decide whether the contradictions in Lou's arguments constitute an element of bad faith. It is certainly disturbing to find her trumpeting out the conventional opinion of the time that *Liebesrausch* and *Lebensbund* were 'zwei grundverschiedene Methoden des Erlebens der Liebe' (p. 139) whilst she kept herself aloof from the destiny of mother which she prescribed for others. As Michaela Wiesner points out, Lou's use of the word *Lebensbund* rather than *Ehe* in 'Die Erotik' indicates a certain malaise.[28] There is certainly a sense in which the logic of Lou's argument strains against her conclusion that the glories of erotic pleasure cannot survive into marriage. Her reinforcement of woman's conventional role is even stronger in her fictional work. We must conclude that Lou's authorial stance can be viewed as dubious; the next question is, does that matter?

In answer to that, we should remember that the veneration of the 'sexless' mother figure in German society was to prove curiously resilient and would be manipulated by Hitler and the National Socialists to their own advantage.[29] One could even argue that the drastic reduction in the birth rate in the former West Germany is a final act of rebellion on the part of German women, who still see their life roles as clearly defined as wife/mother or career woman, and opt for the latter. Lou's 'erotic' writings therefore illuminate a fascinating area of German cultural life, even if there is little to be learnt, factually, from her comments on female sexuality. For feminists, however, these writings, sadly, constitute a missed opportunity.

Biographical Note

Lou Andreas-Salomé was born in St Petersburg in 1861. She was the daughter of a Russian general of Huguenot extraction. An excessively independent-minded woman from very early on, she was loved by both Nietzsche (whom she jilted) and Rilke, with whom she had a passionate affair. She was much admired by Freud, whose colleague she became. In spite of protestations that she would never marry, she became the wife of the Oriental scholar Fred Charles Andreas in 1887; their (chaste) marriage lasted until his death in 1931. Lou travelled widely in Europe and became well known for her writing of both fiction and non-fiction. Her major novels include *Fenitschka* (Stuttgart: Cotta'sche Buchhandlung, 1898), *Menschenkinder* (Stuttgart: Cotta'sche Buchhandlung, 1899), *Ma* (Stuttgart: Cotta'sche Buchhandlung, 1901), *Im Zwischenland* (Stuttgart: Cotta'sche Buchhandlung, 1902), *Das Haus* (Berlin: Ullstein, 1919) and *Rodinka* (Jena: Eugen Diederichs, 1923). Her most important non-fictional works include *Henrik Ibsens Frauengestalten* (Berlin: Hugo Bloch, 1892), *Friedrich Nietzsche in seinen Werken* (Vienna: Carl Konegen, 1894), *Rainer Maria Rilke* (Leipzig: Insel Verlag, 1928) and *Mein Dank an Freud* (Vienna: Internationaler Psychoanalytischer Verlag, 1931). She died in Göttingen in 1937.

NOTES

[1]See Biddy Martin, Woman and Modernity. The (life-)styles of Lou Andreas-Salomé (Ithaca and London: Cornell, 1991), p. 6, where Martin argues that much of Lou's ambivalence towards questions of gender arose from her desire to remain on good terms with her masculine colleagues. She dubs this Lou's "affirmative femininity".
The definitive text on Salomé remains, however, Rudolph Binion's *Frau Lou: Nietzsche's Wayward Disciple* (Princeton: Princeton University Press, 1968).

[2]F.N. Mennemeier, 'Widersprüche weiblicher Emanzipation: Lou Andreas-Salomé', *Literatur für Leser*, 4 (1987), p. 274.

[3]M. Foucault, *Histoire de la sexualité*, 2 vols (Paris: Gallimard, 1976), I: *La Volonté de savoir*, p. 158.

[4]Richard von Krafft-Ebing, *Psychopathia Sexualis* (Stuttgart: Ferdinand Enke, 1886), p. 10.

[5]Wilhelm Bölsche, *Das Liebesleben in der Natur*, 3 vols (Leipzig: Eugen Diederichs, 1900-1903), III, p. 284. Lou and Bölsche both contributed to A. Dix's collection of essays *Der Egoismus* (Leipzig: Freund und Wittig, 1899).

[6]Weininger, a homosexual Jew, was also virulently anti-Semitic, and ended by taking his own life.

[7]August Bebel, *Die Frau in der Vergangenheit, Gegenwart und Zukunft* (Zurich: Verlag der Volksbuchhandlung, 1879; the original title of convenience was replaced in 1891, following the repeal of the 'Sozialistengesetz' of 1890, by *Die Frau und der Sozialismus*. The most recent edition, from which I quote, is Berlin: Dietz Verlag, 1980, (here p. 93).

[8]Iwan Bloch, *Das Sexualleben unserer Zeit* (Berlin: Louis Marcus, 1907), p. 93.

[9]Peter Gay, *The Bourgeois Experience. Victoria to Freud*, 2 vols (Oxford: OUP, 1984), I: *Education of the Senses*, p. 169.

[10]Sigmund Freud, 'Die Weiblichkeit' (1933), in *Studienausgabe*, ed. by A. Mitscherlich *et al.*, 10 vols (Frankfurt/M.: Fischer, 1982), I, 565.

[11]Helene Stöcker and Max Marcuse founded the 'Bund für Mutterschutz' in 1905 to help unmarried mothers. It survived only a few years and was censured by right-wing campaigners for women's rights.

[12]Helene Lange, *Lebenserinnerungen* (Berlin: Herbig, 1928; quoted here in the Berlin, 1930 edn), p. 269. Working-class men were suspicious of equal rights for women as they feared for their jobs.

[13]See Carol Diethe, 'Nietzsche and the Woman Question', in *History of European Ideas*, 11 (1989), special issue: *Turning-Points in History*, pp. 865-76 *passim*.

[14]Friedrich Nietzsche, *Ecce Homo*, VI, 3. Of course, the concept originated with Goethe at the close of *Faust*, Part II.

[15]H. Schrenck-Notzing, *Die Suggestions-Therapie* (Stuttgart: Ferdinand Enke, 1892), p. 32: 'Die häufigste Folge leichterer Formen von Nymphomanie ist die Prostitution.' Dramatists such as Wedekind — who were viewed as enlightened men — held this view, too: the result is female characters such as Lulu.

[16]Cordula Koepcke, *Lou Andreas-Salomé* (Frankfurt/M.: Insel, 1986), p. 202.

[17]A. Livingstone, *Lou Andreas-Salomé* (London: Gordon Fraser, 1984), p. 62.

[18]I.S. Mackey, *Lou Salomé inspiratrice et interprète de Nietzsche, Rilke et Freud* (Paris: Nizet, 1959), pp. 140-41.

[19]Andreas-Salomé, *Lebensrückblick* (Frankfurt/M.: Insel, 1968), p. 213.

[20]Mackey, p. 140.

[21]E. Forster-Nietzsche, *Friedrich Nietzsche und die Frauen seiner Zeit* (Munich: Beck, 1935), pp. 108-32 *passim*.

[22]Andreas-Salomé, *Die Erotik. Vier Aufsätze*, ed. by E. Pfeiffer (Frankfurt/Main and Berlin: Ullstein, 1985). This volume contains 'Der Mensch als Weib' (1899); 'Gedanken über das Liebesproblem' (1900); 'Die Erotik' (1910); 'Psychosexualität' (1917).

[23.]'A Woman is a Branchy Tree' by James Stephens (1882-1950):

> A woman is a branchy tree
> And man a singing wind;
> And from her branches carelessly
> He takes what he can find:
>
> Then wind and man go far away,
> While winter comes with loneliness;
> With cold, and rain, and slow decay,
> On woman and on tree, till they
>
> Droop to the earth again, and be
> A withered woman, a withered tree;
> While wind and man woo in the glade
> Another tree, another maid.

[24]Joseph Campbell, *The Power of Myth* (New York: Doubleday, 1988), pp. 165-167.

[25]Mackey, p. 154.

[26]Pfeiffer, 'Nachwort', *Die Erotik*, p. 188.

[27]Martin, p. 231 (see note 1).

[28]Michaela Wiesner, 'Leben in seinem Ursinn — Lou Andreas-Salomés Essays zur Erotik', *Blätter der Rilke-Gesellschaft*, 11/12 (1984/85), pp. 39-41.

[29]See C. Koonz, *Mothers in the Fatherland: Women and the Family in Nazi Politics* (London: Jonathan Cape, 1987).

Elsa Bernstein

3

Elsa Bernstein: Germany's Major Woman Dramatist?

Peter Skrine

Elsa Bernstein is one of Germany's most unjustly neglected woman writers; she may also well be the most accomplished woman dramatist to have used the German language. Such claims may seem bold: but who else is there to set beside her? She stands almost alone even in the rich and exciting cultural period from 1893 to 1911 during which she was most active, and when women were making a greater and more original contribution to literature than they had perhaps ever done before. Of course other women were also writing plays at the turn of the century. For instance there was Elspeth Meyer-Förster, whose *Heimkehr* (1894) and *Käthe* (1896) were written to expose the social and psychological implications of the inadequate upbringing of women and of the crippling dependence on the men in their lives which was its result. Hilde in *Heimkehr* is an ordinary young woman, intimidated by her husband and crippled by her background, while Käthe's emotional balance is upset when her father has an affair with a married woman. Then there was Dora Duncker, something of a *Frauenrechtlerin* in the theatre and always eager to attack the social attitudes that conditioned women's lack of independence. And of course there was Klara Viebig, a novelist whose strong dramatic talent is revealed to fine, many-faceted effect in *Der Kampf um den Mann* (1895), a set of four impressive one-acters which highlight contrasting instances of female inadequacy, vulnerability and exploitation in the Germany of the time. But Meyer-Förster's achievement was short-lived and soon overshadowed by the box-office success of Wilhelm Meyer-Förster's *Alt-Heidelberg* (1903), which became even better known as *The Student Prince*: Duncker's reputation faded as her subject-matter dated; and Viebig made her reputation with novels and stories such as *Kinder der Eiffel* (1897), *Das Weiberdorf* (1900), and *Die Wacht am Rhein* (1902).

At the turn of the century there can be no doubt that Elsa Bernstein was the most serious as well as the most productive woman dramatist working in Germany. Now and then she wrote poems and stories, but these were entirely subordinate to her creative purpose, which was to show that a woman, too, could write a good play. The image she presented belied that purpose. It combined charm, modesty and determination in almost equal measure. She managed to avoid antagonising the male literary hierarchy of Germany by presenting a profile that was quintessentially feminine but never abrasively feminist.[1] Rilke, who knew her, noted 'wie zart und weiblich die blasse, blonde Frau ist'; he was one of the many artists and men of letters who enjoyed attending the 'Sonntag-Nachmittags-Tees' at her Munich home in the Briennerstrasse.[2] Indeed as a society hostess she occupied a commanding position in the cultural life of the Bavarian capital and was personally acquainted with many literary and musical figures whose names are now better known than hers, amongst them Richard Strauss, Hans Pfitzner, Weingartner, Rilke, Sudermann, Eduard Graf Keyserling, Michael Georg Conrad, Ludwig Thoma, Ludwig Ganghofer, Fontane, Ricarda Huch and Gerhart Hauptmann, whose third son, Klaus, married her daughter Eva in 1919. There was also Thomas Mann, whom she introduced to Katia Pringsheim in 1904. It is all the more astonishing that this remarkable woman has left so little trace in the annals of German literary history, and that no-one has thought her worthy of a biography.[3]

Elsa Bernstein was born in Vienna on 28 October 1866, the cherished daughter of cultivated parents who both came from Prague and were Jews converted to Lutheran Christianity. Her father, Heinrich Porges (1837-1900), was a close associate and champion of Richard Wagner, on whose recommendation he was appointed to the Royal School of Music at Munich in

1867; her husband, Max Bernstein, was a lawyer of liberal views as well as being an ardent Ibsenite and spare-time author of light plays about Munich life. His support meant much to her and must have played a key role in her career: she was spared the humiliating fate of the professor's wife in Paul Heyse's bitter Munich Novelle *Himmlische und irdische Liebe* (1885), whose literary aspirations are killed stone-dead when her husband reads and condescendingly dismisses the literary efforts she has submitted to him anonymously for his opinion. Elsa Bernstein, too, adopted the convention of a pseudonym, but whom it hid was soon open knowledge. She also had another asset which should not be overlooked because it played a crucial part in moulding her literary career. Her remarkably unprejudiced parents had allowed her to defy middle-class prejudice and go on the stage, and from 1884 to 1887 she worked as an actress in Brunswick. Her acting career may not have been a great success, if only because an eye complaint from which she was to suffer for the rest of her life forced her to give it up. But what her Brunswick years gave her was something few other German women writers of her time possessed, namely first-hand experience of the theatre. This distinguishing feature of her art shows up time and again in the command of stage-craft that characterizes her dramas and which, for a while at least, placed them almost on a par with those of Hauptmann himself.

Bernstein's published dramatic oeuvre falls into three parts which are roughly chronological in order and reflect her wide range as a playwright. She first attracted critical attention in 1893 with two plays which are usually, if inadequately, described as belonging to the naturalist school: these are *Wir Drei* and *Dämmerung*. The fact that they were published in Munich and Berlin respectively is a clear indication of her rapid rise to contemporary fame. Both appeared under the pseudonym 'Ernst Rosmer', with its audible echo of Ibsen and indirect allusion to Rebecca West, and they established her (or Rosmer!) as a disciple of Hauptmann of much the same level as Georg Hirschfeld. Unlike Hirschfeld, however, Ernst Rosmer had stamina and went her own way. She became a Fischer author and tried her hand at different kinds of semi-naturalist drama: *Tedeum* (1896) is a 'Gemütskomödie' close in subject and spirit to Hauptmann's *Kollege Crampton* and *Peter Brauer*, while *Johannes Herkner* (1904) is an artist tragedy with affinities to *Michael Kramer*.

Meanwhile *Königskinder* (1894), entitled 'Ein deutsches Märchen', showed her wholeheartedly embracing the possibilities of neo-romanticism, just as Hauptmann was to do in 1896 in *Die versunkene Glocke*. It was followed by a second essay in the neo-romantic symbolist mode, *Mutter Maria*, which appeared in 1900 with the tellingly evocative subtitle 'Ein Totengedicht in fünf Wandlungen'.

During the first decade of the twentieth century, Bernstein changed direction. She began to lay claim to a very different conception of drama which brought her close to the neo-classicism of Hofmannsthal and set free in her a vein of vibrant, colourful poetry; it also revealed a passionate intensity which more realistic works had tended to conceal. This Grecian dimension first emerged in *Themistokles* (1897) and is represented at its best by the verse tragedies *Nausikaa* (1906) and *Achill* (1910). Yet she never ceased to face up to the challenge of realism – a finely-tuned realism that sought to capture every movement of the body and the psyche, every nuance of emotion, each telling gesture and every detail of décor, all imagined with meticulous cinematographic accuracy. Her masterpiece in this vein appeared between the two Greek verse plays: *Maria Arndt* (1908) is a contemporary and indeed intensely personal drama. I would suggest that it is also her most original achievement as a woman writer: a play which calls out for rediscovery and sensitive modern production.

The ten plays that have been mentioned constitute Bernstein's complete published dramatic oeuvre; they are thus her lasting contribution to German drama. But they are not the only plays she wrote. Another nine are known to have existed, but unfortunately they were never published, and it seems highly unlikely that their manuscripts survived the traumatic events which befell her later in her life. Before turning to what happened to Bernstein or attempting a more detailed description of the plays she published, their stage history should be considered, because this is the factor which distinguishes a dramatist's achievement from that of the novelist or poet – the categories to which, it should be remembered, the vast majority of women writers belong. As things stand, we only know the dates of first performances and of one or two other isolated revivals. Much work needs to be done on the repertoires of theatres and stage societies in the German-speaking countries before Bernstein's practical contribution to the German stage can be properly assessed.

It will have become evident that although Bernstein's life was a long one — from 1866 to 1949 — her creative span as a playwright was very much shorter, running from 1893 to 1911. Of the ten plays she published during those eighteen years, a total of seven are actually known to have been performed, which is a remarkably high incidence for a woman author. She made her debut as a writer for the theatre when *Dämmerung* was presented by the Freie Bühne in Berlin on 30 March 1893, the association's only other production that season being Hauptmann's *Die Weber:*[4] the coupling is in itself a token of the high regard in which she was held in some quarters even at the outset of her career. It would be interesting to know how the play fared elsewhere and how long it held the stage. Despite the enthusiasm of Frau Bernstein's admirers, it did not go down well in her home town when it was put on by the Akademisch-dramatischer Verein at the Munich Volkstheater on 9 April 1897 in a production directed by Ernst von Wolzogen.[5] On the other hand, *Dämmerung* seems to be the only Bernstein play to have been translated into English.[6] Whether this translation, which appeared in Boston in 1912, had any impact in the United States or in Britain it is not yet possible to say. In 1895 her lighter naturalist work, the comedy *Tedeum*, was premiered at the Deutsches Theater in Berlin and revived in a revised version by the Burgtheater in Vienna in April 1899. Like *Dämmerung, Mutter Maria* was also premiered by the Freie Bühne: in fact it was its very last production and took place on 19 May 1901. Later it was taken into the repertoire of the Deutsches Theater, which also staged *Johannes Herkner.* Two of Bernstein's finest plays received their premieres in Munich: *Achill* (Hoftheater, 17 March 1911) and *Maria Arndt* (Schauspielhaus, 17 October 1908). But her greatest theatrical success was to be *Königskinder.* Its first performance as a 'melodrama' took place on 23 January 1897 at the Munich Hoftheater, with accompanying music specially written by Engelbert Humperdinck, fresh from his success with *Hänsel und Gretel,* first performed in Weimar in 1893 under Richard Strauss. Its successful run in Munich led to production by some 130 other theatres during the next few years, making it one of the biggest box-office successes of the period. Bernstein's German fairy tale received a new lease of life when it was refashioned as a full-scale opera, again in collaboration with Humperdinck. This operatic version of *Königskinder* captured an international public from the moment it was premiered at the Metropolitan Opera House, New York, on 28 December 1910, with Geraldine Farrar singing the role of the goose-girl, Hermann Jadlowker as the prince and Louise Homer as the witch. Within the next two to three years the opera was staged in Berlin (14 January 1911), Vienna (21 December 1912) and London (Covent Garden, 27 November 1911) as well as Prague, Budapest, Milan, Moscow, Boston and Buenos Aires.[7] The collaboration with Humperdinck was to carry the poetry of Elsa Bernstein and her imaginary fairy-tale world to a wider, more international audience than any German woman dramatist had ever reached.[8] It was the climax as well as the end of her creative career.

Königskinder is a fairy tale for modern folk who no longer believe in happy endings; the golden years could not last, as its author must have sensed. By the mid-1930s the precocious little girl who had been presented to Wagner at the 1876 Bayreuth Festival had begun to fall foul of the race laws introduced by a regime which claimed to champion the German cultural values she stood for. Winifred Wagner, the composer's masterful English daughter-in-law, put in a good word for her, but her efforts to procure a visa for her to leave Germany were of no avail. Because her sister was not to be included and would have to stay behind, Bernstein resolved to stay in Germany and share her fate. It was probably when they expelled her from her home and sent her to the notorious concentration camp of Theresienstadt that her unpublished manuscripts disappeared. Soon her sister was dead. But the pale blonde authoress of *Dämmerung* and *Königskinder* had resilience. Frail and virtually blind, she became a tower of strength and a source of comfort to many of the camp's inmates – and she survived. She died in Hamburg in 1949, aged over eighty. There was a bitter irony in her relationship to the Third Reich. The only work of hers that was officially tolerated during the Nazi period was *Königskinder*, a creation so impeccably and quintessentially German that its actual authorship could be overlooked: ironically the name 'Ernst Rosmer' with its nordic connotations came to her rescue at last. It is more sadly ironic that, like so many other German authors of Jewish extraction who were popular and highly regarded before 1933, Elsa Bernstein has lost out on both counts since 1945: the one work that was tolerated now seemed tainted and out-of-date, while those that were banned have not been reinstated to their proper place in the publishers' lists, let alone the repertoire of German theatres.

Although she survived until 1949, Bernstein published no more plays after the First World War, with the result that she is essentially a playwright of the pre-war period. Writing in 1917, the drama critic Alfred Kerr remarked: 'Sie hat vielleicht Hoffnungen, die man vor einem Jahrzehnt auf sie setzte, nicht erfüllt.'[9] At the time such an observation must have seemed justified, but seen from the perspective of today it is pertinent to ask what these hopes might have been and what was the promise Bernstein fulfilled or failed to fulfil. The unique qualities of her art were already clearly discernible in her first plays, *Wir Drei* and *Dämmerung*, and their quintessence is to be found in her most personal and most 'feminine' work, *Maria Arndt*. Her neo-classical plays, fine though they are, might pass for the work of a man of letters with the sensitivity, poetry and passion of a Hofmannsthal and with his understanding of the female psyche, while the fairy-tale dramas might, on superficial reading, be taken for the work of one or other of her male contemporaries. But *Maria Arndt* and the two earlier semi-naturalist dramas are of quite a different kind. In them she invites us to step through the looking-glass of accepted realism and forget the stereotyped, male-oriented views of how men and women behave as we enter another, stranger, much less familiar dimension of reality: the reality of a world experienced by women and seen by a woman.

In the 1890s *Wir Drei* and *Dämmerung* were measured by Hauptmann's naturalist yardstick and were found wanting despite their obvious merits. Of course resemblances to plays such as *Einsame Menschen* can be detected. The sensitivity and empathy of Hauptmann's treatment of Käthe Vockerat and Anna Mahr was great, but it would be quite mistaken to see Bernstein's *Wir Drei* as a pale imitation of Hauptmann's masterly presentation of a superficially similar threesome of contemporary young people. It would also be quite wrong to imagine that *Dämmerung* has anything in common with *Vor Sonnenaufgang* except for a similar instinctual sense of the dramatic relevance of lighting. The gradations of light – light increasing, fading and passing away

— reflect a dimension of the drama of the 1890s which was a clear response to technical innovations being made in the theatre to exploit the new potential of electricity; but lighting was something which only the greatest and most creative writers could transform into a vital element of drama alongside poetry and movement. In fact if *Dämmerung* bears any deeper similarity to the drama of its day it is to Maeterlinck's *Les Aveugles* (1890) or, more literally and closely, to D'Annunzio's *La Città morta* (1898). Failing eyesight is its theme, a physically induced failure that brings about an increasing sensitivity to sound and touch and, above all, to the motivations concealed in what people say; the words and movements of the central figure, Isolde, and the characters around her seem to be feelers put out as they grope for love and reassurance in a dimly lit world of half-truths and half-held values where nothing categorical can ever be said because truth lies between the lines, in the domain of the unspoken.[10] There are of course traces of trendy Naturalism here: at one notorious point concession is made to the contemporary concern with heredity. Structurally *Dämmerung* clearly owes something to Ibsen's *Ghosts*, of which it is a kind of reverse image, focusing on the relationship of a father and daughter. Such features locate Bernstein's play in time and place. But its dialogue and poetic texture are no more concerned with shedding light on the workings of heredity and disease in accepted naturalist fashion than the author is. Hers is not a play 'about' heredity and the connection between a father's syphilis and his daughter's progressive loss of eyesight: it shuns doctrinaire statement because its aim is to convey a reality that lies beyond such considerations, a reality which requires vision rather than documentation. The world of *Dämmerung* is an intimate one of emotional needs and their subtle effects on human relationships; it is one which thoughtful production could effectively re-create.

Bernstein had already made her artistic intentions clear in *Wir Drei*. In Act 1, one of its three main characters, a young woman writer named Sascha Korff tells her two friends, Agnes and Richard, about her artistic mission. The ensuing dialogue brings one up short. Were these words not being heard the very same year that Edvard Munch painted *The Scream*?

> SASCHA   Man muß aus der wehen Seele des
> unschuldigen Weibes heraus ein Wort finden,
> einen Laut, einen Schrei.

AGNES   Man kann doch einen Schrei nicht schreiben.

SASCHA   Aber man kann ihn fühlen! Und...und...und
         muß dieses − dieses Gefühl so − in die
         literarische Darstellung bringen, daß es auf
         den Leser übergeht.

It would be perverse to claim that the young woman who wrote this exchange was an expressionist writer in the making. Her artistic career was to take her in different directions. Yet the aim outlined by Sascha Korff was one to which Bernstein remained true: hers was the task and the duty to make audible the suppressed cry of so many of her sex. She was surely stating her own artistic creed when she made her first suffering yet ultimately triumphant heroine proclaim: 'Man muß überhaupt viel mehr von seinen Menschen wissen, als man ausspricht.' It is Bernstein's insight into the plight of her characters that enables their cries to be heard.

The sequence of 'realist' dramas Bernstein wrote between 1893 and 1908 show how she set about achieving this objective. *Wir Drei* is hardly 'ein sehr verworrenes, sehr langes und in der vorliegenden Form unspielbares Stück', as Ulrike Zophoniasson-Baierl maintains.[11] It is set in the present, and the action runs from February to September as it traces the breakdown of a young marriage. Sascha had brought her friends Agnes and Richard together: friendship, that favourite theme of the period, unites them, but despite its emotional intensity and exuberance, it leaves the deeper, less conscious depths of their sexuality unfulfilled. Ironically it is just as they begin to realize that this is the case that Agnes finds out she is pregnant. Bernstein was advancing into taboo territory few of her male contemporaries would have dared to tread. But she goes further with a feminine honesty that is astounding even a century later. It is Sascha's account of a poem she has written about a 'schöne Dirne' that acts as the catalyst, not the news of Agnes's pregnancy. The poem arouses Richard and he tries to embrace her: today some would probably even say rape her ('Lassen Sie mich los!' 'Los − versuch's. Ich bin stärker als du!', p. 60). This incident leads immediately to the decisive moment in the play. Oblivious to Agnes's state as she returns from the doctor's surgery, Sascha jubilantly confesses that her husband has declared his love for her and that she let him do so. This remarkable sequence leads to the expected scène-à-faire between the two women and an

Act II dénouement in which it is clearly the characters, not Bernstein herself, who relapse into the stereotyped attitudes their straightforward, honest new generation would expect of them: 'Wir müssen uns scheiden lassen.' One senses that for Bernstein herself this reaction to what has happened is as inadequate and banal as its Victorian middle-class alternative: frankness to the point of gross oversimplification instead of the discreet veil of a respectable lie.

By May, Agnes's pregnancy has become obvious and her position *vis-à-vis* Sascha and Richard is clearer, too: 'Ich will das Weib eines Mannes sein. Nicht seine Geliebte.' Amidst all the intensity Bernstein's brand of humour is also heard, as when Agnes, sewing nappies, laconically observes: 'Kannst du dir die Venus von Milo in andern Umständen vorstellen?' Only now does it strike Sascha that Agnes may have known that she was pregnant before 'it' happened. Of course Agnes did, and of course she sees through Sascha's 'sisterly' kindness: Sascha is only offering to help her because the child she is carrying is *his*. Three times Sascha solemnly swears she does not love him. The only response she gets is Agnes's murmured 'Ich bin sehr traurig'.

The fourth Act, which takes place in August, shows Richard out of his depth as the birth of his child approaches. He faints ludicrously at the onset of her labour, and Bernstein's estimate of her drama's hero is made even plainer when Sascha empties a vase over him to bring him round from his swoon in a reversal of conventional roles. By September (Act V), this jubilantly satirical, almost light-hearted note has given way to a darker mood. All in black, Agnes returns from the graveyard where her baby lies buried, and Richard realizes that she only really became his wife when she gave birth to it. His anguished cry 'mein Weib ist tot' provokes a response in her that promises a happier life together, while Sascha, realizing the impossibility of the eternal triangle she had tried to create, leaves them to get on with their lives. She has chosen her destiny: life on her own.

Written in 1891, *Wir Drei* has clear analogies with Hauptmann's masterly *Einsame Menschen*, which appeared that year, and not only to its disadvantage. While Hauptmann emphasizes the rootedness of his three young people in the social and intellectual climate of their time, Bernstein leaves almost all such circumstantial detail out, because it is irrelevant to her

central purpose, which is to present human relationships and the breakdown
of marriage from the woman's point of view. In Hauptmann's drama, the
independent, intellectual Anna Mahr comes close, if unintentionally, to
becoming the predatory 'other' woman as perceived by Johannes Vockerat,
while Käthe, his wife, surprises us when she reveals that she is not just the
'little' woman her husband always treats her as. But in *Wir Drei* there is no
male centre of gravity to lend ambivalence to the two women characters: the
tragedies of Agnes and Sascha are at once more straightforward and more
subtle because the man in their lives is incapable of comprehending it.
Hauptmann's male sentences himself to suicide, Bernstein's lives happily ever
after.

    Dämmerung, which followed *Wir Drei*, received from Wilhelm Bölsche
the critical appraisal which it deserved. Well aware that Ernst Rosmer was a
woman and that accusations of triviality and superficiality might therefore be
levelled at her by some, Bölsche observed in *Freie Bühne* IV (1893) that
'Jedenfalls ist das Drama "Dämmerung" eine verheißungsvolle Erstlingsarbeit
wie wenige. Es regt durchaus tiefe Gedankenprobleme an. Und es verrät in
jeder Faser den gestaltenden Dichter, der zu Vollendetem reift.' To
discerning critics such as Bölsche, the strengths of her work were evident. His
essay ends with a glowing praise for her handling of dialogue, a new type of
dialogue of an unobtrusively brilliant kind which required a different pace
from that of Ibsen or the mainstream modern German playwrights. Ibsen's
presence may still be felt in Act I, when Sabine Graef, a young eye-specialist
and an early representative in drama of the new, efficient professional woman,
is sent in an emergency to treat the ailing Isolde on behalf of Professor Berger,
her normal consultant. She seizes the opportunity to find out more about the
background to Isolde's complaint; firing direct questions at her astonished
father, the eminent musician Heinrich Ritter, and taking his answers down in
shorthand, she makes her remorseless way to the most leading question of all.
Watching Ritter intently, she comes to the point:

    SABINE   Sie haben nie ein ernsteres körperliches
                Leiden gehabt?
    RITTER   Nein.

SABINE	*sieht in ihr Notizbuch.* Sie heirateten mit – siebenundzwanzig. Sie werden wohl vorher gelebt haben wie alle jungen Leute –
RITTER	*dunkelrot, unterbricht sie heftig.* Bitte mein Fräulein. Ich war fünf Jahre mit meiner Frau verlobt.
SABINE	Eine so lang dauernde Verlobung ist gewöhnlich kein Hindernis.
RITTER	*springt auf.* Hören Sie mal – Sie haben schöne Ansichten.
SABINE	Ich habe keine Ansichten. Nur Erfahrungen.
RITTER	*heftig, jedoch bemüht, sich zu beherrschen.* Sie haben mich zu fragen, was ins ärztliche Gebiet gehört. Aber es gibt Dinge, die man als Geheimnis zu betrachten hat.
SABINE	Es gibt Dinge, denen man das Geheimnis und den Nimbus nehmen muß. Darin liegt ihre Gefahr.
RITTER	Ich sehe gar nicht ein, weshalb das zwischen uns zur Sprache kommen soll. Sinnlos! *Vor ihr stehen bleibend.* Genieren Sie sich denn nicht?
SABINE	Sie verstehen mich nicht oder wollen mich nicht verstehen.
RITTER	*hilflos die Hände zusammenschlagend.* In Kuckucks Namen, ich verstehe Sie nicht.
SABINE	Sie sollen mir sagen, ob die Möglichkeit einer spezifischen Belastung väterlicherseits ausgeschlossen ist –
RITTER	Sie meinen wohl, ich weiß, was spezifische Belastung ist?
SABINE	*schweigt einen Augenblick, dann so gleichmäßig wie alles Vorangegangene.* Lues.
RITTER	*die Hände in den Hosentaschen, sieht sie immer noch verständnislos an. Wiederholt gleichgültig.* Lues – *Langsam den Klang des Wortes sich erinnernd.* Was?? *Fährt empor mit beiden Händen an die Stirne, wütend.* Sind Sie verrückt? *In zorniges Gelächter ausbrechend.* Vielleicht trauen Sie mir noch zu, daß ich silberne Löffel gestohlen habe.
SABINE	*unbeirrt.* Also nein?

RITTER	Lächerlich! Einfach lächerlich! Und Sie mußten wissen, daß man bei einem gebildeten Menschen —
SABINE	*mitleidig lächelnd.* Ach! die gebildeten Menschen —
RITTER	So, und die sittlichen Grundlagen —
SABINES	*Gesicht wird ernst und finster.* Das Schwächste im geistigen und körperlichen Organismus sind die sittlichen Grundlagen, das weiß jeder Arzt.
RITTER	Dann würde ich an Ihrer Stelle voraussetzen, daß ich lüge.
SABINE	*schaut ihn an.* Lügen — Ihr Kind vielleicht blindmachen, das können Sie nicht. Ihre Unkenntnis der Krankheit hat mich irregeführt, darum mußt' ich fragen. Sie haben geantwortet — ich glaube Ihnen.

The pace of this interview is finely gauged, the characterization closely observed; and it is of course a dialogue geared to a specific end and one which was bound to create shock waves in the audience as well as on stage. Bernstein's uncanny ability to generate dialogue out of almost nothing and to incorporate silences and movement into its fabric in such a way that they play an almost more eloquent part than the words themselves in articulating what is on the characters' minds is better exemplified in the following passage from the extended dialogue between father and daughter in Act 5. Some months have now passed, and Isolde has lost her sight despite Sabine's bold last-minute surgical intervention. She is sitting in an armchair painstakingly trying to sort peas, beans and lentils into different containers. But her therapy has also got to take effect at a different level. Self-pity and moral blackmail are never far away:

RITTER	Das ist doch mein einziger Trost, daß ich bei dir bin.
ISOLDE	Das ist recht schön. Du kannst aber doch nicht immer bei mir bleiben.
RITTER	Ich will immer bei dir bleiben.
ISOLDE	Nein, Papa, das wäre sehr unklug von mir. Da hättest du mich bald satt. Das bildet man sich ein am Anfang, daß es mit dem Mitleid immer fortgeht. Das ist gar nicht möglich. Eines

> Tages wirst du gewöhnt sein, daß ich — daß
> ich — nicht sehe und an dem Tage werde ich
> dir über sein.
>
> RITTER   *wendet sich mit einer verzweifelten Gebärde von*
>   *ihr.*
>
> ISOLDE   *auf eine Antwort wartend.* Nun?
>
> RITTER   Was?
>
> ISOLDE   Ich habe gemeint, du sagest mir was.
>
> RITTER   *schweigt.*

Dialogues of this kind, with their tentative verbal gestures and sudden accelerations, abound in a play which is essentially a conversation piece that generates a maximum of tension from a minimum of action. But Bernstein's conception of drama requires a further visual dimension to complement the audibly articulated words and the movements and gestures that accompany them. This dimension is provided by lighting, a key aspect of her style which Otto Brahm must have relished. Each Act is introduced by stage directions which give a clear indication of the degree of light required, rather as key signatures are given to the movements of a musical work. These introductory markings indicate the tonality or mood of the ensuing sequence or scene, and any departure from it is achieved by subtle modulations of lighting that are part of the organic development of the whole act.

A close examination of the stage directions soon makes the structural importance of lighting evident. As Act I opens, Isolde is suffering from acute eye-strain, which bodes ill for the future: the stage directions unobtrusively underline the situation: 'Die Glastüre ist zugelehnt. Auf den Scheiben ein wenig rotes Abendlicht, rasch verschwindend', and draw attention to 'eine Hängelampe mit verstellbarem grünem Schirm'. Act II takes place while there is something of a remission in Isolde's condition, and the luminosity of the setting conveys this optimism: it is a 'heller Sommertag'. Act III follows Isolde's apparently successful eye operation and opens with the possibility of love between her widowed father and her saviour, Sabine Graef. But this happy prospect is as fleeting as the sunlight, and the obstacle to it none the less great for being as yet unknown: 'Die Vorhänge sind ganz herunter-gelassen. Ein paar Sonnenstreichen auf den Fußboden', reads the stage

direction, subtly suggesting intangible barriers. Act IV brings change: it is a
'grauer Herbsttag' during which Isolde becomes aware that her father is
drawn to Sabine and that there is a real danger that he may abandon her in
her hour of need. The last Act sees father and daughter resigned to coping
with their new situation, and the stage direction 'heller Herbsttag' reinforces
its almost hopeless pathos; as the Act proceeds, the sunlight gradually fades in
counterpoint to the last exchanges in the play:

> *Es dunkelt immer mehr*
>
> ISOLDE   Nun hat's mich müde gemacht − im Garten.
>   Es ist wohl schon zum Abend?
>
> RITTER   Ja. Es ist spät.
>
> ISOLDE   Ist die Sonne noch da?
>
> RITTER   Nein. Die Sonne ist fort.
>
> ISOLDE   Komm' zu mir, Papa. Also finster. Früher
>   hab' ich mich gefürchtet im Finstern und jetzt
>   gar nicht mehr. Weil ich immer drin bin.
>   Kommt heute Mond?
>
> RITTER   Vollmond. Da drüben − grad' steigt er über
>   die Bäume − schau nur − *sich besinnend* Ja
>   so.
>
> ISOLDE   Papa, wenn du mir davon erzählst, seh' ich's
>   inwendig. Ich bin gar nicht blind, ich sehe es
>   in mir. Ganz prächtig. Nur daß es schwarz ist.
>   Es ist gar nicht so schlimm... Man kann auch
>   im Dunkeln leben.
>
> RITTER   *hat sie an seine Brust gezogen.* Ja mein Kind −
>   man kann auch im Dunkeln leben. *Sie stehen
>   fest umschlungen. Das helle Mondlicht fällt
>   über sie.*

There is in all drama of the naturalist kind a tendency to gloom and
doom. Bernstein knew this and turned to the classical mode during the first
decade of the century, eager to embrace sunnier climes and the possibilities of
a type of drama more radiant and more serene. Because such plays are not
rooted in the problems and anxieties of the contemporary present, they may
seem escapist; but in Bernstein's case it is an escape into a more positive view
of life which is very different from the escapism of *Königskinder* and *Mutter
Maria*, where the thwarted emotions and blighted hopes of her realistic plays
are rendered bearable by the make-believe subject-matter and setting. In fact

Bernstein tells us more about herself in the classical plays than in the realistic ones. This is especially true of *Nausikaa* (1906), which uses an episode from Greek mythology to present the awakening of a girl to life and love and thus to self-discovery. There are moments in it when her own experience of adolescence and motherhood can express itself more directly than was possible even in *Maria Arndt*. In Act 2, Queen Arete, young Nausikaa's mother, tries to give her daughter good advice after she has first set eyes on the wandering Odysseus. Her antiquated advice suits the chiselled lines in which it is formulated:

> Dem Mann ward Freiheit, das Gesetz dem Weib.
> Und glücklich ist es nur in seiner Hut.
> Des Mädchens Unerfahrung kann nicht wählen. (p. 68)

She amplifies her viewpoint by restating Sascha's and no doubt Bernstein's trust in feminine intuition:

> Nicht vieles Wissen wird dem Weib gegönnt.
> Doch Ahnung ward ihm, unbeweisbar tief,
> Wie Opferdeutung und wie Vogelschau.
> Mir offenbart in jedem Angesicht,
> Mehr als in lauter Rede, lautem Ton,
> Des Menschen Seele ihr Verborgenstes. (p. 70)

There are echoes of Grillparzer as Arete bids her daughter goodnight, and takes the lamp with her, leaving Nausikaa literally and figuratively in the dark. But the room is inundated with moonlight as the girl awakens to her destiny. Her mother had told her:

> Ich wählte nicht, dein Vater wählte mich.
> Gesenkten Hauptes stand ich stumm vor ihm. (p. 69)

But Nausikaa expresses a modern outlook as she comes to herself and realizes that her mother's conception of the role of woman is not for her:

> ich bin Nausikaa,
> Und will nicht das Geschick der Tausende,
> Ich will ein einzig Schicksal!

She cuts her hair and burns her doll, and as she performs these symbolical acts she invokes the goddess in classical metre:

> Lass mich erfüllen mein Los nicht dumpf nur in stummem Gewähren,
> Lass mich im jauchzenden Arm halten den mächtigen Mann! (p. 74)

The role of mute subservience is rejected. A woman, too, has the right to be herself, to choose, and to seek self-fulfilment. But the way towards that goal cannot be easy or straightforward: Odysseus, too, must prove his own identity in his own masculine way before he can return victorious to claim Nausikaa. His exuberant words contain the quintessence of Frau Bernstein's wisdom: men, too, must be ready to respect women and to make concessions if women are to be truly free:

> Dich nur begehre ich noch – dich nur, du selige Angst –
> Nenne mich, wie du mich ahnst, wie du ihn möchtest, den Mann!
>
> (p. 109)

The promise of *Wir Drei* and *Dämmerung* and the originality of *Nausikaa* were to be surpassed in 1908 with the appearance of *Maria Arndt*. Set 'zu Beginn des 20. Jahrhunderts', it deserves to be recognized as one of the first great German plays of the twentieth century, a masterpiece to set beside Schnitzler's *Der einsame Weg* (1904) and *Das weite Land* (1912). *Maria Arndt* – its action classically contained within the setting of an 'älteres Landhaus, die Rosenau genannt, im Villenviertel einer süddeutschen Universitätsstadt' – towers above most of the German drama of its time not only because of the excellence of its finely articulated, hypersensitive dialogue and inexorably tragic structure: Greek tragedy in Edwardian dress. Bernstein's true success here is that she achieves convincing artistic expression for the experience of many women of her generation. Maria Arndt, sensitive, warm and so intent on being a sensible, enlightened mother to her teenage daughter, Gemma, finds herself tragically unable either to live the lie of her own loveless marriage or to reject convention and her own moral standards by accepting the truth and coming out into the open. Anxious that her daughter shall not suffer and hopeful that hers will be a happier life in the new twentieth century, Maria renounces the promise of happiness and fulfilment with the man she loves, and sacrifices herself for her daughter's sake – a gradual, slowly shaping 'decision' that is quite beyond rational thought and whose contours slowly appear during the course of the play as its ostensibly light, untroubled dialogue reveals more and more of the tensions and heartache lurking unuttered between the lines. Here consummate dramatic writing is at one with women's experience and generates a kind of suspense of its own, essentially different from that of other superficially similar plays.

Why has this remarkable woman dramatist sunk without trace? With so many fine plays to her credit, Ernst Rosmer's once familiar name should have been replaced by Elsa Bernstein's; yet instead both names have disappeared from catalogues of books in print and the indexes of most histories of German literature.[12] Bernstein is no longer performed: but why are there no revivals of her plays? The example of Githa Sowerby, her English counterpart as well as contemporary, provides an interesting parallel and contrast.[13] Prior to 1914, discriminating critics in Germany regarded Ernst Rosmer, alias Elsa Bernstein, as second only to Gerhart Hauptmann as an exponent both of realistic psychological drama and neo-romantic fairy tale, and the public tended to agree when given the opportunity. Is what has happened to Elsa Bernstein a matter of genuine aesthetic judgement? Or is it a glaring instance of prejudice in a literary culture that still tends to view women writers as second-rate and which regards women dramatists with deep suspicion because it is assumed that women cannot write plays? Or could it be that one tenacious prejudice is exacerbated by another which is even more deplorable? She was a Jew by race if not religion, and suffered under the Nazi dictatorship.[14] Is it just an unfortunate oversight that this is not mentioned in the main current handbook on German women writers, the *Lexikon deutschsprachiger Schriftstellerinnen 1800-1945* published by Deutscher Taschenbuch Verlag in 1986?

NOTES

[1]The reproach 'wie kann eine Dame so etwas schreiben?' was often heard in connection with both *Dämmerung* and *Königskinder*. See Ella Mensch, *Die Frau in der modernen Literatur. Ein Beitrag zur Geschichte der Gefühle* (Berlin: Carl Duncker, 1898), p. 96.

[2]Rilke lodged in the same street when he first came to Munich in 1897 and saw the Bernsteins regularly. He may well have known her work before then: *Im Frühfrost*, the drama in naturalist vein he wrote in 1895, is subtitled 'Ein Stück Dämmerung', which may well be an allusion to her play *Dämmerung*.

[3]Fortunately we do now have a critical monograph: Ulrike Zophoniasson-Baierl, *Elsa Bernstein alias Enst Rosmer: eine deutsche Dramatikerin im Spannungsfeld der literarischen Strömungen des Wilhelminischen Zeitalters*, EH, Reihe 1, vol. 903 (Bern: Lang, 1985).

[4]A list of plays presented by the Freie Bühne is given in John Osborne, *The Naturalist Drama in Germany* (Manchester: University Press, 1971), p. 173.

[5]See Rainer Hartl, *Aufbruch der Moderne: Naturalistisches Theater in München* (Munich: Kitzinger, 1976), p. 81.

[6]*Twilight*, an English translation of *Dämmerung* by Paul H. Grummann, was published in *Poet Lore*, xxiii, no. 6, pp. 369-443, in 1912/13 and in book form (Boston: R.G. Badger) in 1912.

[7]See Alfred Loewenberg, *Annals of Opera*, second edition (Geneva: Societas Bibliographica, 1955), cols 1304-1305, and Gerald Fitzgerald, *Annals of the Metropolitan Opera Company 1883-1985* (New York: Metropolitan Opera Guild, 1990), p. 199.

[8]A production of *Königskinder* by David Pountney for the English National Opera opened at the London Coliseum on January 30, 1992. See Peter Skrine, 'Elsa Bernstein and *Königskinder*' in *Königskinder or The Prince and the Goosegirl* (ENO programme, 1992).

[9]Alfred Kerr, *Das neue Drama* (Berlin: Fischer, 1917), vol. I, pp. 315-18; here p. 315.

[10]See May Daniels, *The French Drama of the Unspoken* (Edinburgh: University Press), 1953.

[11]Zophoniasson-Baierl, p. 41.

[12]For instance one might expect to find the name Bernstein in the *Personenregister* of *Deutsche Literatur von Frauen*, ed. by Gisela Brinker-Gabler (Munich: Beck, 1988); in fact she is not even mentioned in the section 'Frauen erobern die Bühne: Dramatikerinnen im 20. Jahrhundert' by Erika Vischer-Lichte, pp. 379-93.

[13]Katherine Githa Sowerby's *Rutherford and Son* (1912), a stark dramatization of the plight of a middle-class spinster daughter, was toured in 1980 by Monstrous Regiment and revived by the Stephen Joseph Theatre in Scarborough in 1991. It is now available in *New Woman Plays*, ed. Linda Fitzsimmon and Viv Gardner (London: Methuen, 1991). At the

time of its first production Sowerby was hailed as the world's first female dramatist of distinction. She died in 1970.

[14]The case of Elsa Bernstein adds a significant further dimension to the various kinds of suppression listed in Joanna Russ, *How to Suppress Women's Writing* (Austin: University of Texas Press, 1983 and London: The Women's Press, 1984).

Bibliography of Principal Published Works

Wir Drei (Munich: E. Albert, 1891 [?] and 1893)
Dämmerung (Berlin: Fischer, 1894)
Königskinder (Berlin: Fischer, 1894)
Tedeum (Berlin: Fischer, 1896)
Themistokles (Berlin: Fischer, 1897)
Mutter Maria (Berlin: Fischer, 1900)
Johannes Herkner (Berlin: Fischer, 1904)
Nausikaa (Berlin: Fischer, 1906)
Maria Arndt (Berlin: Fischer, 1908)
Achill (Berlin: Fischer, 1910)
Schicksal (Berlin: privately printed, 1919)
Erlebnis [a *Novelle*] (Munich: Südwestdeutsche Monatshefte, 1928-29)

Reprints:

Dämmerung has been reprinted in *Dramen des deutschen Naturalismus*, ed. by
    Roy C. Cowen (Munich: Winckler, 1981), Vol. 1.

English translations:

Twilight, trans. by Paul H. Grummann (Boston: R.G. Badger, 1912); this
    translation was reprinted in *Poet Lore*, 23, no. 5 (Boston, 1912).
Johann Herkner, trans. by Mary Harned, in *Poet Lore*, 22, no. 5 (Boston, 1911).

Hedwig Landauer-Lachmann

4

Hedwig Lachmann (1865/68-1918)

Brian Coghlan

In setting about the salvaging from near-oblivion of Hedwig Lachmann I am reminded of a nice moment in Neville Cardus's *Autobiography* (London, 1947). He quotes his much younger self reviewing Admiral Sir Percy Scott's *Reminiscences* and in particular Sir Percy's claim that he was the pioneer of the system of director firing. 'His explanation', writes Cardus,

> ...is technical, and a layman cannot pretend to express an opinion on it. But the principle at bottom – which is that you are more likely to hit an object if you know where it is – must be acclaimed a sound one.
>
> (p. 119)

It is fairly clear who Hedwig Lachmann was, where she was some of the time, and the sort of thing she wrote. But it is not easy to establish a firm, clear picture. Why worry? one might well ask, when she is seemingly one of a vast host of sometime minor celebrities who have fallen from historical view, however worthy they may have been.

Hedwig Lachmann, though, is not quite in this category. She appears, if fleetingly or unclearly, at a number of intriguing points, and a few questions are justified. For instance, it was Hedwig Lachmann's translation of Oscar Wilde's *Salome* that Richard Strauss used for his sensational music-drama (1905) which was one of the greatest and – literally – most sensational or scandalous successes in even his controversy-strewn career. As we shall see,

Lachmann's translation was evidently not just any old goodish, workmanlike version which happened to be there, only needing a bit of expert amendment and arranging.   It already had a distinguished history of performance. Secondly: Hedwig Lachmann was the second wife of Gustav Landauer (1870-1919).   Landauer was a man of letters, novelist, socialist of a very individual kind, political jailbird, utopian anarchist, member of the Bavarian revolutionary government in 1919, vilified, tortured and murdered when Munich was (re-)occupied by the *Reaktion* in May 1919. The marriage seems to have been particularly good.   The Landauers, moreover, had some interesting and, possibly, surprising friends. That notorious extremist, utopian socialist and revolutionary Hugo von Hofmannsthal was one.[1]   Thirdly: Hedwig Lachmann not only translated Wilde's *Salome* and some of his poetry and essays.   She also wrote a full-length biography and critical study of him which appeared as early as 1905. I say 'early' for a specific reason. Wilde had died in 1900.   His name, fame and value were, in Anglo-American circles at least, what might be called unfashionable. Lachmann's study is remarkably – but not uncritically – sympathetic, sensitive and positive.   And, important perhaps in this context: Hedwig Lachmann was a woman, and this was not at all how our wives and servants were expected to behave. Her book appeared in the same year (1905) as Hofmannsthal's well-known essay on Wilde, 'Sebastian Melmoth'.[2]

These few selective facts, this contiguity, may constitute a *prima facie* case, at least, for considering the re-classification of Hedwig Lachmann: one can hardly say 'restoration' or 'rescue' or 'rehabilitation' because she never had a great name anyway. Perhaps, though, like but infinitely less than Franz Kafka, she was obscured, almost lost or arbitrarily 'forgotten' during the Nazi period.   Perhaps our present enterprise resembles the work of those 'Kunstrestauratoren' who take some interesting-looking but hopelessly blurred icon/holy picture in an otherwise unremarkable church, and then try to restore – even 'retuschieren' – it to see what it looked like in the first place. Very occasionally you might turn up a Grünewald. It's unlikely but worth the try.

Hedwig Lachmann was born in either 1865 or 1868. Possibly the discrepancy constitutes no great matter. But it seems to set the tone for the odd obscurity of a life which must have seemed public enough, for a while at least. At all events, of four modern bibliographical reference-works, two give 1865, one gives 1868, one gives 1865 or 1868. A fifth and very recent source (1990) gives, unequivocally, 21 August 1865, Stolp/Pomerania, as date and place of birth.[3]

Hedwig Lachmann's immediate environment was cultivated and relatively comfortable. Her early world was the sequestered realm of Jewish orthodoxy, specifically that of the 'Ostjude'. Her father was a member of an established 'Gelehrtenfamilie' in Dubno, south-west Russia. He had fled westward, doubtless as a result of an anti-Semitic riot or pogrom: following Alexander II's great social reforms, characterized by the liberation of the serfs (1861), there was much unrest, opposition, violence, and the Polish uprising of 1863. Thus the family found itself in Pomerania where Hedwig's father Isaak (1838-1900) was appointed cantor and catechist, or teacher of religious orthodoxy, in the local Jewish community. The familiar process of westernization proceeded apace. While Hedwig Lachmann was still a child the family moved to Lauenburg on the Elbe between Schleswig-Holstein and Mecklenburg: the town and dukedom became part of Schleswig-Holstein in 1876. Subsequently the family moved to Hürben near Krumbach, south-west of Augsburg where Isaak had been appointed cantor.

Whatever eastern orthodoxy Hedwig Lachmann may have absorbed as a child, its influence seems to have stopped here. She attended the convent school of the 'Englische Fräulein' in Augsburg. Once can reasonably assume that her parents were remarkably liberal-minded, or realistic, or both. At all events, the confluence of eastern Jewish orthodoxy from the Pale of Settlement with western Christian – and very middle-class – culture was perhaps bound to produce an interesting fusion. As it happened, Hedwig Lachmann seems to have been highly intelligent and linguistically precocious. At fifteen she gained substantial qualifications as a language teacher. In 1882, seventeen years old, she took up a teaching post in England. This was followed by comparable posts in Dresden and Budapest. One senses independence, individuality, self-emancipation, one of Ibsen's 'new women' like Rebecca West (1886) and Hilde Wangel (1892).

It was obviously a drive for personal independence which took Hedwig Lachmann to Berlin in 1889 where, determinedly if reluctantly, she continued to work as a teacher. It was a good time to go to Berlin. 1889 was characterized by unrest and change to an extent which was unusual, perhaps, even in an epoch which was marked by social, political and cultural turbulence. In 1889 Germany in general and Berlin in particular had seen three emperors within less than two years. 1889 also saw the scandalous *première* at the Lessing-Theater of Gerhart Hauptmann's *Vor Sonnenaufgang*, which for many lively spirits and forward-looking thinkers marked the beginning of a new age. Nothing, at any rate, was ever quite the same in the theatre thereafter. 1889 was the last year of Bismarck's era (1862-1890) and was marked by the tensions and stresses between old Chancellor and brash young Emperor which led to the dropping of the pilot a year later. This year, by the way, also saw one of the last great achievements of Bismarck's 'state socialism', the introduction of old-age pensions.

It was thus in many ways a most interesting time for a young, independent woman to come to Wilhelm II's, Gerhart Hauptmann's and Fontane's Berlin. Hedwig Lachmann soon found her way to the circle around Paula and Richard Dehmel and to the Dehmels direct. Dehmel (1863-1920) was at this point only at the beginning of his rapid rise to considerable, if relatively short-lived, fame and artistic notoriety. At first sight it certainly seems an odd constellation: Dehmel with his fervours and ecstasies, priapic masculinity, mystic eroticism, and later, his wildly enthusiastic patriotism, was a very long way, one might think, from everything represented by Gustav Landauer, whom Hedwig Lachmann met some years later. Dehmel seemed to be several dimensions removed from Hedwig Lachmann's emotional world, or at least as much of it as she allowed to disturb the surface presented to the world outside; as far as can be gathered, she personified that almost untranslatable phrase: 'sie tritt hinter sich zurück'; she disappeared behind her own work. The only recent book of any substance which devotes any space at all to her describes her as 'ganz in sich zurückgezogen'.[4]

However, Dehmel was not straightforwardly one-sided either. One recalls his significant and beautifully productive influence on the young Arnold Schönberg in Schönberg's delicately Wagnerian *Verklärte Nacht* (1899), which was based on the poem placed by Dehmel as a kind of foreword or preface to his novel *Zwei Menschen*. And there was another side to Dehmel, that of the 'social' poet: 'Der Arbeitsmann' (1896) — 'Vierter Klasse', 'Traum eines Armen'... This aspect is well depicted in Anetsberger's well-known drawing in *Simplizissimus* (I, 1896). It is simple, direct, heartfelt; Dehmel achieves here his own personal tone:

> Wir haben ein Bett, wir haben ein Kind,
> mein Weib!
> Wir haben auch Arbeit, und gar zu zweit,
> und haben die Sonne und Regen und Wind.

As we shall see, Lachmann's own verse has a warmth of feeling, a preference for concrete — even picturesque — imagery, a tone of voice which recalls Dehmel in his quieter mood. Perhaps it would be fair to say that it recalls his 'social' voice.

This excursus via Dehmel comes about here only because each of the — admittedly very few — commentators on Hedwig Lachmann's developing career draws particular attention to the connection with Richard and Paula Dehmel. Ulrich Karthaus, in the recent Reclam edition of Oscar Wilde/Hedwig Lachmann, *Salome*, is typical. Karthaus, indeed, asserts that Lachmann was stirred to 'eigene poetische Produktion' directly through this contact.[5] From about 1891, at any rate, Hedwig Lachmann was a contributor to various journals. But her early and, such as it was, lasting fame was based, from the start, largely on translation. A volume of Hungarian poetry was followed very soon by *Gedichte E.A. Poes*. This was complemented by translations of Dante Gabriel Rossetti, Swinburne and Verlaine. One senses the direction of her taste and preference.

Hedwig Lachmann met Gustav Landauer in 1899. It was the decisive *rencontre* of her life. What developed was a great and abiding love-affair. It seems to have been a relationship and then, after a few years, a marriage with neither cloud nor blemish. In 1901-2 Lachmann and Landauer had a lengthy stay in England, in Bromley, where friendship with (Prince) Peter Kropotkin seems to have been, for Landauer at least, a decisive experience. At this point the temptation to turn aside into an excursus on Landauer is considerable. His life and career were brilliant, exciting, characterized by extremes, frustrating and unpredictable, and finally, in the literal sense of the word, tragic. He came from a comfortable middle-class background; his father was a successful merchant in Karlsruhe. He studied *Germanistik* and Philosophy in Zurich and Heidelberg, settled in Berlin, was in regular conflict with 'the authorities' and served many months in prison. A later attempt, in Freiburg, to study medicine, was abandoned. By 1896 he was in London at the International Socialist Congress. He was a classic case of the generation conflict: what part his well-heeled family circumstances played, what part the social façades and hypocrisies, the political dishonesties and strains of the mid-to-late Bismarck era played in his development and responses is hard to say. Surprisingly, perhaps, Landauer was not a political activist in the sense that he joined no party; hence, probably, his enthusiasm for Kropotkin. Peter Kropotkin was a Russian aristocrat, geographer and highly placed public servant with great experience in the outer reaches of the Czarist Empire, in eastern Siberia and Manchuria, for example. He was already of mature years – thirty – when in 1872 he joined the International Working Men's Association in Switzerland. He sided with Michael Bakunin against Marx. He served several prison terms, in both Russia and France, for his 'revolutionary' activities. Like Marx and Metternich and Napoleon III, Kropotkin took refuge in England where he lived for more than thirty years before returning to Russia after the February Revolution in 1917. His fame is based largely on his development of 'Communist Anarchism', by which he understood 'mutual aid' as the superior form, a kind of sublimation, of Darwin's 'survival of the fittest' through struggle, devil take the hindmost, etc. Kropotkin rejected the power of the state absolutely. Indeed, he called for the abolition of the state and of private property. His was, I suppose, yet another utopian, millenarian story: perhaps it is reasonable to say that he was the alpha for Landauer's omega. He was of course nearly thirty years – 1842 *vis-à-vis* 1870 – Landauer's senior. He brought name and reputation, experience in the wider world – Goethe's 'große Welt'; his influence on Gustav Landauer was undeniably great. Despite Landauer's ultimately ineffectual career and awful end – the two are linked – one has to believe that Kropotkin's influence was beneficent.

Landauer established the 'Sozialistischer Bund' in Berlin (1908). It is interesting that among its first members were Erich Mühsam and Martin

Buber.[6]   Landauer's friendship and correspondence with Hofmannsthal somewhat antedate this (1905-7). It is clear, though the details are intriguingly obscure, that Hofmannsthal was well acquainted with and had friendly feelings towards Hedwig Lachmann which had originated some time before the correspondence begins.

Landauer, however, − and this is possibly some sort of commentary on the times − never really had a proper job. He was without a doubt immensely talented and energetic: novelist, celebrated lecturer, contributor to various journals, bookseller's assistant, would-be publisher − he hoped to publish *inter alia* Hofmannsthal and Rudolf Borchardt... But his actual earnings were not enough to support his family. He and Hedwig Lachmann had married in 1903; there were two daughters.[7]   Lachmann was evidently the financial mainstay. Towards the end of the war (1917), when the Allied blockade was biting hard and there was great hunger throughout Germany, the family retired to the country.   They left Hermsdorf (Mark Brandenburg), near Berlin, where they had lived for many years, and settled in Hedwig Lachmann's old adopted hometown, Krumbach in Swabia, where she died suddenly early in 1918 (21 February).[8] Later the same year Landauer himself was invited to become *Dramaturg* at the city theatre in Düsseldorf. This was some measure of his repute; his lectures on Shakespeare, for example, were legendary. But he never really 'took to' the job in any consequential sense. He did edit and contribute to *Masken*, the theatre's house journal, but only briefly.

His time was nearly up. It ended horribly. In November 1918 Gustav Landauer accepted Kurt Eisner's invitation to join him in Munich, as a member of the 'workers' council' in the (Bavarian) Provisional National Assembly. It is easy to be wise so long after the event. Omniscient as one is now, it is clear that Landauer was drawing up his own death-warrant with every day he stayed/survived in Munich. He belonged to no party and therefore had no power base. He was neither a 'Münchner' nor a native Bavarian. These things count now and counted then. And he was a Jew. Whether this was a vital factor in the particularly vicious horror of his death is impossible to say. But it seems very likely.

Kurt Eisner was murdered on 21 February 1919. Landauer must have been more isolated than ever. Typically, however, he plunged in even more deeply: 'Mut', as they say, 'hatte er.' The 'Räterepublik' was proclaimed on 7 April. The 'legitimate' majority socialist government of Johannes Hoffmann, Eisner's Social Democratic successor, withdrew to Bamberg. During the short chaotic reign of the 'Räterepublik' Gustav Landauer was a kind of Minister of Education. His actual title was 'Provisorischer Volksbeauftrager für Volksaufklärung'. It must have seemed a long, bitter way from gentlemanly correspondence with Hugo von Hofmannsthal, idyllic evenings in Kent with Prince Kropotkin, and the domestic idyll with Hedwig Lachmann in rural Swabia.

Accounts of his death diverge. Certainly he was apprehended in the home of Eisner's widow.[9] Certainly he was tortured and murdered: whether by professional soldiers of the *Reichswehr* responding to the returning government's request or by the usual *Freikorps* thugs of the Arco-Valley variety[10] is really immaterial. The difference in this case was as academic as that between the *SS* and the *Waffen-SS* (*real* soldiers, as one has been assured so often) twenty years or so later. Equally it hardly matters whether he was killed in a lorry on the way from Starnberg to Stadelheim Gaol or whether he had the luxury of waiting until he got there. He was dead, nastily and very painfully: one of the most original, vital, engaged − if sometimes mercurial and nearly always unpractical − spirits which preceded the war and were, the majority of them, in one way or another, lost in it.

All this seems remote from Hedwig Lachmann. When Landauer was mutilated and murdered she had been dead for fourteen months.[11] And yet: in all the tumult and tragedy of 1918/19 Gustav Landauer found time to edit and publish Hedwig Lachmann's *Gesammelte Gedichte. Eigenes und Nachdichtungen* (Potsdam, 1919). Would he himself have left Krumbach to plunge into revolutionary politics had she lived? Was it despair, distraction, 'blow wind, come wrack...', escape, contented domestic passion on the public rebound? Again one can only hazard a cautious guess. Certainly their life together, nearly twenty years of it, seems to contradict the Byronic dictum: while her love for him was indeed and manifestly her whole existence, his erratic and ultimately disastrous actions after her death indicate that his love for her was, at the very least, not 'a thing apart'.

The marriage, wrote Julius Bab in his study: *Richard Dehmel* (Berlin, 1926), was 'von denkbar tiefster, fruchtbarster Harmonie'. Renate Heuer tells how, describing a long period of 'writer's block' after Hedwig Lachmann's death, Landauer related that everything he wrote was addressed 'to Hedwig'. His love-letters to her have been described as the most beautiful in German literature.[12] There is of course no easy way of determining the degree of truth in this statement. More important is the fact that those who knew Hedwig Lachmann and Gustav Landauer felt their mutual love to be something as lasting and permanent as it was unusual and even unique.

Hedwig Lachmann, as was noted earlier, was a person of strong individuality and unequivocal emancipationist tendency. It is all the more impressive – dare one, in a resolutely post-modern, unsentimental age, say touching? – that she found in Gustav Landauer total personal and artistic fulfilment. 'Ganz in sich zurückgezogen', writes Gisela Brinker-Gabler, 'legt die zu Unrecht vergessene Hedwig Lachmann [...] Zeugnis ab von ihrem nach Jahren des Wartens und Zweifels errungenen Eheglück.' Many of the translations published after she married Gustav Landauer (1903) were done in collaboration with him. Her self-abnegation, though, says nothing about her talent or the talent which others perceived in her. She was clearly a woman of many parts. But access to her work is difficult. As far as can be established, nothing is in print with the continuing exception of her *Salome* translation which was taken over by Richard Strauss, and the occasional poem quoted in the routine studies of 'women writers'. From what can be pieced together, though, certain basic qualities are fairly clear. Perhaps two stand out: the linguistic and historical range of her literary involvement and its wide thematic range, and, secondly, her precise, concrete style or form of expression. It might be trite or obvious to say that this latter was a typically feminine, practical quality. At all events: the quality itself is undeniable:

> Aus deiner Liebe kommt mir solch ein Segen,
> Sie macht mein Herz so sorglos und so fest,
> Ich kann so ruhig mich drin niederlegen,
> Wie sich ein Kind dem Schlafe überläßt.
> ('Für meinen Liebsten', April 1903)

Nevertheless, Hedwig Lachmann's feminine individuality seems to have been rather hard to take even for some of her undoubted admirers. In his once celebrated, pioneering anthology of modern German poetry (1904), Hans Benzmann singles out Hedwig Lachmann as one who 'an Selbständigkeit des Denkens und künstlerischen Empfindens vielleicht alle anderen übertrifft'.[13] From the context it is clear that this superlative is restricted to Lachmann's absolute quality measured against that of other *women* writers. Even so, it is a significant tribute, not least when one notes that Benzmann's anthology includes, by way of comparative example, Ricarda Huch, Else Lasker-Schüler, Agnes Miegel and Lulu von Strauss und Torney. But Benzmann adds thoughtfully:

> Freilich ihre grüblerische paradoxe Natur läßt sie kaum
> zu   künstlerischer   Klarheit   und   poetisch   reinen
> Stimmungen gelangen.
>
>   (p. 72)

He then proceeds, with relief, or so one feels, to take refuge in Hedwig Lachmann's quality and reputation as translator or, he adds graciously, 'Nachdichterin'.

Lachmann's imagery and moods – *Stimmungen* – are *pace* Bergmann notably expressive: the pictures perceived in the outer world seem to be the exact 'objective correlative' of her inner vision or ideal/longing:

> Ein Hügel und darauf ein großer Strauß
> von jungen Eichen überm Ackerland.
> Und im Gebüsch versteckt ein kleines Haus –
> Was ist daran, das dir den Blick so bannt?

It is an ideal of life *à deux*, such as Hofmannsthal, speaking through seventeen-year-old Octavian, puts like this in a famous passage at the end of *Der Rosenkavalier* (1910):

> War ein Haus wo, da warst du drein,
> Und die Leut schickten mich hinein,
> mich gradaus in die Seligkeit!
> Die waren gscheit!

But Hedwig Lachmann's little poem is also a map of life with its bumps, and warts and all:

> Und drüber her das wechselvolle Spiel
> vom Lichte der Sonne vor dem Untergang –

> Was hält dich daran fest? Ein Wunsch, ein Ziel,
> ein Fernhintrieb, dein stiller Heimatshang?

Imagery, rhythm, the actual language 'gesture', anticipate the organic union of symbol with life experience in – say – the much younger/later and better remembered Hans Carossa:

> Zwar kann es einmal sein, wenn du schon mitten
> Im Traume bist, daß Unruh geht ums Haus.
> Der Kies beim Brunnen knirscht von harten Tritten,
> Das helle Plätschern setzt auf einmal aus,
> Und du erwachst – dann mußt du nicht erschrecken!
> Die Sterne ziehn vollzählig überm Land,
> Und nur ein Wandrer trat ans Marmorbecken,
> Der schöpft vom Brunnen mit der hohlen Hand.

Carossa, it could be said, is actually a little complacent, however beautifully consoling and secure:

> Er geht gleich weiter, und es rauscht wie immer.
> O freue dich, du bleibst nicht einsam hier.
> Viel Wandrer gehen fern im Sternenschimmer,
> Und mancher noch ist auf dem Weg zu dir.

Hedwig Lachmann questions her image rather more searchingly. Her inner world has little of Carossa's 'heiler Welt'; it is darker, even threatening:

> Was kommt dich an, wenn plötzlich sich im Raum
> der Abriß einer Welt vor dir erhebt?
> Was ist die Kraft des Bildes, das wie Traum
> und Ahnung sich mit deinem Sinn verwebt?

Lachmann is no Hofmannsthal. Nevertheless, in 'Landschaft', for example, she expresses polarities of experience – security *contra* 'Gefährdetsein' – in nature imagery of solid simplicity which recalls, even though at some qualitative distance, the sharp-edged clarity of 'Manche freilich':

> Die hohen, dichtgedrängten Wälder thronen
> auf Hügeln sanft gewölbt und abgedacht –
> In Heimatschwermut rauschen ihre Kronen.
>
> Sie sind erfüllt von Flucht und Wetterweben
> der zündenden Gewölke, die bei Nacht
> mit schwerem Flügelschlage drüber schweben.
>
> Zu ihren Füßen, wo die breiten Pflüge
> gleichmäßig Furchen ziehn im Ackerland,
> baut still ein enges Dasein sich Genüge.

> Und von der Spanne Leben und dem Sterben
> weht Jahr um Jahr geheimnisvoll ein Band
> zu ihrem Blätterprangen und Verfärben.

Certainly Hedwig Lachmann's *dénouement*, despite the steady rhythmic drive, lacks Hofmannsthal's stark felicity as he gathers in his initially stated metaphor, realizes and then transfigures it:

> Manche freilich müssen drunten sterben,
> Wo die schweren Ruder der Schiffe streifen,
> Andre wohnen bei dem Steuer droben,
> Kennen Vogelflug und die Länder der Sterne.
>
> ...
>
> Doch ein Schatten fällt von jenen Leben
> in die anderen Leben hinüber,
> Und die leichten sind an die schweren
> Wie an Luft und Erde gebunden:
>
> ...

Yet Lachmann's 'Und von der Spanne Leben und dem Sterben' is at least somewhere in the same top league, even if her/its place, slightly to traduce Hofmannsthal's metaphor, is not quite 'gerichtet/Bei den Sibyllen, den Königinnen'.

One might perhaps essay a very cautious summary of Hedwig Lachmann's effect as a lyric poet: her sensitivity to the passing moods of nature is fine, detailed and delicately percipient; but it is constantly related back to human realities. Gisela Brinker-Gabler describes this ability and quality with notable precision as 'Das Sichversenken in die Kreatur, das Mit-leiden mit allem Geschundenen, aber nicht auf die Natur, sondern auf die Menschen bezogen' (p. 340).

In Hedwig Lachmann's expression of 'Mit-leiden mit allem Geschundenem, [...] auf die Menschen bezogen' one senses her awareness of her feminine individuality, her essence as a woman. This is strikingly apparent in some of her poems written during the war where she publicly and courageously says aloud and unequivocally what, doubtless, many people thought, but only in secret, for fear of retribution or scandal, of publicly exhibited patriotism, brutish jingoism and the intimidating, guilt-inducing effect produced by both. On occasion, though quieter in tone, devoid of sarcasm and satire, Lachmann seems to anticipate the young, bitter Brecht:

Preist Ihr den Heldenlauf der Sieger, schmückt
sie mit dem Ruhmeskranz, Euch dran zu weiden –
Ich will indessen, in den Staub gebückt,
Erniedrigung mit den Besiegten leiden.

Gustav Landauer was understandably guilty of loving hyperbole when he said that 'fast jedes ihrer Gedichte ist Vollkommenheit, und diese vollendeten kleinen Schöpfungen werden leben, solange die deutsche Sprache lebt'. Julius Bab said that she was 'eine Dichterin von zarter und fester Eigenart'.[14] 'Eigenart' seems the operative word here. Gisela Brinker-Gabler may well be correct in believing that Hedwig Lachmann learned much from the example of Stefan George. Her range of metaphor and sense of tightly controlled, crystalline form may, indeed, point to this. But, as Brinker-Gabler herself points out, there is no sign of or desire for George's aspirations to be master, preacher and teacher; and no trace whatever of his exclusivism. Lachmann's simple clarity of expression points in the opposite direction.

Despite the protestations and assurances of her few standard-bearers, Hedwig Lachmann's poetry is virtually forgotten, which seems a pity. Not, I think, that there are submerged masterpieces awaiting haulage to the surface. To continue the analogy used earlier in these remarks: there is no whitewashed or plastered-over Grünewald here. On the other hand, one thinks of Friedrich Hebbel reviewing Gentz's correspondence with Adam Müller:

Dasselbe Gefühl, das Lessing trieb (seine *Rettungen* zu
unternehmen), hat mir diesmal die Hand geführt; mein
Zweck ist erreicht, wenn ich durch meine Beleuchtung
des neuen Aktenstücks bei dem Freund der Wahrheit
einige Zweifel erregt habe.[15]

Such reputation as still sticks to Hedwig Lachmann's name is the result of her translations or, more precisely, her translation of Oscar Wilde's *Salome* (1891, translation 1903). The lasting success of this, in the hands of Richard Strauss, has pushed her other work to the background. Yet it too was considerable. Her range was remarkable. In addition to Poe, Rossetti, Swinburne, Verlaine, she translated several works of Balzac, Napoleon's letters, Malory's *Morte d'Arthur*, Rabindranath Tagore, Benjamin Franklin, Frederick the Great, Joseph Conrad; and a three-cornered effort involving David Friedrich Strauss, Renan and Carlyle.

Salome then: it was Hedwig Lachmann's translation that was used by Max Reinhardt for his Berlin production in 1903. It was a sensational success and was an important factor in advancing the name and fame of Reinhardt's new 'Kleines Theater' following the break with Otto Brahm and the 'Deutsches Theater' the previous year. It is interesting to note that the title role was played by the brilliant and intense Gertrud Eysoldt for whom Hofmannsthal created the title role of *Elektra*, which also had its *première* under Reinhardt's direction in the 'Kleines Theater' (30 October 1903). It too was an enormous success. It is not only for the piquant proximity of what were shortly to become Richard Strauss's 'scandalous sisters' that this fact or coincidence is mentioned here. It is rather to indicate Lachmann's evident repute. Her artistic/literary standing was clearly high enough for her to appear virtually alongside a Hofmannsthal *première* and for her work to be presented by Max Reinhardt, who was rapidly emerging as the most discussed, innovative and − in the positive sense of the word − sensational producer/director of the day. Moreover, the most celebrated contemporary composer in all Europe would soon take her work, virtually unaltered apart from cuts, and give it an immortality − or so it has seemed for many years − of its own.

It is worth noting here that Hedwig Lachmann's translation was only one of several on offer.[16] This in itself is some indication of the great interest in Oscar Wilde, who of course had died quite recently (1900). Certainly there were elements of scandal and sensation in this interest. But it is at the same time fair to note that the qualities of shocked horror, somewhat dubious/spurious moral outrage and indignant hypocrisy which characterized Oscar Wilde's reception in England were generally absent, or at least markedly less evident, in his reception on the European mainland. In a word the interest in him there was genuine enough and relatively free of the lip-licking which typified Wilde's home community.

The circumstances attending the aborted English *première* of *Salome* with Sarah Bernhardt in the title role are well documented.[17] It is sad to recall that of noteworthy English critics only Archer and Shaw espoused Wilde's cause. It hurts particularly, perhaps, to recall that Irving himself supported the censorship.[18] In the event *Salome* was not performed in

England until several years after its qualified success in Paris (1896) and its lasting triumph a few years later in Berlin. In passing it is interesting to observe that the first performance in England (May 1905) took place barely six months before Strauss's triumphantly successful setting of Lachmann's text was presented in Dresden (December 1905). The contrast could hardly have been more striking. The English production was made possible by that fine old answer to the Lord Chamberlain and the Licenser of Plays, the private theatre club, in this case the New Stage Club. There was, not so incidentally perhaps, a second performance – also private – a few months later (July 1906) when *Salome* was presented by Granville-Barker's Literary Theatre Society, with stage *décor* by Charles Ricketts which was evidently 'marvellous'. Ricketts had designed the original stillborn production at the Palace Theatre.

There were none of these complications at the Berlin production of Hedwig Lachmann's translation. Fortified by public praise from such luminaries as Mallarmé, Pierre Loti and Maeterlinck, soon to be confirmed by the overt approval of both the intelligentsia and the general theatre public, *Salome* looked set for a long career in the theatre, at least in its German garb.

Robert Ross must necessarily be regarded as *parti pris*. Close friend of Oscar Wilde himself – the 'Robbie' of Betjeman's banal but curiously moving poem on Wilde's arrest[19] – Ross was his literary executor, debt-payer, recoverer of his copyrights, and befriender of his children. All the same, though we may wish to mute the superlatives somewhat, the thrust of Ross's summary in respect of *Salome* seems reasonable:

> ...it was produced in Berlin; from that moment it has held the European stage. It has run for a longer consecutive period in Germany than any play by any Englishman, not excepting Shakespeare. Its popularity has extended to all countries where it is not prohibited. It is performed throughout Europe, Asia and America. It is even played in Yiddish. This is remarkable in view of the many dramas by French and German writers who treat of the same theme. To none of them, however, is Wilde indebted. Flaubert, Maeterlinck (some would add Ollendorff) and Scripture are the obvious sources on which he has freely drawn for what I do not hesitate to call the most powerful and perfect of all his dramas. – But on such a point a trustee and executor may be prejudiced because it is the most valuable asset in Wilde's literary estate.
>
> (see note 16 [pp. x-xi])

These theatrical details are not perhaps as superfluous as they might seem. They all point to a very substantial success. Even the early English performances already noted, although imperfect, obviously made a great impact. Robert Ross notes, for example:

> No one present will have forgotten the extraordinary tension of the audience on that occasion, those who disliked the play and its author being hypnotized by the extraordinary power of Mr Robert Farquharson's Herod, one of the finest pieces of acting ever seen in this country. My friends the dramatic critics (and many of them are personal friends) fell on *Salome* with all the vigour of their predecessors twelve years before. Unaware of what was taking place in Germany, they spoke of the play as having been 'dragged' from obscurity. The Official Receiver in Bankruptcy and myself were, however, better informed. And much pleasure has been derived from reading those criticisms, all carefully preserved along with the list of receipts which were simultaneously pouring in from the German performances.
>
> (op. cit., pp. xi-xii)[20]

In brief then: Max Reinhardt's production, Gertrud Eysoldt's performance, and Hedwig Lachmann's text were the triple jewel in the crown of a notable theatrical achievement.

But what happened then? Was it simply a *coup de théâtre*, a nine-days-wonder which hit some transiently exposed nerve of the theatrical *Zeitgeist* only to disappear, forever it seems, as soon as its ephemeral relevance/impact/scandal had passed? – Hardly. Recent experience of *Salome* on the stage, in English translation (Wilde is of course meanwhile well and truly out of Commonwealth and English copyright) – indicates that the old theatrical Adam moves still.[21]

So what happened then? The answer, paradoxically enough, is probably to be found in Strauss's success two years after he had seen Reinhardt's production (1903). For Strauss, via his publisher Adolph Fürstner, simply bought the total German rights to *Salome*. His business acumen is well documented. It lives on in anecdote factual and apocryphal, always expressed in the mixture of good-humoured cynicism, *bonhomie* and dry practicality which were his personal protection against the intrusions of the outside world: his peculiarly sensitive temperament – this is a personal view — deliberately set up a 'stacheldraht wider unberufene' as George put it. His laconic remark about the connection between the Kaiser's objections to *Salome* and the money with which he built the villa in Garmisch is as typical as it is specific. It will be recalled that *Salome* and *Elektra* are connected on this business/financial level and in this context, too: with the success of Strauss's setting (1909) Hofmannsthal's stage version of Sophocles's *Electra* also disappeared from the theatre except in the form discussed by the famous pair — who soon became the 'old firm' personified — in their well-known correspondence.[22]

We cannot assess the lasting impact of Hedwig Lachmann's version of *Salome* on the 'spoken' stage simply because there is no further, later evidence. Fürstner's wording in the first edition of Strauss's/Hofmannsthal's libretto is formidably comprehensive and unequivocally exclusive. It must have been approved by Strauss himself. Thus, as far as can be established, Hedwig Lachmann's original stage text is still under German copyright. The half-century of Strauss's death (1949) comes round only in 1999 and with it, presumably, *Salome*'s availability for the spoken stage in Germany. So we must wait a few more years to see whether or not Reinhardt's success on the German stage will be repeated nearly a hundred years on: *Salome* as a centenary offering and celebration is a nice thought... Certainly Lachmann's version does not 'date' in the mid-/late-Victorian way. It is mercifully free of deliberate, contrived 'biblical' atmosphere or vocabulary. It stays conscientiously close to Wilde's French original and achieves simple, direct dramatic force. This is perhaps most marked at the various famous, even notorious climaxes. Salome hovering above the cistern as the executioner hacks off the head of John the Baptist beneath it is a good and typical instance:

Wilde:

    Salome   (Elle se penche sur la cisterne et écoute.)

                    Il n'y a pas de bruit. Je n'entends rien. Pourquoi ne crie-t-il pas, cet homme? Ah! si quelqu'un cherchait à me tuer, je crierais, je me débattrais, je ne voudrais pas souffrir. Frappe. Frappe, Naaman. Frappe, je te dis... Non. Je n'entends rien. Il y a un silence affreux. Ah! quelque chose est tombé par

terre. J'ai entendu quelque chose tomber. Il
a peur, cet esclave! Il a laissé tomber son
epée. Il n'ose pas le tuer. C'est un lâche, cet
esclave! Il faut envoyer des soldats.

(Elle voit le page d'Hérodias et s'adresse à lui.)

Viens ici. Tu as été l'ami de celui qui est
mort, n'est-ce pas? Eh bien, il n'y a pas eu
assez de morts. Dites aux soldats qu'ils
descendent et m'apportent ce que je
demande, ce que le tétrarque m'a promis, ce
que m'appartient.

(Le page recule. Elle s'adresse aux soldats.)

Venez ici, soldats. Descendez dans cette
cisterne, et apportez-moi la tête de cet
homme.

(Les soldats reculent.)

Tétrarque, tétrarque, commandez à vos
soldats de m'apporter la tête d'Iokanaan.

Lachmann:

Salome   (an der Cisterne lauschend).

Es ist kein Laut zu vernehmen. Ich höre nichts. Warum
schreit er nicht, der Mann? Ah! Wenn einer mich zu
töten käme, ich würde schreien, ich würde mich wehren,
ich würde es nicht dulden!... Schlag zu, schlag zu,
Naaman, schlag zu, sag ich dir... Nein, ich höre nichts.
(*Gedehnt*) Es ist eine schreckliche Stille! Ah! Es ist
etwas zu Boden gefallen. Ich hörte etwas fallen. Es war
das Schwert des Henkers. Er hat Angst, dieser Sklave.
Er hat das Schwert fallen lassen! Er traut sich nicht, ihn
zu töten. Er ist eine Memme, dieser Sklave. Schickt
Soldaten hin! (*Zum Pagen*) Komm hierher, du warst
der Freund dieses Toten, nicht? Wohlan, ich sage dir:
Es sind noch nicht genug Toten. Geh zu den Soldaten
und befiehl ihnen, hinabzusteigen und mir zu holen, was
ich verlange, was der Tetrarch mir versprochen hat, was
mein ist!

(Der Page weicht zurück, sie wendet sich den Soldaten
                                                      zu.)

Hierher, ihr Soldaten, geht ihr in die Cisterne hinunter
und holt mir den Kopf des Mannes! (*Schreiend*)
Tetrarch, Tetrarch, befiehl deinen Soldaten, daß sie mir
den Kopf des Jokanaan holen!

Lachmann, as both poet and critic, was deeply immersed – one is tempted to say involved – in Wilde's style and artistic purpose. It was noted earlier that her approach to Wilde was both sympathetic and sensitive. Her comment on the ultimate value of *Salome* seems as valid now as it was nearly ninety years ago:

> Die Bedeutung der *Salome* liegt nicht in dem, was den Ewigkeitswert andrer Dramen großen Stils ausmacht: daß die Bewegungen der menschlichen Leidenschaften in festen Gedankenbildern niedergelegt sind, die sich als dichterische Formeln durch die Jahrhunderte vererben – da ist kein Niederschlag an Reflexion, ja, die Lyrik der Sprache, so schwungkräftig sie ist, verflattert und hinterläßt keine bleibenden Umrisse. Der Wert dieser Dichtung ist vor allem der, daß darin große Typen von singulärer Art in vollendetem Stil mit einer zwingend ausdrucksvollen Physiognomie hingestellt sind. Da ist keine Charakteristik im kleinen, kein Moment, das nicht zum wesentlichen hinlenkte. Wie in einem antiken Steinrelief stehen die Gestalten gleichsam mit einer einzig intensiven Spannung ihrer Lebensfibern aufgefangen.

Her eye for the intricacies of character is particularly acute. She notes the 'Bruch' in Herodes compared with the 'willensstarke, unzerspaltene Natur' of Salome whose 'Lebensenergien im vollen Einklang mit der Größe ihres Schicksals und ihres Verbrechens sind'. 'Herodes', she writes,

> hält die Mitte zwischen dem skrupellosen Sinnen- und Tatmenschen und dem gefühlskranken Fatalisten. [...] Er ist durchaus tragisch, vom Dichter in eine grandiose Untergangsstimmung gehüllt. Eine feine Ironie liegt darin, wie er im naiven Schutzbedürfnis seines abergläubischen Gemüts voll Ehrfurcht zum nüchternen Rationalismus der Römer aufblickt. Eine leise Wendung zur Satire charakterisiert ihn sogar als einen Fürsten von humanen Regungen mit einem Zug ins glatt Weltmännische, Diplomatische, was die poetische Wirkung nur verstärkt, wenn er gleich darauf aus dieser künstlichen Gehaltenheit in die Haltlosigkeit der Angst- und Wollustriebe hinabsinkt.[23]

This is not the place for a detailed critique of Lachmann's monograph. Even less is it the place to re-animate the dust around battles long ago. It is perhaps enough to say that Lachmann's views in matters social/conventional, sexual, psychological and literary/aesthetic are expressed in a remarkably balanced, humane, progressive and sensitive way:

Die Stellung, die der Mensch zum Triebhaften in seiner
Natur einnimmt (diesen Begriff in seinem ganzen
Umfang mit allen Abzweigungen gedacht), die Art, wie
er die impulsiven Kräfte erkennt, auslegt, nützt oder
mißbraucht, sie dem allgemeinen Sittengesetz anpaßt
oder eigenmächtig davon absondert und nach eigener
Maßgabe walten läßt, bestimmt seinen ethischen Wert.
Dabei kommt es nicht auf das objektive Werturteil an –
nur auf die Intensität, mit der ein sich selbst
vertrauender Sinn einer vermeintlichen Wesenserfüllung
zustrebt. So kann, was sich uns als Missetat, Gewaltakt,
Verbrechen dartut, für den, der es verübt, einer
sittlichen Handlung gleichkommen; wenn er die volle
Verantwortlichkeit dafür übernimmt, und ein Ideelles in
ihm der Anstoß dazu gewesen ist, so kann ein
Außerordentliches im Menschen, das uns durch seine
Bizarrerie, Fremdartigkeit, Abnormalität abstößt, durch
eine besondere Natur seine Rechtfertigung finden. Aber
freilich: nur, so lange das seelische Äquivalent für das
äußere Tun vorhanden ist, so lange ein intellektuelles
Urteil der persönlichen Willkür zustimmt, bleibt die
Einheit gewahrt, die auch den heterogensten Charakter
der Gesamtheit gegenüber zu einer selbständigen Größe
abstempelt. Reißt das Band, das das triebhafte
Begehren an den bewußten Willen knüpft, geht die
innere Freiheit verloren, wird Zwang der Leidenschaft,
was ungebundenes Spiel der Kräfte war – dann lockert
sich auch der Kreis, der mit feiner Grenze das einzelne
Individuum von der Welt abschloß und ihm eine
Ausnahmestellung gewährte und unrettbar verfällt es
den Gesetzen der Allgemeinheit.[24]

Hedwig Lachmann's account of Wilde's life, work, downfall and moral
significance appeared in 1905. It seems to have marked the *apogée* of what
might be called her public life. Thereafter, as was noted earlier, she withdrew
almost wholly from view. She was as 'productive' as heretofore; this includes
of course the various joint ventures with Gustav Landauer. But she was
apparently content with the role of sheet-anchor, headquarters and provider-
in-emergency. That such a free, individual and enlightened spirit found such
fulfilment in marriage, relative anonymity, children and seclusion will seem
remarkable to some, admirable to others, fascinating and puzzling to all. She
is of course only one of many 'Verschollene und Vergessene' – most of them,
probably, Jewish – who disappeared from view, especially in Germany and
Austria, as a result of the hiatus and amnesia brought about by the National
Socialist episode. Quite evidently, she is not a forgotten major figure. But a

full-length biography, including Landauer's 'Privatdruck' on her death, would be worthwhile, to say the least. A joint biography of Lachmann and Landauer, with its diverse perspectives on life, art, theatre, *mores* and politics, could be very much more than just another 'life and times'.

Warm appreciation is due to Ninette Ellis, Barr Smith Library, University of Adelaide, for vital help in the preparation of this essay. Her enthusiasm and expertise in a difficult and fragmentary bibliographical situation were invaluable.

NOTES

[1]Norbert Altenhofer gives an excellent and detailed account of the relationship between Hofmannsthal and Gustav Landauer: see 'Hugo von Hofmannsthal und Gustav Landauer: Eine Dokumentation. Mit dem Briefwechsel Hofmannsthal-Landauer und Landauers Essays über Hofmannsthal', in *Hofmannsthal-Blätter* 19/20 (1978), 43-90.

[2]*Oscar Wilde* (Berlin/Leipzig, 1905), Vol. 34, *Die Dichtung* ed. Paul Remer, 88pp. This also includes Hedwig Lachmann's translation of three Wilde poems: 'Taedium Vitae', 'Sonett an die Freiheit', 'Das Hurenhaus'. Hofmannsthal's essay 'Sebastian Melmoth' (1905) is in *Reden und Aufsätze I: 1891-1913* (Frankfurt: S. Fischer, 1979), pp. 341-344.

[3]Ulrich Karthaus, postscript to Oscar Wilde, *Salome* (Stuttgart: Reclam, 1990), p. 65.

[4]Gisela Brinker-Gabler, *Deutsche Literatur von Frauen*, 2 vols (Munich: Beck, 1988), Vol. 2, p. 336.

[5]Karthaus, p. 65.

[6]The close and productive relationship between Martin Buber and Gustav Landauer is a topic in itself. Buber's commemorative editorial efforts on Landauer's behalf were as admirable as they were noteworthy. *Inter alia* he edited and published Gustav Landauer's *Meister Eckarts Mystische Schriften* of 1903 (1922), *Der werdende Mensch* (1921), *Beginnen* (1924) and *Gustav Landauer: Sein Lebensgang in Briefen* (2 vols, 1929). See also Martin Buber's memoir 'Erinnerungen an einen Tod (Dem Gedächtnis Gustav Landauers)', in *Von Juden in München* ed. H. Lamm (Munich: 1958), pp. 166-169.

[7]Subsequent family history offers yet another bitter-sweet commentary on the course of German history this century. One of Hedwig Lachmann's daughters (Brigitte) married a Russian doctor (medical) — 'Nikolaievich Peschkoisky'. They emigrated to the United States in 1939 and changed the family name to Nichols. Their son Michel Igor became Mike Nichols and a celebrity in the entertainment world ('Mike Nichols & Elaine Stich'). See Robert Zeschin, 'Ladies of the Libretto' in *Opera News* (USA), 18 March 1972, 27. (A word of caution, though: Mr Zeschin's essay is informative and valuable, but it is also inaccurate in at least three places. He calls Gustav Landauer 'head of the German Social Democratic Party', and says Hedwig Lachmann died 'in 1938, a year before Landauer was felled by a Nazi assassin's bullet'. I can only trust that his data on the Landauer family are correct otherwise.) Mike Nichols went on to considerable success as a film director, particularly noted perhaps for the screen version of Edward Albee, *Who's Afraid of Virginia Woolf?* (with Elizabeth Taylor as Martha and Richard Burton as George).

[8]Gustav Landauer's *Wie Hedwig Lachmann starb* (1918) was evidently a 'Privatdruck': I have been unable so far to see a copy. See *NDB*, Vol. 13 (Berlin 1982), p. 494.

[9]See Wolfgang Stoll, 'Gustav Landauer' in *Lexikon der deutschsprachigen Literatur* (Munich, 1981), p. 315, also Ernst Toller, *Eine Jugend in Deutschland* (1933).

[10]'Leutnant' Graf Arco-Valley was a nationalist student, political reactionary and 'officer' in the *Freikorps*. He shot Kurt Eisner.

[11] 21 February 1918 – 2 May 1919.

[12] *NDB*, Vol. 13.   Renate Heuer's source for this view of Landauer's letters is attributed to H. Blüher, *Werke und Tage* (1953).

[13] *Moderne Deutsche Lyrik* ed. by Hans Benzmann (Leipzig: Reclam, 1904). Benzmann's foreword, introduction and biographical notes offer a fascinating and detailed account of how it all seemed at the time.

[14] See *NDB*, Vol. 13, p. 494.

[15] Quoted by Hofmannsthal (1926) in a *Gedenktafel* for Friedrich von Gentz (1764-1832): *Reden und Aufsätze III: 1925-1929* (Frankfurt/M.: S. Fischer, 1980), p. 106.

[16] In February 1908 Robert Ross published an edition (London: Methuen) of *Salome* in English translation. This volume also included *La Sainte Courtisane* and *A Florentine Tragedy*, together with Walter Ledger's extensive bibliography of translations, into English and other languages, of *Salome*. Not included in the latter, however, doubtless because, as far as can be established, it was never published, was a fragmentary version or scenario by Anton Lindner. The story is worth telling because it bears on the quality of Hedwig Lachmann's version. Norman Del Mar gives an excellent account in his authoritative biography of Richard Strauss (3 vols, London 1962/69/72).

> ...in 1901, it was given in Breslau in a translation by Dr Kisper. The following year it was produced with enormous success [...] in Berlin, where it played for the unheard-of run of two hundred performances.
>
> Meanwhile a certain Anton Lindner, a young Viennese writer, had already had the perception to send the play to Strauss who had, in fact, set a poem of his, 'Hochzeitlich Lied', as one of the songs op. 37. Nevertheless his ingenious rewriting of the opening scene pleased the composer more in its choice of subject than its handling. Strauss's letter to his parents telling them of this new project of a Pendant to *Feuersnot* (!) reflects his qualms as to the successful outcome of Lindner's aspirations. Fortunately Strauss was able at once to perceive the vast possibilities in Wilde's text as it stood without alteration other than extensive cuts. [...] He began making a few preliminary sketches, and then early in 1903 took the opportunity of the Berlin production to go and see the play for himself. [...] At the theatre he encountered a close friend, one Heinrich Grünfeld, who immediately commented that here would be some real material for an opera for him. Strauss at once replied that indeed he was already at work on it, for the visit had confirmed him in his determination to set Wilde's original text. Hedwig Lachmann's translation, which was the one used in Reinhardt's Berlin production, was accordingly cut to his specifications and the composition of the music went forward like lightning.

> (Vol. I, 242-243)

Strauss, in fact, made very few changes to the Lachmann version beyond the extensive cuts needed to reduce it to music-theatre dimensions.

[17]See, for example, Richard Ellington, *Oscar Wilde* (Harmondsworth: Penguin, 1988), pp. 350-353.

[18]Ibid., p. 353.

[19]'The Arrest of Oscar Wilde at the Cadogan Hotel', in (for example) *The Best of Betjeman* (Harmondsworth: Penguin, 1978), pp. 22-23.

[20]Ross's specific reference is to the first production, noted in the text above, by the New Stage Club. This is perhaps a suitable point at which to remind the reader of the intrigue, censorship, outrage, etc. which attended the English *première* of *Salome* in Strauss's setting at Covent Garden in 1910. In his autobiography *A Mingled Chime* (London: Hutchinson, 1944) Sir Thomas Beecham, who was producer/*Intendant*/conductor as well as chief negotiator and 'fixer', gives a hilarious and detailed account which has justly become a classic. See especially pp. 97-99 (Beecham's dealings with the Prime Minister, Mr Henry Asquith) and pp. 102-103 which deal with the Lord Chamberlain's Office, the composition of a bowdlerized text and the performance itself. Interestingly enough one has the impression that Hedwig Lachmann's text was not used. The point at which the much tried singers took refuge in her 'original' might be quoted here:

> For about half an hour all went just as had been planned, everyone singing their innocent phrases accurately, if somewhat frigidly. But gradually I sensed that telepathy which exists between the conductor of the orchestra and the artists onstage, a growing restlessness and excitement of which the first exhibition was a slip on the part of Salome, who forgot two or three sentences of the bowdlerized version and lapsed into the viciousness of the lawful text. The infection spread among the other performers, and by the time the second half of the work was well under way they were all living in and shamelessly restoring it to its integrity, as if no such things existed as British respectability and its legal custodians.
>
> (p. 104)

[21]For example, Steven Berkoff's recent production of *Salome* at the Adelaide Festival (Her Majesty's Theatre, Adelaide, 17-21 March 1992). This production was originally staged at the Gate Theatre, Dublin, and re-created for the Royal National Theatre, London.

[22]*Richard Strauss — Hugo von Hofmannsthal: Briefwechsel — Gesamtausgabe* ed. by Franz and Alice Strauss and rev. by Willi Schuh (Zurich: Atlantis, 1952; augmented edn, 1964).

[23]*Oscar Wilde*, op. cit., pp. 46-48.

[24]Ibid., pp. 64-66.

Hedwig Lachmann: A Bibliography

E.A. Poe. *Ausgewählte Gedichte* (Berlin: Verlag des Bibliographischen Bureaus, 1891; further edn 1902).

Ungarische Gedichte (Berlin: Verlag des Bibliographischen Bureaus, 1891).

Im Bilde. Gedichte und Nachdichtungen (Berlin and Leipzig: Schuster & Loeffler, 1902, including translations of Dante Gabriel Rossetti, Swinburne and Verlaine).

Oscar Wilde. Der Sozialismus und die Seele des Menschen. Aus dem Zuchthaus zu Reading, Aesthetisches Manifest, tr. by Hedwig Lachmann and Gustav Landauer (Berlin: Juncker, 1904; reissued Zurich: Diogenes, 1970).

E.A. Poe. Heureka (Berlin: Minden: Bruns, 1904).

Oscar Wilde. Das Bildnis des Dorian Gray, tr. by Hedwig Lachmann and Gustav Landauer (Leipzig: Insel, 1907; reissued Frankfurt/M: Suhrkamp, 1983 and Frankfurt/M: Insel, 1985).

Napoleon. Briefe (Leipzig: Insel, 1912).

Sir Thomas Malory. Der Tod Arthurs (Leipzig: Insel, 1913).

Rabindranath Tagore. Der König der dunklen Kammer, tr. by Hedwig Lachmann and Gustav Landauer (Leipzig: Wolff, 1919).

Gesammelte Gedichte, ed. by Gustav Landauer (Potsdam-Berlin: Gustav Kiepenheuer, 1919).

E.A. Poe. Hans Pfaalls Mondfahrt (Regensburg: Habbel & Neumann, 1922)

H. de Balzac. Sarrasine (Vienna, Hellerau: Avarun, 1922; also appearing together with *Facino Cane* as *Zwei Novellen,* Leipzig: Insel as number 19 of the Inselbücherei).

Joseph Conrad. Lord Jim tr. by Hedwig Lachmann and Ernst W. Freissler (Berlin: Fischer, 1927; reissued as a *Lizenzausgabe* Frankfurt/Main: S. Fischer, 1935 and Heidelberg and Marbach a. N.: Palladium, 1952).

Lachmann was responsible for the Insel Verlag Balzac edition translations *Verlorene Illusionen, Die Frau von dreißig Jahren, Die alte Jungfer* 1908- .

From 1911 to 1914 she worked with Hedda Moeller-Bruck on an edition of Poe in translation for J.C.C. Bruns Verlag, Minden.

She wrote a volume on Oscar Wilde in 1905 (see note 2).

There is an unpublished correspondence with Richard Dehmel.

The German Translations of Wilde's *Salomé*

Salome tragoedie in einem akt von Oscar Wilde (facing which is:) Übertragung von Hedwig Lachmann. Zeichnungen von Marcus Behmer (Leipzig: Insel, 1903). There were five editions in all, not including the 1990 Reclam edition (see note 3).

Lily Braun

5

'Dissonance is the Voice of the Future'
Lily Braun's *Memoiren einer Sozialistin*

Ricarda Schmidt

In recent years, a great number of studies have been devoted to autobiographical writing by women.[1] Methodologically, one can discern two tendencies in these studies which developed diachronically and may now often be found simultaneously. First, by exposing the male bias of traditional definitions and studies of the genre, they open up space for the analysis of autobiographies by women which – due to women's status in patriarchy – could not correspond to the received notion that autobiography deals with an individual's relationship to the public world, and is supposed to be representative of its period as well as portraying an individual's uniqueness. Women's lives, by definition, were *not* to extend beyond the private sphere, and those women who did play a role in public life were the exception, i.e. not representative.[2] Moreover, it has been argued, following Nancy Chodorow's analysis in *The Reproduction of Mothering*, that women's sense of self is shaped less by separation and difference from others (= uniqueness) than by contiguity (= relatedness).[3] Thus an extension of the definition of the genre was called for to accommodate women's experience of life: genre was to be problematized and modified by gender. This methodological revision has led to fascinating studies of hitherto marginalized women's autobiographies which emphasize private life and interrelatedness with other women, and make use of unconventional forms.[4]

Secondly, in developing a conception of the "autos", the self, of autobiography, feminist studies of women's autobiographies are increasingly based on poststructuralist theories which dispute the unity of the subject, the referentiality of language and a teleological development of history. Thus poststructuralist analysts of women's autobiographies look for signs of a non-harmonious self and a non-teleological perspective and evaluate them positively, in both a political and an aesthetic sense, since, as Goodman points out, a unified self 'would almost necessarily be one that conformed to a conception of dominant history'.[5] This approach often leads to interesting discoveries of contradictions and traces of the multiplicity of self in the very autobiographies whose authors endeavoured to follow the patriarchal pattern of unified, rational subjectivity.[6] But it can also lead to critics adopting a teleological stance at the same time as they criticize the teleological perspective of autobiographers. For, ironically, the achievement of women's autobiographies in the past is often judged by their closeness to or distance from current conceptions of a non-harmonious self and a non-teleological view of history.[7]

While nowadays we cannot analyse the concept of the self which is developed in autobiographies without taking into account the poststructuralist critique of the harmonious self-identical subject and of the teleological view of history, I would argue that poststructuralist methodology should be supplemented by an increased consideration of historicity. For the history of events, ideas and genres in which both male and female autobiographers are embedded (albeit in different ways) will not allow them to create forms and ideas which are entirely free from the prevailing order. Yet the degree to which any writers are interesting is measured by the extent to which they add something new to existing ideas and aesthetic forms. Should it not be the task of literary critics to explore texts for manifestations of this tension between the perpetuation of the existing order and attempts at its modification, rather than looking for the manifestation of a contemporary ideal in texts from a different age? I would argue, moreover, that the poststructuralist idea of a decentred, non-harmonious subjectivity is difficult to practise even nowadays, since we have all been brought up on the idea of harmony. Women autobiographers in the past, who modelled their text on the prevailing norm of an integrated self, may well have been able to accommodate within it not an entirely liberated self but aspects of themselves which did not conform to the male order, and they may have dealt with tensions inherent to this norm which we still experience today.

I shall now turn to Lily Braun's *Memoiren einer Sozialistin*, first published in two parts in 1909 and 1911. Not only did the genre designation 'Roman' contradict the expectations raised by the title *Memoiren*. It was also well known − and this contributed to the commercial success of the work − that this 'novel' was Braun's thinly disguised autobiography. Indeed, it went far beyond the concentration on the public persona characteristic of memoirs, devoting great attention to emotional and psychological development. Thus, Lily Braun's *Memoiren* are evidence of that blurring of genre distinctions which Patricia Meyer Spacks describes as typical of the twentieth century:

> Twentieth-century autobiographies deliberately adopt the techniques of novels. Twentieth-century novelists write thinly veiled autobiography, call it a novel, then complain if readers suspect some direct self-revelation. [...] The multiplying confusions of genre are encouraged and publicized, becoming part of the general confusion of our times.[8]

I shall look at Braun's *Memoiren* as an example of female autobiography which does not set a model for poststructuralist concepts of subjectivity and writing, yet consciously and unconsciously gives voice to a woman's contradictory experiences in private and public life. Aware of heterogeneity as dissonance, Braun strives for harmony in homogeneity. While working for socialism (i.e. the collective good), she insists on the development of the individual as part of it, trying to combine Marx with Goethe and Nietzsche. Equating religious dogmatism with socialist dogmatism and rejecting both, Braun nevertheless desires and believes in the quasi-religious teleological determinism of socialism. Although writing at a time when she was rejected by the Socialist Party, she does not denounce the idea of socialism. While stressing her commitment to public life, she insists that motherhood was her most important experience. While arguing that women are only free when every one of them has the chance to take part in public life and realize her biological potential (both in free sexuality and motherhood), she remains convinced that submission is women's sexual 'nature'.

Lily Braun was long neglected by the second Women's Movement. Only from the mid-eighties onwards has she received more attention.[9] Her autobiography was reprinted by two different publishers in the same year, though in one case in an abridged version.[10] The most important work on Lily Braun is the excellent book by the historian Alfred G. Meyer on her political development, which situates her thinking in the contemporary debate within the SPD and the Women's Movement in order to show that she held positions whose importance we have only now come to appreciate.[11] Meyer has also edited and translated a selection of Braun's articles.[12] But he is primarily interested in her as a political thinker and in the impact of her ideas on her life, whereas I intend to analyse problems of gender and genre, subjectivity and textuality as they manifest themselves in Braun's fictionalized autobiography. What kind of subjectivity does Braun project in her text? What textual strategies does she employ for her purpose? Does the text reveal anything about the problems and conflicts of her subjectivity which she did not wish to reveal to the reader or of which she was unaware? In what way is the tension between being part of her time (tradition) and being ahead of her time (rebellion) inscribed in the text?

The title of Lily Braun's autobiography recalls two other titles which stand for mutually exclusive perspectives on life. On the one hand, *Memoiren einer Sozialistin* echoes the title of Malwida von Meysenbug's *Memoiren einer Idealistin*, published in Berlin in 1876. In this three-volume autobiography, Meysenbug gives an account of the evolution of her individuality which led not to her integration into society but to her isolation. The autobiography ends with Meysenbug's withdrawal from political action, after public and personal defeats, into a pessimistic 'apotheosis of philosophical resignation and self-negation'.[13] Braun's striving for the development of her individuality, her experiences of separation and isolation, as well as some of her political aspirations, are all reminiscent of Meysenbug. Yet the evaluation of these ideals and experiences is shaped from another perspective to which the subtitle *Lehrjahre* of Braun's first volume alludes: Goethe's *Wilhelm Meisters Lehrjahre* and its concept of the development of the individual, through mistakes and errors, towards maturity and an active contribution to the shaping of his environment. It is this optimistic and activist concept that Braun tries to take out of its male context and to appropriate for her feminist purposes, rather than the pessimistic and resigned perspective of her female predecessor. However, this entails certain problems. For while Wilhelm Meister himself is a 'softy', the structure of the novel confirms patriarchal values. His relationships with different women serve as a means to an end; women have to die (innocently) in order to move the hero's education on. Moreover, admirable (sic!) Lothario's path is 'littered' with rejected lovers who are criticized for their failure to accommodate their feelings to his rapid loss of interest. The fact that Lily Braun models her autobiography on Goethe's novel indicates that she identifies with Wilhelm without even noticing the objectification of women in *Wilhelm Meister*. Yet her appropriation still carries with it the very aspects it has left unexamined: the assumption of a desire for submission to the superior male as part of women's nature is perpetuated in Lily Braun's feminism, as I will show.

Lily Braun wrote her autobiography at a time when she found herself extremely isolated. Her SPD comrades were shunning her and her second husband, Dr Heinrich Braun, for their 'revisionism'.[14] They had closed the Brauns' access to publication in party newspapers and thus to earning a living. The Brauns' attempt at founding a new journal, *Neue Gesellschaft*, in which to publish their unorthodox views of socialism failed after a few years and all the capital they had invested in it was lost. Not only were they financially ruined; Lily Braun was also questioning the commitment which had led her to renounce the privileges of her aristocratic background in favour of becoming a socialist, only to find herself cold-shouldered by her fellow socialists.[15] In the preface to her memoirs Braun refers to this situation metaphorically:

> Auf steilem Felsenpfad bin ich bis hierher gestiegen,
> meinem wegkundigen Blick, meiner Kraft vertrauend,
> weit entfernt von den Lebenssphären, die Tradition und
> Sitte mit Wegweisern versah, damit auch der
> Gedankenlose nicht irre gehe. Jetzt aber muß ich stille
> stehen, muß Atem schöpfen, denn die große Einsamkeit
> um mich her läßt mich schaudern. Wohin nun? Hinab
> zu Tal, zu den Wegweisern? Oder weiter auf selbst-
> gewähltem Steige?
>
> (I, p. 3)

The very conventionality of these metaphors and the binary opposition Braun sets up between a dull conformist life (Tal, Wegweiser) and the risky life of individual self-realization she has chosen (steiler Felsenpfad, selbstgewählt) indicates that these memoirs are going to be a vindication of her life rather than a serious questioning of her motives and choices that might lead to a decisive change of direction. Her choice of metaphor indicates, moreover, that she will adopt a teleological perspective on her life: since she likens the path of her life to the lonely climbing of a mountain, a teleological closure is assumed – the summit – any divergence from which must be regarded as failure.

Lily Braun describes with great detail and seriousness, and in strictly chronological order, her childhood as the daughter of an impulsive Prussian officer and his cold dutiful wife.[16]   Thinly disguised fictional names camouflage the first-person narrator and important people in her life to the uninitiated reader of today, but would hardly have fooled contemporary readers of this then well-known political figure or misled them into taking the stated genre of the book, 'Roman', for a factually accurate designation. Indeed, Braun's *Memoiren* were extremely popular and had sold over 50,000 copies by the early 1920s.

Alix von Kleve, alias Lily von Kretschman, portrays herself as an outsider from childhood onwards. Physically frail and sensitive, she develops a vivid fantasy life. Idealistic and rebellious, yet subject to feelings of guilt, she experiences psychosomatic illnesses as a result of these unresolvable conflicts. The split between rebellious behaviour and a guilty conscience for not conforming to social norms continues into her girlhood. She rejects Christianity, for example, yet agrees under pressure to be confirmed. Her alleged naivety in flouting the cramping conventions for girls' behaviour serves to make readers aware of the injustice of these conventions. But when her unorthodox behaviour and her flirtatiousness mislead men into believing she loves them, she feels guilty for having hurt their feelings. Torn between desire and duty, she attempts to suppress desire (not only for erotic adventures but also for knowledge and education, and for personal liberty) in order to fulfil the feminine duties expected of her, especially by her mother. Furthermore, contradiction even shapes her desire: the adolescent girl feels sexually attracted to beautiful men but spiritually drawn to thoughtful men whom she often finds physically repulsive. This confirms that the conflict between desires and social norms is an intra-personal as well as an inter-personal one. It is precisely the sharp painfulness with which she experiences this dissonance which makes her strive for a homogeneity of self.

Braun evokes vivid images of her childhood and youth in Wilhelmine Germany, of which she saw a great deal because her father was stationed in many different parts of the country. Apart from brief moralistic generalizations typical of the tone of nineteenth-century literature (e.g. 'Zu fragen hatte ich nicht den Mut; es gehört echte Bildung dazu, Unwissenheit einzugestehen', I, p. 219), Braun rarely comments from a later perspective on her younger self. On the contrary, she attempts to let the reader participate in her development as it was experienced at the time, withholding any subsequent insight and changes of view for the sake of vivid immediacy. While this technique promotes empathy and identification on the part of the reader, it precludes the possibility of critical distance which Braun's model, Goethe, had explored. Especially at the beginning of *Wilhelm Meisters Lehrjahre*, the narrator contrasts Wilhelm's naive enthusiasm with his own superior insight and exploits the incongruity between them to ironic effect. But Braun's style of vivid immediacy also accounts for the absence of the didacticism and moralizing which is so prominent in Goethe's autobiography *Dichtung und Wahrheit*.

In both volumes of her *Memoiren*, Braun skilfully integrates the depiction of social and historical developments into the narration of the life of her alter ego Alix Brandt. Thus social problems and theoretical positions are made part of the 'action'. The text achieves a novelistic unity of plot and design typical of the nineteenth-century *Bildungsroman*, confirming that both the allusion of the subtitle 'Lehrjahre' to its prototype and the genre designation of Braun's text as a novel are not arbitrary, and that they influenced the way the author looks at and presents her own life: the individual is representative of her times, her times are presented through her direct experiences. Everything is supposed to be part of an overall design and to serve a purpose, even though it may not be obvious at the time to the individual concerned.

Immersed for years in the lifestyle of meaningless amusement typical for girls of her class while waiting for a husband, the protagonist is finally jolted by both internal and external events into a different direction. An unhappy ending to a great love affair and the family's pecuniary difficulties change her expectation of pursuing the conventional feminine path of her time and class. She begins to work for money, to earn an income from writing. She edits her grandmother's papers and, since her grandmother was acquainted with Goethe, attracts the attention of Goethe scholars. She is invited to Weimar and to further editorial work on Goethe memorabilia. But she declines a safe career as a research scholar and protégée of the Duke of Weimar because it would not allow her active spirit sufficient influence on the world.

The protagonist's acquaintance with Georg von Glyzcinski, alias Georg von Gizycki, leads to her introduction to reformist ideas. Her marriage with him, 'keine Liebes-, sondern eine Freundschafts- und Arbeitsehe' (I, p. 575) because of his paralysis, achieves her emancipation from her parents, her intellectual education, and her first reformist activities in the 'ethische Gesellschaft' which the couple founded. While the first volume ends with her first husband's death, thus marking the end of her formative years and leaving her to pursue her own way, the second volume is devoted to her troubled relationship with the German Socialist Party which she joins after his death.

Braun's narrator-protagonist, on joining the SPD in order to change the world and to help the oppressed, soon finds herself confronted with the demand to bow to party discipline. Wanda Orbin (alias Clara Zetkin) tells her: 'wenn Sie aber zu uns gehören wollen, so haben Sie Ihre Person der Allgemeinheit unterzuordnen' (II, p. 170). Alix first tries to conform, but her attempts to initiate action and to influence party politics (especially in a feminist direction) are frustrated time and again by the demand that she toe the party line, any divergence from which is branded as a betrayal of the working class. Alix Brandt's difficulties within the SPD multiply during the discussion of Bernstein's revisionism, which is hotly contested by the party leadership and the rank and file members alike. Braun's alter ego Alix attributes the acrimonious effect of Bernstein's theses to the fact that they destroy the religious root of many people's socialist conviction:

> Auf uns, die wir durch die Erkenntnis des Elends in der
> Welt zum Sozialismus geführt worden waren, die wir von
> ihm in einem in seiner Wurzel religiösen Glaubensüber-
> schwang die Erlösung von allem Übel erwartet hatten,
> wirkte die kühle Klarheit der Bernsteinschen Beweis-
> führung niederschmetternd. [...] Die Zeiten meiner
> religiösen Kinderkämpfe schienen wiedergekehrt zu
> sein. Nur daß ich jetzt mit allen Fasern meines Innern in
> dem Glauben wurzelte, dem ich meinen ganzen Lebens-
> besitz geopfert hatte, aus dem ich alle Kräfte sog. Was
> stand noch fest, dachte ich verzweifelt, wenn so vieles
> schwankte?
>
> (II, p. 245)

Here, Alix recognizes that, like so many other socialists, she has merely replaced God by Socialism. She has maintained the same structure of subordination, self-sacrifice and duty of the individual to the higher being/thing which she had rebelled against in her youth (see II, pp. 534-535). She is now prepared to distance herself from the quasi-religious structures in socialism (see II, pp. 290, 326, 494). But while she repudiates the individual's subordination in return for the promise of paradise, as a 'Kinderglauben' (II, p. 246) she (unlike the others) is now willing to overcome, she herself is as unable to live without the teleological certainty which is characteristic of both religious belief and belief in Socialism:

> Mein Glaube an die Entwicklung im Sinne des
> Sozialismus ist das einzig Feste, was mir noch nach all
> dem Zusammenbruch geblieben ist. Wenn ich nur das
> Geringste entdecke, was ihn zu stützen, zu kräftigen
> vermag, so macht mich das stärker.
>
> (II, p. 537)

She does not renounce teleology, but merely the certainty of the way towards it. This alone causes her agony and makes others view her as a traitor. With her teleological certainty, Braun stands in the tradition of classical auto-biography, in spite of the twentieth-century issues involved. Yet her autobiography also testifies to the modern experience of the gap between, on the one hand, hopes and efforts, and, on the other, the result as 'something that never happens'.[17] For not only does Braun never see her socialist ideals realized, she also suffers from the SPD's dogmatism and is made an outcast by the very party through which she hoped to realize her ideals.

Braun's fictionalized autobiography is remarkable in that it thematizes an individual's experience of the impossibility of a harmonious integration into the collective, but still sustains this concept as an ideal. While nowadays we might want to question the ideal itself, Braun's concept is more typical of a transitional period in which she assumes an outstanding position because her belief in the ideal does not blind her to the circumstances preventing its realization, as happened to so many socialists and communists later in the century, at least for long periods of their lives. Rather than refuse to see things that do not fit in with cherished beliefs, Braun's protagonist risks dissent, disharmony and isolation in the pursuit of intellectual honesty. Her unique ability to recognize the practices of the party, whose proclaimed ideals she shares, as a violation of these very ideals, and to admit this violation both to herself and the public at large, manifests itself in the prophetic insight: 'da wußte ich, daß die Partei der Freiheit Scheiterhaufen zu schichten imstande sein würde' (II, p. 291). Of course, Braun takes care to portray her alter ego as individualistic and rebellious from childhood onwards, in order to motivate this behaviour in later life as a 'natural' expression of her personality. In short, she projects an idealized version of herself. Moreover, she draws strength in her struggle against dogmatism from two very different thinkers. First, Goethe and his idea of the individual's development to the full of all his faculties provided her with the basis of a utopian ideal, one which she did not renounce for the socialist one but tried to fuse with it: for her Socialism means full personal development for everyone rather than the dictatorship of the proletariat. However, while Goethe could still portray positively the culmination of this development as the individual's integration into a society whose values he accepts and which he in his turn shapes towards further perfection, at the beginning of the twentieth century this ideal can only be presented as a hope, no longer as a reality, even on a fictional level.

The other thinker who provides Braun with a standard against which to measure the Social Democrats' interpretation and practice of Marxism is Nietzsche. Given his explicitly anti-socialist stance and his repeated denunciation of socialists as 'flat-headed', Nietzsche may seem an odd philosopher for a socialist to draw on.[18] In recent times Nietzsche's anti-democratic stance has been virtually explained away, and everybody has appropriated their bit of Nietzsche for a progressive cause, but at the turn of the century the combination of Marxism and Nietzsche was Lily Braun's unique invention.[19] She anticipated the modern view that Nietzsche was arguing for the diversification of individuality and understood individuality as something that has not yet been realized. Nietzsche provided Braun with arguments not only for the critique of Christianity, but also for the importance of a qualitative change in each individual – a change which was all-encompassing and not restricted to the orthodox Marxist view of the economic revolution from which everything else would follow as a matter of course. It was the Nietzschean insistence on individuality which helped her to resist the socialists' demand for the submission of the individual to the cause of Socialism. For her, the development of individuality became the precondition and the ultimate aim of Socialism.

Towards the end of the second volume of her *Memoiren*, the protagonist Alix makes a speech in a café to a group of socialists who are debating the way forward; this speech can be taken as Braun's summary of her views on Socialism. Interruptions and contradictions from her comrades provide a vivid image of the prevailing theoretical positions in the SPD against which Alix develops her dissenting position in a dreamlike state which associates her words with those of a seer. She draws on the aesthetics of religious writing in order to give the following view of how to achieve for Socialism the authority of a quasi-religious vision:

> Mit dem Ziel des größten Glücks der größten Anzahl, – an das ich glaubte, wie Sie alle, – schaffen wir eine Gesellschaft behäbiger Kleinbürger [...] Den Weg zu unserem Ziel finden wir nur, wenn die Idee der ethischen Revolution der Idee der ökonomischen Umwälzung Flügel verleiht.
>
> (II, pp. 653-654)

With this belief, Alix has found her absolute truth – one which isolates her from her comrades, but contains the summit of her insight and provides her with the ultimate certainty so that she can close her memoirs with the reassuring sentence: 'Und ich erkannte, daß ich nicht irre gegangen war' (II, p. 657).

With hindsight, we can today recognize Braun's insistence on individuality within Marxism as a radical demand whose adoption might have made Stalinism impossible. Yet that part of Nietzsche which Alix dismissed (see II, p. 653), the Nietzsche of the master and slave morality, is also present in her, without her recognizing it. Repeatedly the narrator reports that one of her desires and exhilarating experiences when speaking publicly is the power to unify the masses and to impose her will on her audience: 'Zu *einer* Riesenkraft wollte ich die schwarze Menschenmasse vor mir zusammen-schweißen, von *einem* unbeugsamen Willen beseelt' (II, p. 109). The emphasis on 'einer' and 'einem' stresses her goal of homogeneity. It is to be achieved, on her part, by excluding emotions in favour of iron determination: 'kein weiches Gefühl konnte mich überwältigen, eiserne Entschlossenheit beherrschte mich' (II, p. 109). Today, we cannot read this passage on iron determination and on imposing *one* unshakable will on the masses without thinking of fascist rhetoric and practice.

Braun was an outsider in her party because of her individualism, and her feminism also marginalized her. For among Marxists feminist issues were classed as minor problems which would be solved automatically after the revolution. Braun refused to accept the orthodox classification into 'Haupt-und Nebenwidersprüche'. Her ideas on the women's question, too, were shaped by her Nietzschean approach – again ironically so, since Nietzsche's misogyny excluded women from the unfolding of individuality he argued for, and reduced them to mere matter against which the male mind could rise undisturbed. Braun's un-Nietzschean application of the Nietzschean concept of self-development to women led her to fight for women's suffrage, economic independence, free sexuality, maternity leave, rights for servants, the abolition of the patriarchal household, and so on. The fact that Braun's *Memoiren* are so delightfully free from the usual party jargon reflects her unorthodoxy and the originality of her approach. Furthermore, the readability of this text is increased by her portrayal of the feminism of her protagonist Alix as an integral part of her socialist perspective and of her personal experience of life. Thus the narration of Alix's first tentative steps towards the SPD is intertwined with the narration of her scandalous love story with the divorced and recently remarried Heinrich Brandt, alias Heinrich Braun. While the good old combination of politics and romance accounts for the hold the narrator manages to have on her reader, the conventional nature of this romance is remarkable, coming as it does from a radical feminist. For when Braun writes about erotic experiences (as opposed to theoretical positions on sexuality, on which she can be very enlightening, daring and in advance of her time), she becomes clichéd and tends to overwrite:[20]

> Mein Herzblut, das ich bereit war, restlos für ihn zu vergießen, hatte es [i.e. ihr Festgewand] mit roten Rubinen bestickt, Schnüre, an denen die Tränen meiner Sehnsucht schimmernd gereiht waren, schmückten mir den Nacken, mit Smaragden der Hoffnung waren die seidenen Schuhe besetzt an meinen Füßen, die ihm entgegengingen, und auf meinen Armen, die ihn umfassen wollten, funkelten, alle Farben und allen Glanz der Welt in sich vereinend, die Diamanten meiner Leidenschaft.
>
> (II, pp. 94f. Similar instances of *Kitsch* on pp. 129, 143f. to take only a few examples)

Things become even worse when Braun, perhaps in a clumsy imitation of Goethe's nature poetry from his storm and stress period, uses the sun, the earth and the seasons as sexual metaphors. Immediately before she decides to have sex for the first time with her husband-to-be, the narrator invokes the following imagery:

> Und sie [i.e. die Sonne] war da. Glühend in junger Liebe, als küsse sie die Erde zum erstenmal. In der heißen Umarmung ihrer Strahlen ward die keusche Braut zum Weibe, das sich dem Geliebten schrankenlos hingibt. Sie warf die dunklen Schleier von sich, in die sie sich eben noch scheu gehüllt hatte, und auch die letzten weißen duftigen Hüllen zerriß sie. In ihrer prangenden Schöne stand sie vor ihm, die schimmernde weiße Stirn stolz gen Himmel gehoben, den schneeigen Busen rosig überhaucht von dem Gruß dessen, der sie erlöste.
>
> (II, p. 143)

Yet this overwritten and cloying scene, embarrassing in its predictability of stock images and stock feelings and its pseudo-elevated style ('ward', 'prangende Schöne', 'gen Himmel'), was composed by the same writer who opposed the institution of marriage with the concept of free love and women's development towards self-realization. In a public discussion Alix contradicts a speaker who proclaims that the Women's Movement will serve to improve family life since the emancipated woman will be able to share her husband's intellectual life so that he will not have to look for stimulation outside the home. Alix cuts straight through the illusion of the reconcilability of old and new moralities:

> Je mehr sich das Weib zur selbständigen Persönlichkeit
> entwickelt, mit eigenen Ansichten, Urteilen und
> Lebenszielen, desto mehr ist die alte Form der Ehe
> bedroht. Ihr Glück beruhte nicht auf Gleichheit,
> sondern auf Unterordnung, nicht auf Arbeitsgemein-
> schaft, sondern auf Arbeitsteilung. [...] Es kommt aber
> auch gar nicht darauf an, daß wir mit heißem Bemühen
> die Ehe retten; mag sie an der Entwicklung zerschellen,
> wie manche andere Lebensform, wenn nur der Kern
> erhalten bleibt: die Liebe.
>
> (II, pp. 539 and 540)

Here, an original and provocative point of view is put across in fluent and persuasive language. It is, in fact, the language of Lily Braun, the political journalist. For what is passed off in the autobiography as Alix's spontaneous intervention in a feminist discussion repeats verbatim Braun's article 'Das Problem der Ehe', which appeared in the Brauns' journal *Neue Gesellschaft* in 1905.[21] Braun skilfully inserts this and others of her articles into her auto-biography, slightly rearranging the order of paragraphs, cutting, adding situational description, and combining the presentation of her theoretical positions with that of her personal life and concrete experiences. In this instance, the experience of marital problems of her own forms the background to her theoretical statement.

Braun demonstrates both the interconnectedness of private experience and political positions and the contradiction between them. For while she argues for and lives a life in which a woman develops all her faculties and tries to exert an influence on the world, she longs erotically for the woman's submission to a superior male:

> — daß ich mich ihm, dem Starken, unterwerfen durfte, —
> welche tiefe Seligkeit war das!
>
> (I, p. 280)

> Je stärker ich die Überlegenheit seines Willens empfand,
> desto mehr liebte ich ihn.
>
> (II, p. 361)

Like the men who influenced her thinking, Goethe and Nietzsche, Braun transforms the traditional relationship between the sexes into an ontological truth. Goethe cast the unequal relationship between the sexes into the form of a natural complementary harmony in which man is assigned a Promethean position and woman is his clay:

> Denn einem jungen Paare, das von der Natur
> einigermaßen harmonisch gebildet ist, kann nichts zu
> einer schöneren Vereinigung gereichen, als wenn das
> Mädchen lehrbegierig und der Jüngling lehrhaft ist. Es
> entsteht daraus ein so gründliches als angenehmes
> Verhältnis. Sie erblickt in ihm den Schöpfer ihres
> geistigen Daseins, und er in ihr ein Geschöpf, das nicht
> der Natur, dem Zufall oder einem einseitigen Wollen,
> sondern einem beiderseitigen Willen seine Vollendung
> verdankt; [...].[22]

Nietzsche envisaged gender relations as equally natural and eternal, but antagonistic rather than harmonious:

> Sich im Grundproblem 'Mann und Weib' zu vergreifen,
> hier den abgründlichsten Antagonismus und die Noth-
> wendigkeit einer ewig-feindseligen Spannung zu
> leugnen, hier vielleicht von gleichen Rechten, gleicher
> Erziehung, gleichen Ansprüchen und Verpflichtungen zu
> träumen: das ist ein *typisches* Zeichen von
> Flachköpfigkeit, und ein Denker, der an dieser
> gefährlichen Stelle sich flach erwiesen hat – flach im
> Instinkte! –, darf überhaupt als verdächtig, mehr noch
> als verrathen, als aufgedeckt gelten: wahrscheinlich wird
> er für alle Grundfragen des Lebens, auch des
> zukünftigen Lebens, zu 'kurz' sein und in *keine* Tiefe
> hinunter können. Ein Mann hingegen, der Tiefe hat, in
> seinem Geiste, wie in seinen Begierden, auch jene Tiefe
> des Wohlwollens, welche der Strenge und Härte fähig ist,
> und leicht mit ihnen verwechselt wird, kann über das
> Weib immer nur *orientalisch* denken: er muss das Weib
> als Besitz, als verschliessbares Eigenthum, als etwas zur
> Dienstbarkeit Vorbestimmtes und in ihr sich Vollendetes
> fassen, [...].[23]

Unlike Goethe and Nietzsche, however, Braun asserts an essential inferior femininity in the erotic sphere, while at the same time arguing in all other spheres for the change of woman's position towards equality: 'Weibesliebe ist Hingabe an den Höherstehenden, [...]. Darum wird die erotische Treue um so seltener sein, je stärker das Weib sich geistig und seelisch individualisiert' (II, p. 362).

The contradiction between her demand for women's individuation and her assertion of a natural female desire for submission is never consciously reflected on by Braun. But it is perhaps the unconscious impact of this insoluble dissonance which makes her discriminate so harshly against other views of the male-female relationship: 'Nur die Halbgeschlechtlichen, die der

Natur Entfremdeten konstruieren künstlich eine Weibesliebe, die den
Gleichen begehrt. Den Höherstehenden will sie; denn blindes Vertrauen und
kindliche Schutzbedürftigkeit ist ihres Wesens Inhalt' (I, p. 384).

Braun's *Memoiren* are designed to construct her life as whole and to
progress teleologically, thus aiming to achieve homogeneity for an existence
torn by heterogeneous impulses, and to vindicate a career which led to her
isolation both from her class of origin and from the socialists to whose cause
she had devoted herself. And yet, despite her attempt to present herself as
'whole' and in control, the reader perceives 'dark corners' in her life which
speak of unresolved conflicts and contradictions. Apart from her desire for
erotic submission, the mother-daughter conflict springs to mind as an example
of such a corner where conflict has been stifled rather than resolved.

This is not to say that Braun is entirely repressed. She does face her
dissonant feelings on other issues, voicing doubts about the possibility of
uniting love and marriage (II, pp. 232-233), and professional life and
motherhood (II, pp. 226-228, 363-364) − both of which Alix argues for
passionately, yet experiences practical difficulties with. Braun's narrator-
protagonist realizes how both she and her husband unconsciously pursue
traditional role-expectations of each other (cf. II, p. 293). But her overriding
desire for a harmonious self makes Braun turn a blind eye to the existing
dissonance and end her fictionalized autobiography with a double novelistic
closure. Not only does Alix find peace of mind in her vision of the true way to
Socialism, even though this isolates her from her comrades; she also creates a
happy ending for her personal life − her marital problems are overcome and
both husband and wife see their son as the harbinger of the future, expressed
in the imagery of light and vegetation:

> Wo die dunkle Allee sich der weiten, sonnenbeglänzten
> Wiese öffnet, tauchte die schlanke Gestalt unseres
> Sohnes auf. Er hielt einen Zweig jungen Grüns in der
> hocherhobenen Hand. Der wehte über ihm wie eine
> Fahne.
>
> (II, p. 657)

To summarize, I would argue that by applying the male genre of the
'Bildungsroman' to her fictionalized autobiography of a feminist socialist,
Braun succeeds in constructing a female life in the public limelight as
meaningful in a spiritual sense although she lacked practical success. This

sense of pursuing a teleological course in her life enables her, paradoxically, to insist on both individualism and feminism within Socialism, which at the time regarded these as alien. To some extent, the construct of a homogeneous life enabled her to support heterogeneity. It is also due to her individualism and her feminism that Braun's language is, for the most part, free from party jargon, lively, evocative and very readable – that is, as far as rational and theoretical topics are concerned. However, when she talks of erotic desires and experiences, her language becomes encrusted with clichéd metaphors. While this may reflect the difficulties women had at the beginning of this century in talking publicly of their sexuality, it seems to me that it is also an indication of the fact that Braun's strengths lie rather in the realm of political thought than in that of art – although she has enough artistic sensibility to write a book which gives a fascinating picture of her times and of a woman who in many respects refused to be bound by their accepted limitations.

Braun's *Memoiren* also offer interesting points as regards theories of autobiography and subjectivity, showing as they do that homogeneity and heterogeneity of the subject, a teleological perspective and the absence of its fulfilment, may coexist in a complex relationship, instead of being mutually exclusive. Furthermore, Braun's *Memoiren* exemplify how a woman writer, in drawing on the male tradition of philosophy and literature, expands and transforms some aspects of this tradition successfully in order to apply it to a feminist context, and, at the same time, is herself caught up in some of this tradition's misogynist assumptions. Genre is indeed *modified*, but not overcome, by gender.

NOTES

[1]See bibliographical appendix.

[2]See Sidonie Smith, *A Poetics of Women's Autobiography. Marginality and the Fictions of Self-Representation* (Bloomington and Indianapolis: Indiana UP, 1987), pp. 7-8.

[3]Nancy Chodorow, *The Reproduction of Mothering* (Berkeley: University of California Press, 1978).

[4]See Doris Sommer, '"Not Just a Personal Story": Women's Testimonies and the Plural Self', in *Life/Lines*, ed. by Bella Brodzki and Celeste Schenck (Ithaca and London: Cornell UP, 1988), pp. 107-130, and Mary Lowenthal Felstiner, 'Taking Her Life/History: The Autobiography of Charlotte Salomon', ibid., pp. 320-337, among many other interesting analyses in this volume.

[5]Katherine Goodman, *Dis/Closures: Women's Autobiography in Germany Between 1790 and 1914* (New York/Berne/Frankfurt/M.: Lang, 1986), pp. 209-10.

[6]See for example Sara Friedrichsmeyer, 'Women's Writing and the Construct of an Integrated Self', in *The Enlightenment and Its Legacy*, ed. by Sara Friedrichsmeyer and Barbara Becker-Cantarino (Bonn: Bouvier, 1991), pp. 171-180; and Annegret Heitmann, 'Zwischen Macht und Marginalität. Leonora Christines Autobiographie *Jammerminde* als Zeugnis eines gesellschaftlichen Umsturzes', in *Frauen – Literatur – Revolution*, ed. by Ingeborg Singendonk-Heublein et al. (Pfaffenweiler: Centaurus, 1991), pp. 188-98.

[7]See Goodman, pp. 209-210 (note 5).

[8]Patricia Meyer Spacks, *Imagining a Self. Autobiography and Novel in 18th-Century England* (London and Cambridge, Mass.: Harvard UP, 1976), p. 300.

[9]Braun is mentioned in Marielouise Janssen-Jurreit's seminal work *Sexismus. Über die Abtreibung der Frauenfrage* (Munich: Carl Hanser, 1978[3] (1976)), but Braun's antagonist, Clara Zetkin, is given far more attention. See also Richard J. Evans, *The Feminist Movement in Germany 1894-1933* (London and Beverley Hills: SAGE Publications, 1976); Evans analyses Braun's political impact within the Women's Movement. Bärbel Clemens, *"Menschenrechte haben kein Geschlecht!" Zum Politikverständnis der bürgerlichen Frauenbewegung* (Pfaffenweiler: Centaurus, 1988), pp. 42-49, analyses the theoretical assumptions of Lily von Gizycki's (= Lily Braun's) arguments for female suffrage. See also the first full-length study of Braun since the second Women's Movement began, Ute Lischke McNab, *Lily Braun and the German Women's Movement. 1865-1916* (PhD thesis, Cambridge, 1984). Unfortunately this study does not go beyond paraphrase and facile generalization.

[10]Lily Braun, *Memoiren einer Sozialistin*, intr. by Monika Kramme, repr. of the 1926 edition (Bonn: Dietz, 1985), and *Memoiren einer Sozialistin* ed., abridged and intr. by Elisabeth Fetscher (Munich and Zurich: Piper, 1985). See also the reprint of Lily Braun, *Die Frauenfrage. Ihre geschichtliche Entwicklung und ihre wirtschaftliche Seite*, intr. by Beatrix Wrede-Bouvier (Bonn: Dietz, 1979 (1901)). In this article I am quoting from the oldest unchanged reprints that were available to me. Since Braun's autobiography was published in two separate full-length volumes, they were reprinted according to demand, and it appears that the second volume was the more popular one: Lily Braun, *Memoiren einer Sozialistin. Lehrjahre* (Munich: Albert Langen, 1923 (1909)) and *Memoiren einer Sozialistin. Kampfjahre*

(Munich: Albert Langen, 1922 (1911)), here called I and II. My title is an allusion to the following observation on an SPD party conference in the Hanover 'Ballhof': "'...Auch auf diesem Parteitag hat es sich gezeigt, daß die Partei über ihre Grundsätze und ihre Taktik einheitlich denkt und auch fernerhin in voller Einmütigkeit handeln wird...,'' sagte Singer zum Schluß. Die Arbeitermarseillaise brauste durch den Ballhof. Hörte niemand die Dissonanz? Es waren nicht die Geister der Vergangenheit, die Prinzessinnen, die Kurfürsten und die Könige, die sie hervorriefen. Es war der Geist der Zukunft.' (II, p. 329)

[11]Alfred G. Meyer, *The Feminism and Socialism of Lily Braun* (Bloomington and Indianapolis: Indiana UP, 1985). See Meyer's condensation of the early chapters of his book in his article 'The Radicalization of Lily Braun', in *German Women in the Nineteenth Century. A Social History*, ed. by John C. Fout (New York and London: Holmes and Meier, 1984), pp. 218-33.

[12]Lily Braun, *Selected Writings on Feminism and Socialism*, trans. and ed. by Alfred G. Meyer (Bloomington and Indianapolis: Indiana UP, 1987).

[13]Goodman, p. 141 (note 5).

[14]For an account of revisionism within the context of the Socialist Party and an evaluation of Lily Braun's revisionist ideas in particular, see Meyer, *The Feminism and Socialism of Lily Braun*, pp. 77-112.

[15]Meyer, pp. 163-64.

[16]See Marianne Schuller's criticism of the absence of laughter in feminine discourse in 'Wenn's im Feminismus lachte...', in her *Im Unterschied. Lesen/Korrespondieren/Adressieren* (Frankfurt/Main: Neue Kritik, 1990), p. 207: 'Das Lachen also bringt das Heterogene, Zwieschlächtige und Unreine ins Spiel; das Materielle, Körperliche, das dem Wissen widersteht. In einer paradoxalen Wendung könnte man sagen: das Lachen ist das Zeichen ohne Bedeutung. In dem Maße aber, wie es einen Riß in die Sinnfunktion einführt, muß jedes sich zur Weltanschauung schließende Sinnkonzept das Lachen fürchten wie der Teufel das Weihwasser.' While this critique highlights certain tendencies which lead to the absence of laughter, it also remythologizes laughter as a subversive force per se. Yet laughter, provoked by humour or satire, can also contribute to the perpetuation of the status quo, as is shown by Dagmar C.G. Lorenz in her essay 'Humor bei zeitgenössischen Autorinnen', *The Germanic Review*, vol. LXII, no. 1 (Winter 1987), pp. 28-36.

[17]W.B. Yeats, *Reveries over Childhood and Youth* (1915). Quoted from Roy Pascal, *Design and Truth in Autobiography* (London: Routledge and Kegan Paul, 1960), p. 137.

[18]See Friedrich Nietzsche, *Jenseits von Gut und Böse*, in *Nietzsche. Werke. Kritische Gesamtausgabe*, ed. by Giorgio Colli and Mazzino Montinari (Berlin: Walter de Gruyter, 1968), vol. VI/2, fünftes Hauptstück, no. 203, pp. 129f.: 'Die *Gesammt-Entartung des Menschen*, hinab bis zu dem, was heute den socialistischen Tölpeln und Flachköpfen als ihr "Mensch der Zukunft" erscheint, – als ihr Ideal! – diese Entartung und Verkleinerung des Menschen zum vollkommenen Heerdenthiere (oder, wie sie sagen, zum Menschen der "freien Gesellschaft"), diese Verthierung des Menschen zum Zwergthiere der gleichen Rechte und Ansprüche ist *möglich*, es ist kein Zweifel! Wer diese Möglichkeit einmal bis zu Ende gedacht hat, kennt keinen Ekel mehr, als die übrigen Menschen, – und vielleicht auch eine neue *Aufgabe*!...' See similar statements on socialism in *Jenseits von Gut und Böse*, zweites Hauptstück, no. 44, p. 57; fünftes Hauptstück, no. 202, p. 127; neuntes Hauptstück, no. 265, p. 229; see also Nietzsche's *Zur Genealogie der Moral* in vol. VI/2, erste Abhandlung, no. 5,

p. 278 and *Die Fröhliche Wissenschaft*, in *Nietzsche. Werke. Kritische Gesamtausgabe*, vol. V/2, fünftes Buch, no. 356, p. 279.

[19]See for example Georges Bataille, 'Nietzsche (1949)', in *Nietzsche*, ed. by Jörg Salaquarda (Darmstadt: Wissenschaftliche Buchgesellschaft, 1980), pp. 45-49; Wolfgang Müller-Lauter, 'Nietzsches Lehre vom Willen zur Macht (1974)', in *Nietzsche*, pp. 234-287. See also the essays collected in *90 Jahre philosophische Nietzsche-Rezeption*, ed. by Alfredo Guzzoni (Königstein: Hain, 1979). See *Friedrich Nietzsche. Zur Genealogie der Moral*, ed. by W.D. Williams (Oxford: Blackwell, 1972), introduction, pp. vii-xxi.

[20]In my view of Lily Braun's language I differ from Alfred G. Meyer who, in *The Feminism and Socialism of Lily Braun*, pp. 109-111, evaluates it in wholly positive terms.

[21]See Lily Braun, 'The Marriage Problem', in *Selected Writings on Feminism and Socialism*, pp. 124-28 (note 12).

[22]Johann Wolfgang von Goethe, *Aus meinem Leben. Dichtung und Wahrheit*, in *Sämtliche Werke*, ed. by Ernst Beutler et al. (Munich: dtv, 1977), vol. 10, p. 207.

[23]Friedrich Nietzsche, *Jenseits von Gut und Böse* (note 18), vol. VI, 2, siebentes Hauptstück, no. 238, p. 181.

Bibliographical Appendix

1) Work on women's autobiographies:

Shari Benstock (ed.), *The Private Self: Theory and Practice in Women's Autobiographical Writings* (Chapel Hill: University of North Carolina Press, 1988).

Bella Brodzki & Celeste Schenck (eds.), *Life/Lines. Theorizing Women's Autobiography* (Ithaca and London: Cornell UP, 1988).

Sara Friedrichsmeyer, 'Women's Writing and the Construct of an Integrated Self' in *The Enlightenment and Its Legacy*, ed. by Sara Friedrichsmeyer and Barbara Becker-Cantarino (Bonn: Bouvier, 1991), pp. 171-80.

Katherine Goodman, *Dis/Closures: Women's Autobiography in Germany Between 1790 and 1914* (New York/Berne/Frankfurt/M.: Lang, 1986).

Mary Grimley Mason & Carol Hurd Green (eds.), *Journeys: Autobiographical Writings by Women* (Boston: G.K. Hall, 1979).

Annegret Heitmann, 'Zwischen Macht und Marginalität. Leonora Christines Autobiographie *Jammersminde* als Zeugnis eines gesellschaftlichen Umsturzes' in *Frauen – Literatur – Revolution*, ed. by Ingeborg Singendonk-Heublein et al. (Pfaffenweiler: Centaurus, 1991), pp. 188-98.

Estelle C. Jelinek, *The Tradition of Women's Autobiography* (Boston: Twayne, 1986).

Estelle C. Jelinek (ed.), *Women's Autobiography: Essays in Criticism* (Bloomington: Indiana UP, 1980).

B. Martin /A. Lixl, 'Zur Politik persönlichen Erinnerns. Frauenautobiographik um die Jahrhundertwende', in *Vom Andern und vom Selbst*, ed. by Reinhold Grimm and Jost Hermand (Königstein: Hain, 1985), pp. 94-115.

Patricia Meyer Spacks, *Imagining a Self. Autobiography and Novel in 18th-Century England* (London and Cambridge, Mass.: Harvard UP, 1976).

Barbara Saunders, *Contemporary German Autobiography. Literary Approaches to the Problem of Identity* (London: Institute of Germanic Studies, University of London, 1985).

Sidonie Smith, *A Poetics of Women's Autobiography. Marginality and the Fictions of Self-Representation* (Bloomington and Indianapolis: Indiana UP, 1987).

Domna C. Stanton (ed.), *The Female Autograph* (New York: New York Literary Forum, 1984).

Gudrun Wedel, 'Rekonstruktionen des eigenen Lebens. Autobiographien von Frauen im 19. Jahrhundert' in *Deutsche Literatur von Frauen.* Zweiter Band. *19. und 20. Jahrhundert*, ed. by Gisela Brinker-Gabler (Munich: C.H. Beck, 1988), pp. 154-65.

2) Work by men on autobiography:

Philippe Lejeune, *Je est un autre* (Paris: Seuil, 1980).

Philippe Lejeune, *Le pacte autobiographique* (Paris: Seuil, 1975).

Georges May, *L'Autobiographie* (Paris: Presses Universitaires de France, 1979).

Georg Misch, *Geschichte der Autobiographie* (1907 and 1955; repr. Frankfurt/M.: G. Schulte, 1969).

Bernd Neumann, *Identität und Rollenzwang: Zur Theorie der Autobiographie* (Frankfurt/M.: Athenäum, 1970).

Günter Niggl, *Geschichte der deutschen Autobiographie im 18. Jahrhundert: Theoretische und literarische Entfaltung* (Stuttgart: J.B. Metzler, 1977).

James Olney (ed.), *Autobiogaphy: Essays Critical and Theoretical* (Princeton: Princeton UP, 1980).

James Olney, *Metaphors of Self: The Meaning of Autobiography* (Princeton: Princeton UP, 1972).

Roy Pascal, *Design and Truth in Autobiography* (London: Routledge and Kegan Paul, 1960).

Wayne Shumaker, *English Autobiography: Its Emergence, Materials, and Forms* (Berkeley and Los Angeles: University of California Press, 1954).

William C. Spengemann, *Forms of Autobiography: Episodes in the History of a Literary Genre* (New Haven and London: Yale UP, 1980).

Jo Mihaly with her grandmother and a friend

6

Jo Mihaly and her War Diary
...da gibt's ein Wiedersehn!

From the game 'Krieg' to the dance 'Der tote Soldat'; from the child who welcomed war to the pacifist

Andrea Hahn

Und kein Wiedersehn in der Heimat, o nein; kein Wiedersehn.
Leere Worte, Lügen. Wie ich das alles hasse!

(p. 365)

These are the sober words of a sixteen-year-old girl at the end of the First World War, summing up what few had the courage to recognize. Honesty and a commitment to oppose war, National Socialism and the stupidity and cruelty of so-called 'good' citizens on the one hand, and to support oppressed individuals and social outcasts on the other – these qualities characterize the life and work of this girl, later to become the writer and dancer Elfriede Kuhr, who wrote under the name of Jo Mihaly.

Elfriede Alice Kuhr, also known as Piete, was born on 25 April 1902 in the West Prussian town of Schneidemühl (today the Polish town Pita) in the province of Posen. Her mother, Margarete Kuhr née Golz, ran a 'Meisterschule für Bühne und Konzert' in Berlin; her father, Richard Kuhr, was an architect in Danzig. The two elder sons lived with him, but Elfriede and her brother Wilhelm grew up with their maternal grandparents in Schneidemühl. After attending a school for young ladies, which she left without taking the final examination, and training as a nurse for infants, Jo Mihaly went to Berlin in 1920 to study ballet, fencing and acrobatics with Hans Gérard and Max Terpis. From 1923 to 1925 she toured Germany as a member of various ballet groups. From 1925 to 1933 there followed contracts as a solo dancer in the Dreistädte-Theater Königshütte-Beuthen-Gleiwitz and the Volksbühne Berlin. Encouraged mainly by Mary Wigman, she put on her own dance matinées, in which social criticism played a large role. In 1929, the year of her marriage to the actor Leonhard Steckel, her first poetic work appeared: *Die Ballade vom Elend*, a novel about two tramps in prison. From 1931 to 1933 she was a member of the 'Rote Gewerkschaftsopposition' of actors and of the 'Rote Hilfe' and in 1933, listed as one of the 'verbrannte Dichter', she had to emigrate with her husband and their newborn daughter Anja to Switzerland, where she lived first in Zurich.

In exile she was active in various ways against National Socialism: from 1934 to 1938 she was the leader of the 'Neuer Chor' in Zurich, which aimed by means of words and dance to draw attention to the situation in Germany and the roots of fascism, as she saw it, in capitalism. For years she performed her own dance numbers with political content in Zurich and Paris, sometimes together with the singer Ernst Busch. In 1938/39 she supported the banned German Communist Party, forged links with resistance groups and produced leaflets against the Nazis which were distributed in South Germany. The 'Kulturgemeinschaft der Emigranten in Zürich' was founded under her chairmanship in 1943; it continued the political fight against National Socialism, and above all took up the case of refugees interned in Swiss camps. After the end of the war she became important as the co-founder and for a time (1945) president of the 'Schutzverband deutscher Schriftsteller in der Schweiz'. In Frankfurt am Main she devoted herself in 1945/46 to the rebuilding of cultural life and initiated the 'Freie deutsche Kulturgesellschaft'. From 1949 she lived as an independent writer in Ascona, where she was co-founder of the 'Werkkreis der Literatur'. In the eighties she took part in the film '*Fantasmi & Ospiti*' under the direction of Isa Hesse-Rabinovitch (released 1989). Jo Mihaly died on March 29th 1989 in Seeshaupt. She received awards from the city of Zurich in 1948, 1958 and 1960, and from the city of Ascona in 1980.

As in her dances, Jo Mihaly tried to draw attention to abuses within society in her poetic works – poems, stories, novels and children's books. She also tried to encourage sympathy for those deprived of their rights, for those on the fringes of society to whom it gladly turns a blind eye and for those stigmatized as outsiders. Examples of this are *Hüter des Bruders* (1942), the story of a freedom fighter on the run who is offered hospitality by gypsies at the risk of their own lives; the novel *Die Steine* (1946) in which she portrayed the misery of German emigrants; and the collection of stories *Das Leben ist hart* (1954) in which she depicted the harsh life of mountain peasants in the Ticino. Increasingly the author concerned herself with innocent, often helpless animals, creatures often dependent on man, as for example in *Der weiße Zug* (1957), in the stories *Von Mensch und Tier* (1961) and in *Der verzauberte Hase* (1971).

Jo Mihaly's social involvement can be traced back to her experiences during the First World War. Later, in 1983, an interviewer reported:

> Prägende Erfahrung dieser Zeit sei Mitleid gewesen, [...]
> Mitleid mit den *'nebenher Schlechtbehandelten'*, es habe
> am Anfang ihres Engagements gestanden und sie ein
> Leben lang motiviert und begleitet.[1]

She documented this phase, which was crucially important for her emotional development, in a diary, written during the First World War and first published in 1982 under the title *...da gibt's ein Wiedersehn! Kriegstagebuch eines Mädchens 1914-1918*.[2] The remainder of this essay traces the maturing of the child Piete who at first believes the German nationalist ideas of her mother and then grows into a pacifism that respects human beings, nature and the animal kingdom.

On 14 August 1914 Germany declared war on Russia and the First World War began officially. The European nations were in a state of feverish enthusiasm, the soldiers marched out to battle borne along by the general euphoria and romantic dreams. Europe before the war had been riven with tensions: political crises were the order of the day; nationalist thinking had led to separatism and to the start of the collapse of the Austro-Hungarian

Empire; industrialization had sharpened class distinctions and animosity between the proletariat and the bourgeoisie as well as between rich and poor countries; the interests and aims of a comparatively small number of industrialists and the authoritarian state stood out against broadly based claims for more democracy and more social justice.[3] Fear of poverty and of social decline, stagnation and a crippling everyday life, wearying struggles and resignation among a large part of the European population, feelings of meaninglessness and a sense of doom among intellectuals, imperialism on the part of the rulers, all of these escalated; the tension rose to its peak in the July crisis of 1914 and made the outbreak of war seem like a release: government and people revived the illusion of forming a unity, a unity of purpose against the common enemy, the supposed aggressor; the chance to break out from the monotony of everyday life seemed to be close at hand; victory, honour, heroism beckoned. The greatest fear now was that the war might be over before one had taken part in it. Novels, stories, poems, letters and diaries in increasing numbers bear witness to this. Whether Rupert Brooke or the characters in Erich Maria Remarque's pacifist novel *Im Westen nichts Neues* (1928), Ernst Jünger spoke for all at the start of the war when in his *In Stahlgewittern* (1920) he recalled:

> Der Krieg mußte es uns ja bringen, das Große, Starke, Feierliche. [...] Ach, nur nicht zu Hause bleiben, nur mitmachen dürfen.[4]

The intoxication and dreams of victory also reach the West Prussian garrison town of Schneidemühl, as Elfriede − Piete − Kuhr, twelve years old at the time, records in her first diary entry (1 August 1914): 'In der Stadt sind alle Häuser beflaggt, als feierten wir ein Fest' (p. 14). Like most adults, the children welcome an event that enables them to identify with the feelings of the grown-ups and holds out the prospect of a great adventure. Each morning on waking Piete looks forward to another day with something new and interesting in prospect. All the greater is her disappointment when, on the second day of the war, she gets just as many good things to eat and goes for her walk as usual: 'Ich bin traurig. Ich möchte dort sein, wo Krieg ist, um zu wissen, wie er ist' (p. 16). And whilst adult men can serve the fatherland, a child feels excluded and useless:

Ich ärgerte mich sehr, weil ich erst zwölf Jahre alt und
kein Mann bin. Was nützt es, ein Kind zu sein, wenn
Krieg ist. Ein Kind ist im Krieg gar nichts wert. Man
muß Soldat sein.

(p. 15)

But Piete and her friends know how to console themselves: if one can't join
the war, then one can play it. Drill is performed strenuously in the courtyard;
dolls lose their interest and the answer to the question 'what is your favourite
game?' is 'Soldat' (p. 97), or 'Leutnant von Yellenic und Schwester Martha'
(p. 150). At school one can draw battleships, move little flags on maps and −
fairground memories come flooding back − one can hammer nails into a cross
at the cost of a contribution towards the war effort: 'Es macht Spaß' (p. 94).
And, best of all, every time a great victory is to be celebrated, there is a day off
school. The following dialogue needs no comment. When 10,000 Russian
prisoners have been taken after a battle, Piete's friend Gretel asks:

'Hast du dann morgen schulfrei?' [...] 'Nee', sagte ich,
'erst bei fünfzigtausend.' 'Schade!' sagte Gretel.

(p. 65)

However, the war did not look all that romantic for long. The high-
flying expectations of magnificent parades and quick campaigns à la 1812-15
and 1870-71 were soon disappointed − the soldiers were not back home for
Christmas.   After an initially successful offensive by German troops,
particularly on the Western front, the advance soon came to a halt; already in
December 1914 the lines in the West and the East were drawn and a grinding
war of attrition set in. There was no marching out with flags and fanfares; the
modern machinery of war replaced this with an inhuman slaughter: trenches,
mud; waiting in the heat and the cold; hunger; poison gas, machine-gun fire
and mass attacks, and at most a few yards of territory won or lost at great
human cost − such was the daily fare of the soldiers.

At home everyday life looked different. Propaganda tried to obscure
the truth, but people were not spared the effects for long. In a town close to
the front like Schneidemühl with a garrison, hospitals and a prisoner-of-war
camp, a railway station where thousands of soldiers in transit stopped for a
break, and where the ground often vibrated with the commotion of nearby
fighting, the population came into close contact with the effects of war.
Personal deprivations could not be avoided: food became first expensive, then

scarcer and scarcer, until the inhabitants often no longer knew where their next meal was coming from; fuel posed the same problems. The Golz family, originally well-off, becomes poor during the course of the war. Piano lessons for the children can no longer be paid for, the servant girl has to be given notice, an old rep door-curtain has to do for a confirmation dress and black shoes from the undertaker stand in for accessories. Yet more sacrifices are necessary: Piete's friend Dora Haensch has to send her dog as a first-aid dog to the front, a loss that hits animal-loving Piete particularly hard and makes clear to her that war destroys not only people but also animals and plants.

In the early days there was a great sense of unity, but soon hostility towards individual sections of the population becomes increasingly fierce. As so often, the Jews are harried as scapegoats; at the first signs of disillusion-ment they are accused of causing the war in order to make money. Piete's schoolfriend Sibylla Löwenstein is reviled and ostracized as 'Judsche' (p. 49) and 'Judensau' (p. 56); Piete herself, who is the only one to remain friends with her, is abused as a suspected Jewess. The girl innocent of all such prejudice, and later not able to imagine why the Germans and the Poles can no longer be friends, feels confused. Although her mother supports her tolerant attitude and reassures her with the comment that the growing anti-Semitism is only the result of a general nervousness, she is irritated by the discrepancy between the hostility towards those accused of starting the war and the public displays of enthusiasm for it:

> Und dann, wenn die Juden den Krieg gemacht haben
> und man sie so deswegen verachtet — warum schreien
> dann alle hurra und sagen, der Krieg sei Ehrensache und
> es sei herrlich, fürs Vaterland zu fallen?

(p. 70)

The unanswered questions and contradictions increase. Newspaper accounts and eye-witness reports frequently contradict one another; rumours do the rest.

The everyday scene is filled not by exultant victors and romantic heroes, but by the dead and wounded. As assistant and companion to her grandmother Piete is drawn into the lives and the stories of the soldiers who report to the Red Cross post at Schneidemühl railway station or lie in the military hospitals and later sometimes write letters to her from the front. In the process she learns things that are absent from the sanitized newspaper accounts: how inhabitants of the border region were maltreated and had to flee from their homes; about the horrifying mutilations of the wounded, and about the desperate battle for Verdun. She sees soldiers going mad with physical pain or psychic strain. One of them, who fought in Masuria and had to watch Russians drowning in the swamps,

> [...] rannte vor der Rotkreuzbude auf und ab, raufte sich das Haar, schlug mit der Stirn mindestens zehnmal gegen einen eisernen Laternenpfahl und brüllte: 'Ich hab sie schreien hören, mir kann keiner was erzählen! Ich hab sie schreien hören, hab sie schreien hören!' Dann schrie er selber mit weitoffenem Mund: 'Aaaaah... aaaah...aaaah...', bis ein paar Sanitäter gelaufen kamen und ihm die Arme auf dem Rücken festhielten. Das Gesicht hatte er sich am Laternenpfahl ganz zerschlagen, es rieselte Blut von seiner Stirn. [...]
> Als man ihn endlich fortgebracht hatte, sagte ich zu Großmutter: 'Sie schreien ja doch, Großmuttchen! Siehst du, sie schreien in den Sümpfen. Der Soldat lügt nicht!'
>
> (p. 56)

The picture of men crying out and drowning in the swamps continued to haunt Jo Mihaly; she was to return to it years later in her novel *Hüter des Bruders*.[5] Death strikes down not only strangers but people to whom Piete is close. No member of the Golz-Kuhr family is in fact killed in battle — Piete's uncle Bruno comes back safely and her brother Willi does not have to go to the front at all — but close relatives and friends are on the list of casualties, just as are artists and writers whom Piete admires, like August Macke and Franz Marc, also Hermann Löns, all of whose songs she knows by heart. As a children's nurse she has to see babies waste away and even die for want of nourishment and medicines to save the 'kleine Hungerleichen' (p. 342). Worst of all, before she enters the nursing service she is shattered in December 1917 by the fatal aeroplane crash of Lieutenant Werner Waldecker, her first love. With the news of his death her world collapses: 'Ich dachte bloß immer: "Tot!" Ein gähnend schwarzes Loch' (p. 297). And she asks again and again: 'Was soll ich nur machen?? [...] Warum hast du das zugelassen, lieber Gott? *Warum?*' (p. 299) Piete's schoolwork deteriorates. She does not qualify for a leaving certificate. Her attitude towards war changes irrevocably.

Chaos and death, the constant confrontation with experiences threatening people's very existence, the consequent uncertainties, anxiety and pain that must be overcome if they are not to lead to madness or suicide – all demand appropriate strategies in response. In the literature on the First World War, most of it written after the event, two trends are evident: first the attempt to find a direct and positive counterbalance to the terrible experiences, and second concern with questions of meaning.

Escape into the idyll of everyday things and the little pleasures of life brings moments of respite or oblivion. This applies just as much to soldiers at the front as to people at home and it plays an ever greater role as the war continues and the feeling grows that it will never come to an end.[6] Piete finds distractions in the cosiness of the Red Cross post where it is 'wie bei Muttern' (p. 72), in the garden with the steadfast old apple tree, in looking after Minka the kitten and Rebecca the slow-worm, later in party games with their boisterous joviality, in flirtations, in looking after the sick and in music:

> Ich bat sie [Gretel], gleich zu uns nach oben zu kommen; sie könne mit uns Abendbrot essen; dann würde ich ihr alle Lieder von Gil singen, die ich auf >El bobo< [Pietes Gitarre] spielen kann. So kam sie zum erstenmal wieder zu mir. Wir aßen mit Großmutter Pellkartoffeln mit süßsaurer Apfelsoße und saßen nachher am offenen Ofenloch, und ich spielte und sang alle Gil-Lieder. Die Glut im Ofenloch sprühte manchmal wie rote Sterne auf. Es war wie früher. Ich war so glücklich.
>
> (p. 368f)

Together with Gretel, Piete contrives for herself a further means of escape: the game 'Leutnant Yellenic und Schwester Martha', which is continued as a form of serial story throughout the duration of the war. Each time, topical themes and situations, particularly Werner Waldecker's death, are taken up, lived through again as fiction, and given expression:

> Krieg, Verwundung, Lazarett, Gesundung, Kasinobälle – und wieder Krieg und Front und Flugzeugabstürze und so weiter. Auch Begräbnisse. Aber wir konnten ja gar nichts anderes spielen als Krieg, weil es keinen Frieden gab.
>
> (p. 349)

In this way, reality, so hard to come to terms with, can be worked out to some extent in play. Nature, too, becomes a protective wall against destruction, for nature is innocent in contrast to man. Thus Piete reacts with characteristic passion to the threat by Willi's friend Androwski that he will one day have had enough 'von diesem rotzigen Leben', disillusioned as he is by the war:

> 'Nein!' [...] 'Das dürfen Sie nicht sagen. Das Leben ist schön, ich meine: die Natur. Die Tiere. Der Wind, das Gras − '
>
> (p. 226)

With her little flights into make-believe Piete creates for herself small refuges where harmony is set against chaos, and which provide support and protection from despair. Retreat into 'little pleasures' only produces moments of respite, however, and is not enough to assimilate the war experience; it cannot make sense of the chaos and bloodshed:

> Die Sinnfrage, die sich in dieser Situation stellt, verlangt nach einer Antwort, die dem eigenen Leben Sinn verleiht oder zumindest in der gegenwärtigen Lage soviel Halt und Orientierung gibt, daß das Weiterleben möglich ist.[7]

The answers given in literature range from arguments justifying the war to admissions of meaninglessness. The categories that Ernst Jünger establishes in his war story *Sturm*, which appeared in 1979, make this clear:

> Wenn ich mit anderen darüber sprach, merkte ich, wie wenig der Mensch im Grunde in sich zu Hause ist. Die einen suchten das Getane zu heiligen, die anderen zu entschuldigen, die dritten verdammten es.[8]

While Jünger defines war as an unavoidable historical necessity which will lead from chaos to a new and better order, the National Socialist author, Hans Zöberlein, seeks redemption in the struggle for 'Lebensraum' for the German people − if necessary using violence. If no meaning can be found, some lesson for the future must at least proceed from this realization, or one ends in madness like Siegfried Sassoon, cynicism like Robert Graves, or dies like Remarque's protagonist Paul Bäumler[9] and Adrienne Thomas's Katrin.[10] Thus, for many, the only meaning they can wrest from the meaninglessness lies in keeping alive the awareness of the inhuman aspect of war, in order to warn future generations and thereby to prevent further conflict. Art presents a possible way of achieving this.[11]

In Jo Mihaly's diary various responses and reactions are similarly introduced. There is the soldier who goes mad, the cynic Androwski who can only keep a hold on life by hoping that out of the chaos a new society will emerge as it appears to be doing in Bolshevist Russia; the brother who seeks solace in music; the grandmother who looks for comfort in religion; the mother who escapes into enthusiasm for German Nationalism and finally takes refuge in the myth of the 'stab in the back'. During the course of the war Piete herself lives through the complete range from blind faith via denial of the truth to the admission of meaninglessness. Moreover, in her case the question of meaning is linked with a further set of problems. In 1914 she is twelve years old, in 1918 sixteen: the years of war coincide with the time of her puberty. While a world – in Germany the Wilhelmine Empire with its subservience to authority – is falling to pieces, old sets of values being superseded by new ones, she has at the same time to cope with the confusion of identity that goes with her age. She has to free herself from the attachments of childhood, test her own ideals against those of her role models, and develop into an autonomous person.

In the first sections of the diary she introduces her imaginary reader not only to the events of the war, but also to her family and her former circumstances. All we hear about her father is that he lives with his two elder sons in Danzig and that she does not know him; very much later she adds that he in fact never asks about his two younger children and that they have no wish to see him. Her mother's father was the head of the family until his death in 1912, after that her grandmother and mother. Piete's life and that of her much-loved brother Willi are marked by both these women.

The children have a very close relationship with their grandmother, Bertha Golz née Haber, the one who is always there, the educator, carer and provider of a harmonious family life. They owe it to her that their upbringing is free and unrestricted, largely unencumbered by stuffy Wilhelmine conventions. Piete wanders alone through the fields and meadows, goes swimming with her friend in the Sandsee, sets up wigwams in the wood with Willi and plays with the neighbours' children, who are not always 'quite the right class'. She, the child from the white villa, is allowed to eat bread and dripping with the family of her coachman. Snobbery seems to be unknown to her grandmother, the widow of an architect and local councillor, and from her Piete has inherited the leftish streak – the 'rote Ader' (p. 121) – that her mother recognizes with such horror in her daughter. For Bertha Golz, a deeply religious woman, the commandment to love one's neighbour and the principle of respect for others still apply even in war. Whether friend or foe, 'es sind alles Menschen, man soll damit nicht spotten' (p. 147). As head of the Red Cross post at Schneidemühl station she works selflessly throughout the war, to the point of exhaustion, for the welfare of the soldiers and the wounded, and despite increasing impoverishment distributes her belongings generously among them. Her commitment springs not from approval of the war but from purely humanist convictions. She is the only member of the family not to be carried away on a wave of enthusiasm; she rejects it from the first, not being prepared to understand that 'die Menschen nicht Frieden halten können − !' (p. 15). Even during the first days of the war she horrifies those around her with her views:

> Die Soldaten sollten die Gewehre hinwerfen und sagen:
> 'Wir machen nicht mehr mit' und sollten nach Haus gehen!
>   [...] Die Mütter sollten alle zum Kaiser gehen und sagen: 'Jetzt aber Frieden!'
>
>   (p. 86)

Piete's mother Margarete Kuhr represents the opposite pole to Bertha Golz. Piete correctly assesses her relationship with the two women when she states:

> Großmutter ist wie meine Mutter, während Muttchen in Berlin eine Art Fee ist, eine Königin, die wir anbeten.
>   (p. 222)

She runs a singing school in Berlin, and can only make rare visits to Schneidemühl, which then turn into family celebrations. Not only does this beautiful and adored woman keep at a physical distance, she signs her letters 'Eure Grete Kuhr' (p. 364): Piete sometimes thinks she is too modern to make use of old-fashioned words such as 'Mutter' or 'Mama' (p. 365). In the capital, she moves in aristocratic and high military circles. She objects to Piete's friends, who are recruited from a quite different social level. She mistrusts her 'Hang nach unten' (p. 75) and her 'Umgang mit der Straße' (p. 121), always admonishing Piete 'der Gasse etwas mehr Reserve gegenüber [zu] bewahren' (p. 75). According to her opinion the 'reds' indeed come from the gutter, and she sees in them agitators among the people 'gegen den Kaiser und alle

Ordnung' (p. 120). The mood of revolution among the soldiers at the end of the war is for her a sign of 'einreißende Verwilderung' and a 'scandal' (p. 364); political passions have dragged German honour down into the mire. She holds on to her doctrinaire German nationalist attitudes until the end of the war. According to her view, the honour of Germany is at stake; it is for this and for the preservation of their country that men are willing to die a hero's death (p. 76). Her view coincides with the teachings of two further institutions that determine Piete's life: church and school.

Priests and teachers are active as propagandists for the fatherland. From the pulpit the clergy preach a 'holy war', the German 'Kampf der Gerechtigkeit' (p. 15) which is approved by God; they praise the victors who at the battle of Tannenberg took more prisoners and lives than at Sedan, and afterwards say the Lord's Prayer including the line '...as we forgive those who trespass against us' (p. 54). The teachers forbid their pupils to use foreign words and demand that they learn by heart the songs that glorify Germany and the war, admonish them 'treudeutsch zu sein und Gott um den Sieg unserer Waffen zu bitten' (p. 18), canvass for war loans and organize collections for the war effort. Piete soon comes to realize 'Am glücklichsten sind die Lehrer' (p. 17), for they achieve their aims: the children regurgitating whatever they are told. Piete's schoolfriends join in the same enthusiasm; they pass on rumours about the war, rage against Jews and socialists, insist that they hate the Serbs without knowing who the Serbs are, want to be soldiers without realizing that this implies killing. The authorities loyally fulfil their task of winning children and young people for the war effort, so that this in turn influences their parents.

In the First World War the young generation was an effective strategic tool because a new form of warfare was being waged by both technological and propagandistic means, and faith in the ability to manipulate human beings was reaching a peak. Without those affected realizing it, the High Command exploited the love of adventure, the enthusiasm and the inexperience of children and young people in order to indoctrinate adults. In the so-called 'vaterländischer Unterricht' churches and schools were consciously used as arenas in which to mould opinion. In the *Richtlinien für die Aufklärungs- und*

Propagandatätigkeit im Bereich des stellv. Generalkommandos des X. AK. of 10 May 1917[12] we read:

> *Unter unbedingtem Ausschluß politischer Streitfragen* will die Aufklärungsstelle des Generalkommandos alle Mittel: Presse, Flugblätter, Flugschriften, Vorträge, *Kirche, Schulen* [author's emphasis], Vereine, Theater, Kino usw. ausnützen, um Klarheit über Ursache und Zweck des Krieges zu verbreiten, der Verhetzung und Verärgerung mancher Kreise mit Erfolg entgegenzuarbeiten, die Zuversicht und Opferwilligkeit der Bevölkerung zu stärken und das Verständnis für die Kriegsereignisse zu erhöhen.
>
> (p. 816)

And below:

> *Die Schulen* haben in hohem Maße dazu beigetragen, das Verständnis der Bevölkerung für manche Schwierigkeiten unserer Kriegswirtschaft zu erhöhen und haben, um nur ein praktisches Beispiel zu erwähnen, in Verbindung mit der Geistlichkeit für die Unterbringung der Stadtkinder auf dem Lande durch ihre aufklärende Tätigkeit dankenswerte praktische Arbeit geleistet. Die Aufklärung in den Schulen ist schon deshalb von großer Bedeutung, weil sie von den Kindern auf die Eltern weiterwirkt.
>
> (p. 820)

Pacifists such as Robert Graves and Erich Maria Remarque accuse the older generation in their writings of having brought destruction on innocent youth from 1914 to 1918. In *Goodbye to All That* (1929) Graves observes that war is 'a sacrifice of the idealistic younger generation to the stupidity and self-protective alarm of the elder'.[13] Remarque sees teachers in particular — and his Kantorek stands for them all — as guilty of sacrificing their pupils to their own German nationalist ideals that glorify war, while neglecting their responsibility, disseminating empty slogans and refusing to see the mass destruction at the front:

> Es gab ja Tausende von Kantoreks, die alle überzeugt waren, auf eine für sie bequeme Weise das Beste zu tun.
>
> Darin liegt aber gerade für uns ihr Bankerott.
>
> Sie sollten uns Achtzehnjährigen Vermittler und Führer zur Welt des Erwachsenseins werden, zur Welt der Arbeit, der Pflicht, der Kultur und des Fortschritts, zur Zukunft. Wir verspotteten sie manchmal und spielten ihnen kleine Streiche, aber im Grunde glaubten wir ihnen. Mit dem Begriff der Autorität, dessen Träger sie waren, verband sich in unseren Gedanken größere

> Einsicht und menschlicheres Wissen. Doch der erste
> Tote, den wir sahen, zertrümmerte diese Überzeugung.
> Wir mußten erkennen, daß unser Alter ehrlicher war als
> das ihre; sie hatten vor uns nur die Phrase und die
> Geschicklichkeit voraus. Das erste Trommelfeuer zeigte
> uns unseren Irrtum, und unter ihm stürzte die Welt-
> anschauung zusammen, die sie uns gelehrt hatten.[14]

Although Piete's experience, as for all those remaining at home, is different
from that of soldiers at the front, she goes through the same disillusionment
and disorientation; her faith in the ideals of her parents' generation is also
shattered. In the course of the war she inclines more and more towards the
views of her grandmother – her piety, her commitment and her pacifism –
but at first it is her mother's attitude and that of church and school that form
her opinions.

As mentioned, the first days of the war are completely taken up with
the excitement of a great adventure; people have no idea what is about to
happen to them, the children least of all. The question of guilt seems easy to
resolve; for Piete the answer, in keeping with her mother's opinion, is that it
was the Serbs that started it, the Germans are defending land and honour and
standing alongside their Austrian ally, and soldiers are dying the death of
heroes, which for Piete even in April 1915 means:

> Fürs Vaterland. Für die Birken. Für die Flüsse, für die
> Wiesen. Für eine Stadt, ein Dorf. Für das, was man lieb
> hat.
>
> (p. 163)

With news of the first casualties uncertainty spreads and Piete is assailed by
doubts:

> Wie kann der Kaiser 'froh' zu Feld ziehen? Wenn er
> über das Schlachtfeld geht und hört einen Sterbenden zu
> seinen Füßen 'Mutter!' rufen – was dann??
>
> (p. 45)

There are as yet no far-reaching reflections; the girl avoids discussing whether
the Kaiser does in fact stroll across a battlefield. Naive belief in the Kaiser
and in God provide protection against anxiety. So Piete tries to comfort
refugees with the declaration that the Kaiser is taking care of everyone, they
need have no fears; she counters fear of hunger with confidence that the
fatherland will not let anyone starve. When the expected victory and the end
of the war do not occur in December 1914, she thinks that by writing a petition

to the peace-loving Kaiser he will make peace. A still higher authority, God, is equally invoked. By drawing a chalk cross over the railway tracks, Piete and Gretel believe they will protect the soldiers travelling past, and in place of the Kaiser God is besought on Christmas Eve: 'Bitte, bitte, mach Schluß, lieber Gott, mach Schluß mit dem Krieg!' (p. 117). But increasingly Piete loses her faith in the omnipotence of the Heavenly Father. She cannot see any sign of his intervention or understand how he can allow all this to happen. Again and again the ground beneath her begins to shake, and in despair she looks for a firm foothold:

> Lieber Gott, sieh es bitte ein, daß ich bei deinem ewigen Schweigen manchmal denke, daß du in einem Wolkenkuckucksheim sitzt. Du könntest doch zum Beispiel über diese bluttropfende Erde als Strafe die Plagen Ägyptens loslassen! Wenn du die, die am Krieg schuld sind, furchtbar strafen würdest, dann würden sie vielleicht wieder nach deinen Geboten leben. So steht es jedenfalls im Alten Testament; wir haben es in der Schule gelernt. Gib mir doch endlich ein Zeichen, sprich doch ein einziges Mal zu mir. Aber deutlich, lieber Gott, damit ich dich ganz genau verstehe.
>
> (p. 367)

Piete stands alone with her questions and problems. The inconsistent behaviour of the adults in authority offers no support to a sceptical child. Church and school, far from providing any sense of direction, encourage feelings of uncertainty. Her mother, is equally inconsistent. She declares herself to be a German nationalist and sings the praises of the Kaiser, the war and its gallant heroes, yet she pulls every string to prevent her own son from doing war service. The daughter with her own vision of things is for ever coming into conflict with her mother, for example when mourning the first death of a family friend:

> Wenn einer Mutter der Sohn fällt, wird sie sich die Augen ausweinen, nicht weil er den Heldentod gestorben ist, sondern weil er hin ist, begraben, fort. Er sitzt nicht mehr am Tisch, sie kann ihm keine Stulle mehr abschneiden oder seine Strümpfe stopfen. Da kann sie nicht 'Danke' sagen, daß er den Heldentod gestorben ist. (Bitte, bitte, Muttchen, sei nicht böse!)
>
> (p. 67)

The diary is itself a symbol of the clash between mother and daughter. When at the beginning of the war Piete starts writing her notes, which she continues despite many inner struggles right up to the last day, the impetus to do so comes not from herself but from her mother, who wants her to record in writing 'eine so große, herrliche, erhebende Zeit' (p. 93) and to know it will be handed on to posterity; she intends to have the diary typed and bound, so that she can read it out to her circle of Berlin acquaintances. She wants not a private diary but a war documentary in which the events of the war are recorded. In accordance with these instructions Piete starts out by noting down all the army reports that seem important to her, copying them from daily newspapers at first undigested but then ever more critically. Departing from the intention of her mother, Piete wishes also to show how children experience the war:

> Wahrscheinlich schreiben nicht viele Kinder Kriegstage-
> buch, und es wird vielleicht später wichtig sein zu
> erfahren, wie die Kinder eigentlich durch diesen Krieg
> gekommen sind.

(p. 91)

For this reason she adds to the war reports descriptions of everyday life in Schneidemühl and her own experiences, feelings and reflections; to the horror of Margarete Kuhr these take up more and more space as time passes. Associatively linked and described in clear, sober language, the individual moments fuse into an overall picture which, in keeping with Piete's inner development, is transformed during the course of the war.[15] The newspaper quotations − euphoric war reports at second hand about the momentous battles and victories − are pushed into the background as her own experiences come to the fore. Only occasionally is an announcement recorded in deference to her mother. Ludendorff's resignation is noted in a single sentence, with the following commentary:

> Eigentlich interessiert mich das gar nicht mehr, aber da
> ich ja Muttchen zuliebe immer weiter Kriegstagebuch
> führe, muß ich das notieren.

(p. 363)

Without realizing it, she has long since given up writing a diary for her mother; when her mother wants to browse in it again in July 1917, Piete takes fright and all her 'sins' are revealed: she has been neglecting the war reports and in their place giving expression to intimate secrets about her mental state. These would be better hidden if Piete does not want to risk a conflict, as in

December 1914, when her mother discovers in reading through the diary that her daughter sees the war as not particularly heroic and in addition seems to have a 'red streak' (p. 121). On being challenged, Piete refuses, not being ready to betray her ideal of truth:

> Warum bin ich nicht bei den Soldaten! Warum bin ich nicht tot! Warum lebe ich denn noch dies Leben? Es macht mir doch schon lange alles keinen Spaß mehr, erstens die Schule, zweitens der Krieg. Anders schreiben kann ich nicht. Nein, ich kann nicht, hörst du, Muttchen? Ich will auch nicht! So ist das Leben hier bei uns, und wenn ich es anders beschreiben soll, müßte ich lügen! Lieber schreibe ich überhaupt nicht mehr.
>
> (p. 121)

What was to have been an objective document, penned by an obedient daughter for her mother, has become a private diary, a means of coping with puberty and of articulating and bringing order to her own development and the chaos of wartime. Precisely in this, however, lies the more than just personal significance of these notes. Far from being a transcription of war reports it is an exact description of Piete's inner and outer world, in keeping with her intention to show how those remaining at home, especially herself, came through the war, how they reacted to one another, and what conclusions they drew from the experience.

The relationship between mother and daughter mirrored so clearly in the conflict about the nature of the diary, becomes increasingly fraught. On the one hand, her mother's reproaches wound her self-esteem, and on the other they create in her a dilemma between the need for recognition and the need to preserve her ideals. She repeatedly finds herself longing to get out of it all through suicide. It all comes to a head when the revelation of one event, captured by a short, innocent comment in the diary and thereby betrayed to her mother, causes a storm to break. Piete is playing the piano at the home of the elder sister of a friend while they are drinking coffee in the next room with soldiers: harmless accompanying music to what she thinks is harmless chatter. The reproaches of her outraged mother, who has no faith in the moral integrity of her daughter, hit Piete hard. She refuses to comply with the wishes of her mother that she should break off her relationship with her friend and return to a more factual style in her diary, but for the first time there appears not just a vague death-wish, but a specific thought of suicide. Turning on the gas seems to offer the simple solution to all problems.

The scene just mentioned takes place at the beginning of September 1916, the year that represents a decisive turning-point in Piete's life. With deadlock in the war the Germans, once so enthusiastic, become demoralized and discontented. Despite redoubled efforts at propaganda, feelings of uncertainty and of being at a dead end cannot be laid to rest.

Piete's existential fears, of the chaos of war, the gulf between her mother's attitudes and values and her own, the inconsistent conduct of the three authorities — mother, school and Church — and the complexity of the war situation, all increase her confusion. The feeling of her own worthlessness and uselessness, resulting from doubts caused by the school and lack of support from her mother, aggravate her identity crisis. Finally, on 1 December 1916, she asks God to accept her death as a sacrifice and in return to end the war, with or without victory. On 3 December she writes in her diary:

> Nun will ich sterben, damit das Sterben an den Fronten aufhört. Wenn ein Kind (das bin ich doch noch, nicht wahr, lieber Gott?) sich zum Opfer bringt, dann *kannst* Du den Krieg doch nicht weiter zulassen, dann *mußt* Du alle Soldaten, die jetzt noch gesund sind und eine Zukunft haben, leben lassen! Es ist mir ernst, lieber Gott. Dir auch?
>
> (p. 250)

Having written this, she lies down on her bed and turns on the gas. She is saved only because her grandmother returns home unexpectedly early. Acute headaches remind her later in life of her readiness to sacrifice herself.

After Piete's attempted suicide a decisive change takes place. The relationship with her mother remains problematical. The exchanges between them seem to be based on love, but Piete suffers from the feeling that she is no longer loved as she used to be and that she still has to take second place to her brother:

> Mir scheint, Muttchen hat mich nicht mehr so lieb wie früher. [...]
> Ich weiß, daß Muttchen meinen Bruder Willi (sie nennt ihn jetzt 'Gil') immer lieber gehabt hat als mich.
>
> (p. 254)

To compensate for this she now clings more closely to her grandmother: 'Ich aber bin Großmutters Kind' (p. 254). Whilst she cannot accept the ideals of her mother, her former model, she can identify with the pacifism, humanism and piety of Bertha Golz. On this basis she can construct a system of values suited to herself, a system of coordinates for making judgements and carrying out actions which will give her in the future a sense of direction and enable her to behave consistently and to take on responsibilities.

The war moves further into the background in her diary entries. She still includes news from the front, but the tone has changed. Desolate reports composed in her own words take the place of copied newspaper items glorifying the war. On 20 June 1917 she writes:

> Ein Gespenst in grauen Lumpen ist dieser Krieg, ein Totenschädel, aus dem Maden kriechen. Schon viele Monate lang toben neue schwere Kämpfe im Westen. Es sind die Schlachten am Chemin-des-Dames, an der Aisne und in der Champagne. Alle Erde ist ein Trümmerfeld, alles ist Blut und Schlamm. [...] Ein großes Sterben!
>
> (p. 280)

All in all, Piete's life is ruled by war-weariness; a new teacher, Lieutenant Waldecker and the revolution breaking out in Russia now form the centre of attention. Discussion about the fate of the Tsar's family excites everyone's interest. In her fear that the Romanovs may be shot, Piete articulates for the first time a pacifist point of view: even if they are guilty of making war, that does not justify their being shot, for that would be a further act of war. The fact that she is thereby distancing herself from every form of war, does not seem as yet to be apparent to her. She is still not quite certain of her new position, but finds some support in the Christian commandment 'Thou shalt not kill' (p. 272). After Waldecker's death Piete finally turns away decisively from her earlier affirmation of war; from now on, every form of killing and of violence is rejected by her categorically. In the case of the Romanovs she pleads for leniency: it would be better to let them do hard labour on the fields like their former subjects. By the end of the war there is nothing left of the child eager for war who once played war games in the yard with the neighbours' children. The game 'Leutnant Yellenic und Schwester Martha', which in any case had become more of an acting out of teenage love against the background of war, now comes to a solemn end: Lieutenant Yellenic is carried to his grave. The time for it is past, the protagonists are not children any more; it was a 'Kindertraum' (p. 353) which offered them refuge and protection from a destructive reality. The most that Piete can still summon up is enthusiasm for the return of the survivors, for those who 'aus der Hölle gesund nach Haus kommen' (p. 360). She has only one wish left: 'Raus! Raus!' (p. 360) and 'nie wieder' (p. 314). Piete sees no meaning in the war: 'Millionen Tote für nix und wieder nix' (p. 313). In her view nothing justifies these human sacrifices, animal sacrifices, sacrifices of natural life, not even a revolution and the new order that might possibly result. If death is the price, 'will ich nicht mal 'ne Revolution!' (p. 313).

Piete, who seeks comfort in faith but cannot believe blindly, as a leading clergyman advises her to do, is forever asking why and how and where God stands: what has nature done, why does man destroy it and why does God remain silent? She does not question the existence of an almighty being, rather she defends herself against Androwski's atheism, his view that God is only 'das Wahnprodukt unserer menschlichen Angst' (p. 338). After lengthy searching she finally finds an answer to her questions: the guilt for the war is borne by those who sin by waging it. War is a temptation that they have not withstood:

> Die Strafe ist der Krieg. Vielleicht hat Gott von Anfang an erwartet, daß wir den Krieg beenden, und wir haben es nicht getan, sondern noch obendrein wie am ersten Kriegstag gesungen: 'Nun danket alle Gott'. Wenn das so wäre, dann haben wir bloß immer gesündigt.
>
> (p. 373)

Like Graves and Remarque she sees the older generation as carrying the real guilt, having disregarded their responsibility and seduced the younger generation into welcoming war:

> Aber nun ist es zu spät. Man muß nur aufpassen, daß es später nie wieder einen Krieg gibt. Wir dürfen nicht mehr auf den Schwindel reinfallen, den uns die Alten vorgezaubert haben. Wir waren ja noch Kinder, Schüler. Und alle in der Schule, der Direktor und die Lehrer voran, haben hurra geschrien.
>
> (p. 314)

Piete now adopts a critical tone towards her mother and her mother's brother:

> Bei denen ist 'deutschnational' immer noch Trumpf.
> Und wenn du hurra! fürs Vaterland fällst, krepierst du
> für sie als Held.
>
> (p. 313)

Piete's rebellion against her mother is also apparent in her choice of career. She rejects her mother's plan that she should study singing and succeed her as director of the singing school.

After leaving school without any qualifications, she decides to become a babies' nurse. From the start it is clear that this will only be a temporary stage. When the Bible is consulted and her grandmother opens it at random at a place which is to determine Piete's future, they read that she is called to be a prophet of the Lord, proclaiming the light to those that walk in darkness (p. 324). Hans Androwski, who has no time for divine prophecy, urges her to take up a good cause and place her writing talents at the service of humanity. She decides to combine what she has to do with what she wants to do by going to Berlin to study dance and to write. In December 1915 she expresses for the first time an idea that runs like a leitmotif through the rest of the diary, an idea that will become decisive for her and determine the path her life is to take: she decides she wants to become a dancer and create a dance which she will call 'Der tote Soldat' (p. 201). She takes dancing lessons and in the course of the war collects the necessary equipment: boots from her uncle, the helmet of a Belgian soldier killed in action, the tattered uniform of her brother. In her first plan a dead soldier is to climb out of his grave in blind obedience as soon as he hears the signal for attack at the start of a new war. By the end of the war she is certain of one thing:

> Ich kann alles im Tanz ausdrücken – ein sterbendes
> Kind zum Beispiel oder eine Mutter, die den Sohn
> hergeben muß, oder einen Soldaten, der von einer Kugel
> getroffen wird, oder –
>
> (p. 337)

The realization that war is meaningless awakens in Piete neither resignation nor despair, but opposition. Man must learn from what has happened, he must recognize his responsibility and act accordingly; it is his task to preserve the memory of the horror and see to it that things never reach that point again. She sees her own future task as enlightening people, warning them and making a contribution towards the prevention of a new war which is already looming in the distance on Armistice Day. She wants to fight not with a gun but with other means. Alongside the general humanitarian assistance she already gives as a nurse, she sees in art the weapon tailor-made for her:

> Ich dachte nach und sagte, daß ich allen armen Menschen helfen will, aber auch den Tieren, weil die so oft zu leiden haben und ganz unschuldig sind. [...] Im stillen dachte ich aber auch, daß ich, wenn ich nach Berlin komme, gegen den Krieg und jede Schlechtigkeit, die man den Menschen antut, kämpfen will.
>
> (p. 358)

With this Piete – Jo Mihaly – places herself in the ranks of artists and writers such as Henri Barbusse, Roman Dorgelès, Robert Graves, Erich Maria Remarque and Adrienne Thomas who were passionately committed to the prevention of violence and a new war. She wanted to use art to preserve the memory of what had happened, to stir up feelings and appeal to reason and sympathy. It was with this purpose in mind that Jo Mihaly – Elfriede Kuhr – realized her aim after the First World War. Later her free dances 'Vision eines Krieges' and 'Gas' counted among her greatest successes. She danced them in Switzerland during the National Socialist period and the Second World War.[16]

NOTES

[1]Interview with Andreas Bürgi in *Die Wochenzeitung*, 4 November 1983, p. 13.

[2]Page references are to the new edition by Horst Budjuhn (Munich: dtv, 1986).

[3]See Klaus Vondung, 'Propaganda oder Sinndeutung' in his *Kriegserlebnis, Der Erste Weltkrieg in der literarischen Gestaltung und symbolischen Deutung der Nationen* (Göttingen: Vandenhoek & Ruprecht, 1980), pp. 11-37 (p. 18).

[4]Ernst Jünger, *In Stahlgewittern*. In: *Werke*, Bd. 1, Tagebücher I, Der Erste Weltkrieg (Stuttgart: Klett-Cotta, 1961), pp. 9-310 (p. 11).

[5]*Hüter des Bruders*, op. cit., pp. 184- .

[6]See Roman Dorgelès, *Les Croix de bois* (Paris: A. Michel, 1919):

> Le bonheur est partout; c'est le gourbi où il ne pleut pas, une soupe bien chaude, la litière de paille sale où l'on se couche, l'histoire drôle qu'un copain raconte, une nuit sans corvée... Le bonheur, mais cela tient dans les deux pages d'une lettre de chez soi, dans un fond de quart de rhum.   Pareil aux enfants pauvres, qui se construisent des plais avec des bouts de planche, le soldat fait du bonheur avec tout ce qui traîne.
>
> (p. 132)

[7]See Vondung, op. cit., p. 24.

[8]Ernst Jünger, *Sturm* (Stuttgart: Klett-Cotta, 1979), pp. 82-83.

[9]Erich Maria Remarque, *Im Westen nichts Neues* (Frankfurt/M., Berlin, Wien: Ullstein, 1983), p. 288.

[10]Adrienne Thomas, *Die Katrin wird Soldat* (Berlin: Propyläen, 1930), p. 327. See the essay by Herman Moens in this volume.

[11]See Vondung, op. cit., pp. 31-32.

[12]Quoted from *Quellen zur Geschichte des Parlamentarismus und der politischen Parteien*, 2. Reihe: *Militär und Politik*, ed. by Erich Matthias and Hans Meier-Welcker, Vols 1 and 2, *Militär und Innenpolitik im Weltkrieg 1914-1918*, ed. by Wilhelm Deist (Düsseldorf: Droste Verlag, 1970).

[13]Robert Graves, *Goodbye to all that* (London: Cassell, 1957), p. 217.

[14]Erich Maria Remarque, op. cit., p. 18. Cf. Leonhard Frank, who emigrated to Switzerland for the duration of the war. In his autobiographical novel *Links wo das Herz ist* (Munich: Nymphenburger Verlagshandlung, 1952) he mentions the role of teachers: 'Die Engländer, die Franzosen, die Russen hatten Michael nichts angetan − der Lehrer Dürr war ein Deutscher. Er dachte: "Daß die zehntausend deutsche Lehrer Dürr ihre Schüler nicht für das Leben vorbereitet hatten, sondern für den Kasernenhof, den Krieg, den Tod, würde ein

aufschlußreicher Vorwurf sein für ein Gedicht gegen die Machthaber und den Wahnwitz dieser Zeit.'" (Quoted from the Munich 1967 edn, p. 120).

[15]How much Jo Mihaly revised the diary for publication cannot be gone into here, since the present writer has not had access to the manuscript or found any further information on the subject.

[16]Werner Mittenzwei, *Exil in der Schweiz* (Frankfurt/M.: Röderberg-Verlag, 1979), p. 219 and p. 225.

Jo Mihaly: Select List of Publications

Ballade vom Elend (Stuttgart: Verlag der Vagabunden, 1929).

Kasperltheater (Stuttgart: D. Gundert, 1929).

Michael Arpad und sein Kind. Ein Kinderschicksal auf der Landstraße (Stuttgart: D. Gundert, 1930; new edn Berlin: LitPol-Verlags-gesellschaft, 1981).

Hüter des Bruders (Zurich: Steinberg-Verlag, 1942; page reference is to the new edn with the title *Gesucht: Stephan Varescu*, Reinbek: Rowohlt, 1989).

Wir verstummen nicht. Gedichte in der Fremde (Zurich: Posen, 1945) (written in collaboration with Stephan Hermlin and Lajser Ajchenrand).

Die Steine (Stuttgart: Heinrich F.C. Hannsmann, 1946).

Das Leben ist hart. Drei Geschichten aus dem Tessin (St. Gallen: Tschudy, 1954).

Der weiße Zug (Basel: Gute Schriften, 1957).

Bedenke Mensch... (Winterthur: Gemsberg-Verlag, 1958).

Von Mensch und Tier. Eine Sammlung der schönsten Tiergeschichten (Einsiedeln, Zurich and Cologne: Benziger Verlag, 1961).

Was die alte Anna Petrowna erzählt. Geschichten aus Rußland (Heilbronn: Salzer, 1970).

Gib mir noch Zeit zu lieben. Weihnachtserzählungen (Heilbronn: Salzer, 1970).

Der verzauberte Hase. Tier-Erzählungen (Heilbronn: Salzer, 1971).

...da gibt's ein Wiedersehn! Kriegstagebuch eines Mädchens 1914-1918, with historical foreword by Wolfgang Petter (Freiburg and Heidelberg: Kerle, 1982). New edn Munich: dtv, 1986.

Secondary Literature on Jo Mihaly

Ingeborg Bayer, 'Jo Mihaly', in *Literatur-Lexikon*, ed. Walter Killy (Gütersloh and Munich: Bertelsmann, 1990), Vol. 8 (1990), 162.

Andreas Bürgi, 'Jo Mihaly. Am gründlichsten vergessen!', *Die Wochenzeitung*, 4 November 1983, p. 13.

Wilhelm Kosch, 'Jo Mihaly' in *Deutsches Literatur-Lexikon*, 3rd edn, revised and ed. by Bruno Berger and Heinz Rupp (Berne and Munich: Francke, 1986), Vol. 10, 1071.

Werner Mittenzwei, *Exil in der Schweiz* (Frankfurt/M.: Röderberg-Verlag, 1979).

Carl Seelig, 'Jo Mihaly. Eine Dichterstimme aus dem Tessin', *National-Zeitung*, 19 March 1961, Sunday supplement.

Herbert A. Straus & Werner Röder (eds), *International Biographical Dictionary of Central European Emigrés 1933-1945*, Vol. 1, Part 2 (Munich, New York, London, Paris: Saur, 1983), pp. 818-19.

Hans Teubner, *Exilland Schweiz: Dokumentarischer Bericht über den Kampf emigrierter deutscher Kommunisten 1933-45* (Berlin: Röderberg-Verlag, 1975).

Adrienne Thomas

7

Die Katrin wird Soldat:
A Fictionalized Diary of the First World War

Herman Moens

About the Author

'Hat Ihre Gattin schon die *Katrin* [...] gelesen?' When this question appeared on 3 December 1930 in the *Börsenblatt für den deutschen Buchhandel*, No. 280, it needed no further explanation. Thanks to a comprehensive advertising campaign by the Propyläen-Verlag every bookseller knew this could only mean *Die Katrin wird Soldat* by Adrienne Thomas. It was its author's first book, and a great success for its publisher. Within two weeks of its publication on 13 November 1930 eleven thousand copies had already been printed.[1] Five months later this number had risen to 100,000.[2] The publisher did not hesitate to forecast further sales successes in the relevant periodicals.

Who was the author whose portrait appeared so frequently in newspapers and periodicals during the next few months? In secondary literature only a few facts are given about her development and career. Hertha Adrienne Strauch was born on 24 June 1897 in St Avold, Lorraine, which at the time was part of the German empire. The family was of Jewish origin; her father, Julius Strauch, owned a small business. Adrienne Thomas grew up as a bilingual child in St Avold and Metz, where she attended the grammar school. During the First World War she worked as a Red Cross nurse, first in Metz and later in Berlin-Mariendorf, where she had moved with her parents. After the war she studied singing and acting in Berlin. It was probably at this time that her first marriage took place, though no documentary evidence has yet come to light.[3] After the Nazi seizure of power in 1933, Adrienne Thomas, although only represented by one book, was classified among the undesirable writers.[4] The 1932 and 1934 editions of *Kürschners Deutscher Literatur-Kalender* mentioned her without any biographical detail: in the 1937 edition her name no longer appeared. In 1938 her work was placed on the list of 'unerwünschte Schriftsteller'.[5]

Her life was deeply affected by the events of that period; they led her through many intermediary stages into exile in New York. But despite hostile circumstances, Adrienne Thomas remained active as a writer. She published six novels and two volumes of stories, and sent contributions to newspapers and periodicals (among them the *Neues Wiener Tageblatt*, *Basler Nachrichten*, *Neue Jüdische Zeitung*, *Free World Magazine*, and *Prager Tageblatt*). Oppressed by political developments, she emigrated in 1932 to Switzerland, moving from there in 1934 first to France and then lived from 1935 to 1938 in Austria. After the Anschluß of Austria to the German Empire in 1938 she once again had to cope with persecution:

> In Wien hatte ich Angst. Man brauchte nur das Radio anzustellen und die plebeischen Stimmen der neuen Machthaber zu hören, ihren niedrigen Hohn und ihr beispielloses ordinäres Gejohle. [...] Ich hatte Angst, aber nachts saß ich dann doch an irgend einem Tisch und schrieb. [...] Die Nazis waren gewiß nicht nach Wien gekommen, um mich zu suchen. Da sie mich aber durch einen Zufall entdeckten, befahlen sie mir, mich am kommenden Morgen um sechs Uhr in einer ihrer Kasernen einzufinden.
>
> (*Reisen Sie ab, Mademoiselle!*, Amsterdam, 1947, p. 7)

With the help of French friends she was able to flee to France via Czechoslovakia, Hungary, Yugoslavia and Italy. The manuscript of her novel *Wettlauf mit dem Traum* (Amsterdam, 1939), which she had started to write in Vienna, followed by a roundabout route: after being transported to Berlin in a car bearing the swastika it came via England to Alsace, where its author had found temporary refuge. As a result of a search of her landlady's house in Sèvres near Paris — she had moved there in the spring of 1939 — the manuscript of her largely autobiographical new novel *Reisen Sie ab, Mademoiselle!* was nearly confiscated. Only after the officials looking into this had discovered the foreword by Jean Giraudoux, then French propaganda minister, in the French translation of *Die Katrin wird Soldat* was the house search called off.

As the result of a decree Adrienne Thomas presented herself on 15 May 1940 to the internment camp in the Vélodrôme d'Hiver in Paris:

> [...] es kam der 15. Mai, der Tag, da die Kriegsmaschine Tausende von Frauen, darunter mich, schluckte. [...] Bei Durchsicht meiner Dokumente wunderte sich der Beamte, warum ich mich überhaupt zur Internierung eingefunden hatte. Ich sei in Frankreich geboren, die Maßnahme beziehe sich nicht auf mich. Aber er hatte mich bereits eingetragen, und so mußte ich vorerst bleiben. [...] Indessen vergaß man mich. [...]
>
> (Ibid., pp. 9-10)

She continued to be interned, first in Paris, then a week later in the camp at Gurs in southern France. From there she succeeded in escaping via Dax and Pau to Sauvagnon, where she was able to make ends meet as a laundress. Eventually she heard from the writer Hermann Kesten that the 'Emergency Rescue Committee' he had set up had produced an emergency visa for her and the necessary money to cross from Lisbon to New York, where she landed on 13 September 1940.[6] She met her future husband Julius Deutsch (1884-1968) in the Park Plaza Hotel, where she was staying temporarily. He was a socialist politician who had emigrated from Austria to Czechoslovakia in 1934, fought in the Spanish Civil War in 1936 as a general in the Republican Army and had finally fled to the United States via Great Britain and Cuba in 1940 after a period in Paris (1938).

During her stay in the Park Plaza Hotel Adrienne Thomas cultivated her contacts with old acquaintances from Europe, such as Hermann Kesten, Georg Bernhardt, former chief editor of the *Berliner Vossische Zeitung*, Konrad Heiden, author of a biography of Adolf Hitler, the Communist writer Leo Lania, and the journalist and writer Egon Erwin Kisch. Her novel *Ein Fenster am East River* (Amsterdam: Allert de Lange, 1945) was written during her New York exile and describes her stay in the United States.

After her marriage in 1941 Adrienne Thomas worked as a secretary for the Free World Organization,

> deren Ziel es war, den zu Anfang des Kriegs stark-
> verbreiteten Isolationismus Amerikas zu überwinden
> und das amerikanische Volk für die bewußte Teilnahme
> an einer völkerbindenden, demokratischen Gestaltung
> der freien Welt zu gewinnen.[7]

She used her writing talents as head of the German and Austrian section of the organization's periodical *Free World Magazine*. Julius Deutsch, otherwise very reticent about his wife, highlighted this work in his autobiography *Ein weiter Weg. Lebenserinnerungen* (Zurich: Almathea, 1960), for instance on p. 366. On 2 May 1947 she followed him back to liberated Europe; he had already returned to Vienna in 1946.

Her literary production after the war was not as successful as her earlier work. It included two books for children, *Ein Hund ging verloren* (Vienna, 1953) and *Markusplatz um vier* (Vienna, 1955), a selection called *Da und Dort* (Vienna, 1950) from a series of articles for the paper *Neues Österreich*, and a new edition of the novel *Wettlauf mit dem Traum* (Amsterdam: Allert de Lange, 1949). *Die Katrin wird Soldat* also reappeared in various editions (among others Vienna, 1950; Marbach, 1951; Frankfurt/M., 1962; Gütersloh, 1964; Frankfurt/M., 1987). The paperback edition published by Goldmann Verlag in Munich in 1989 in connection with the filming of the novel was out of print by 1992: *Die Katrin wird Soldat* was serialized on German television early in the evening with Peter Deutsch directing and Claudia Brunnert in the title role.

In recognition of her life's work, the honorary title of professor was conferred on Adrienne Thomas on 25 June 1973 by the Austrian Minister of Education. She died on 7 November 1980 at the age of eighty-three.

Die Katrin wird Soldat – a Synopsis

Die Katrin wird Soldat may be unfamiliar to many readers, so a short synopsis may be helpful. It is in three parts, of which the first two, 'Johann' and 'Zwischen Schangel und Wackes' (Schangel is a derisive nickname for a Frenchman; Wackes for an Alsatian) are much shorter than the third part, which is called 'Die Katrin wird Soldat': this takes up well over half the novel and provides its title. The first part describes the central character's experiences up to the time when she first falls in love; the second ends with her boy-friend volunteering to go to the front. The third part narrates her subsequent experiences, particularly as a Red Cross auxiliary in the garrison town of Metz. The strong autobiographical element is unmistakable. Like Adrienne Thomas herself, Katrin Lentz was born in 1897 and grows up, like the author, in Metz, which was then in German Lorraine. Katrin is given a diary as a fourteenth birthday present on 27 May 1911. She notes down her experiences in this diary until her death in December 1916, at first with child-like naïvety, then more seriously and made bitter and despairing by the horrors of the war. Adrienne Thomas later provided a summary of the first book in the novel *Katrin! die Welt brennt!* (Amsterdam: de Lange, 1938), which might well appear to be its sequel. Katrin Boissier, the main figure in *Katrin! die Welt brennt!*, is introduced as the niece of Katrin Lentz. At the very beginning of the novel Adrienne Thomas refers to her first work as follows:

> Zwischen Tanzstunde und Eisbahn steuert Katrins kleines Leben auf die erste Liebe. Lucien Quirin. Ein unbeherrscht herrschsüchtiger Primaner, in dessen kurzer Lebensspanne sich schon alle Komponenten eines langen Lebens gesammelt haben. Zwischen himmlischer und irdischer Liebe steht er, zwischen 'praktischem Beruf' und seiner Bestimmung zum Maler, zwischen Heimaterde und Vaterland, zwischen Frankreich und Deutschland. All diese Konflikte beendet der Krieg. Lucien meldet sich kriegsfreiwillig. Und auch Katrin – wird Soldat. Zuerst kocht sie nur Obst ein für die Lazarette und näht Wäsche für die Verwundeten. Dann aber steht sie von heut auf morgen dem ganz großen Ernst ihrer Zeit gegenüber... Sie arbeitet auf dem Metzer Hauptbahnhof beim Roten Kreuz, erlebt den brausenden Aufmarsch des ausziehenden Heeres und die geräuschlose Rückkehr zerfetzter Menschen. Katrin ist siebzehn Jahre und lernt den Umgang mit Sterbenden. Begreift, daß man noch ein Lachen schenken kann, wo nicht mehr zu helfen ist. [...] Nachts kann sie oft nicht schlafen vor Sehnsucht und Angst um Lucien, und im Dienst lügt sie dann doch mit Gelächter und Lärm ein paar Bayern, die irgendwelche Vorschriften übertreten haben, bei ihren Vorgesetzten heraus. Alle ihre Freunde fallen. Einer nach dem anderen. Katrin tut weiter ihre Pflicht. Zittert in heißer Angst: wer ist der Nächste? Und eines Tages, natürlich, ist der Nächste Lucien Quirin. Der Krieg hat ihn als ein gebührendes Opfer eingezogen. Eine Weile taumelt noch Katrin durch eine große Lebensleere. Nun trägt sie nicht mehr die übernommenen Pflichten, sondern die Pflichten tragen nun sie. Es müssen wohl nicht die

rechten Krücken für ihre neunzehn Jahre gewesen sein.
Sie hielten sie nicht mehr lange. So fällt sie auch. Die
sogenannte Todesursache war Pneumonie. In
Wirklichkeit ist sie wohl, als man ihr einen Freund nach
dem anderen und zuletzt ihren Lucien wegamputierte,
verblutet.

(*Katrin! die Welt brennt!*, pp. 13-14)

Publication History

Adrienne Thomas told the story of the genesis of her novel in a brochure
issued by Propyläen-Verlag in March or April 1931 when publication figures
had reached 100,000:

> [...] an einem unerfüllten Abend stöberte ich in Notizen,
> Zetteln, Briefen, Kindertagebüchern. In Kriegs- und
> Vorkriegsaufzeichnungen. Eigentlich zu dem Zweck,
> diesen unnötigen Ballast zu vernichten. Also ich
> stöberte, blätterte und las. Fand mich plötzlich am
> Schreibtisch wieder. In dieser Nacht wurden die ersten
> Seiten der *Katrin* geschrieben, und in den nächsten
> Tagen erschien mir mein spontaner Versuch leicht
> komisch — ich wagte gar nicht, das Geschriebene zu
> überlesen, ich war vielmehr fest entschlossen, es nicht
> fortzusetzen. [...] Ein mir befreundeter Schriftsteller
> interessierte sich für meine Arbeit, nannte meine
> Aufzeichnungen, Zettel und Notizen ein gutes Material
> und war der Meinung, das alles könne in seiner
> Gesamtheit ein plastisches Dokument ergeben. [...]
> Dann war die *Katrin* fertig. Lag vor mir und erschien mir
> trotz ihrer Zusammensetzung aus Wirklichkeit und
> Phantasie als eine allzu private Bilanz. Unerhörter
> Optimismus, das ein 'Buch' zu nennen.

In the foreword to her novel *Reisen Sie ab, Mademoiselle!* Adrienne Thomas
describes in detail what happened next:

> Durch Zufall hatte ich erfahren, daß der anglo-
> amerikanische Verlag Harper Brother and Heinemann
> ein Preisausschreiben veranstalte. Die einzigen sich an
> den Wettbewerb knüpfenden Bedingungen waren, daß
> es sich um einen jungen, unbekannten Autor handeln
> müsse. [...] Ende September 1929 sandte ich mein
> Manuskript nach Amerika.

(p. 5)

Encouraged by a 'bekannter Schriftsteller' she had also sent her manuscript to
Ullstein Verlag in Berlin, but from them, as indeed from other major German
publishing houses, all she received was a polite rejection. The fact that it did

finally get published in Germany may well have had something to do with the revelation that her manuscript had achieved third place and an 'honourable mention' from among more than four hundred entries submitted to the Harper Brother and Heinemann competition; 'gleichzeitig erbat sich der Verlag eine Option auf meinen Roman', she recalled (p. 6). Julius Deutsch tells the following anecdote in his memoirs:

> Eines Abends saßen meine Frau und ich mit Siegfried Trebitsch und Erich Maria Remarque beisammen. Das Gespräch drehte sich um die Kurzsichtigkeit von Verlegern, die so oft die Bedeutung eines Werkes verkennen. Adrienne und Remarque überboten sich in humorvollen Schilderungen ihrer Erfahrungen. Wer alles von großen und größten Verlegern hatte die hernach so berühmt gewordenen Erstlingswerke der beiden *Im Westen nichts Neues* und *Die Katrin wird Soldat* abgelehnt!
>
> (*Ein weiter Weg*, p. 386)

Before the novel appeared in book form it was published in the prestigious *Berliner Vossische Zeitung* as a serial, the first instalment appearing in No. 174 on Wednesday 23 July 1930. That day's headline read, 'Hitlervorstoß in Sachsen erfolglos'. Up to the thirty-third and final instalment in No. 207 of 30.8.1930 the text was specifically described as a novel. No biographical data or photographs of the writer were provided. The copyright is still held by Ullstein-Verlag. The fact that the first edition was brought out by Propyläen-Verlag led and still leads to bibliographical confusion, as can for example be seen in the blurb in the 1987 Fischer paperback edition.

The Publishers' Publicity Campaign

The book edition of the novel was announced by the editors of the *Vossische Zeitung* on 28 September 1930 in answer to a reader's enquiry; confirmation by the Propyläen-Verlag followed under the headline 'Die literarische Über-raschung dieses Winters' (*Börsenblatt* No. 251 of 28.10.1930). Presumably to emphasize that the writer was a woman and that the book, in diary form, chronicled a love story, the announcement in the *Börsenblatt* was framed by a design suggesting eight hearts: from 28 November 1930 these hearts were clearly depicted. A similar surround was also chosen for the publishers' own periodical *Der Querschnitt*, including 1930 no. 12 and 1931 no. 4. One week after publication, the *Börsenblatt* carried a full-page portrait photograph of the writer with the invitation to cut it out and display it at once in a window (*Börsenblatt*, no. 269, 20 November 1930). In no. 276 (28 November 1930) advertisements (size: 32 cm x 24 cm and 60 cm x 80 cm) were put on offer, in order to attract orders; these contained extracts from readers' letters such as 'Wundervolle, liebe Adrienne Thomas, Ihr wunderbares Buch gehört in alle reiferen Frauenhände!' and 'War mir doch, als ob ich mein eigenes Tagebuch las [...] so hatte ich's erlebt, als ich in Mülhausen im Elsaß den Bahnhofsdienst versah'.

The synopsis of the novel in the publicity material makes clear that it was being marketed as a love story by a woman: 'Es führt den Titel "Die Katrin wird Soldat" und ist ein Liebesroman in Tagebuchform, Niederschlag aus fünf Lebensjahren eines jungen Mädchens voll Charme und Klugheit. [...] Ein junges Leben voll Wissen und Ahnen, Hoffnung und Verzweiflung und voll unendlicher Liebe wird hier klar und ungekünstelt beschrieben, so, wie nur ein wirklicher Dichter es nachfühlen kann.'[8] Booksellers were urged: 'Geben Sie es Ihrer Gattin! Auf diese Weise prüfen Sie auch gleich, wie das Buch auf Frauen wirkt!'[9] Just before Christmas Propyläen-Verlag quoted a letter from a bookseller saying he intended to give as private Christmas presents two copies of what he called 'dieses nicht nur bezaubernde, sondern den Leser "verzaubernde" Buch'.[10] By making use of readers' letters on the subject, the publishers' advertising also suggested comparisons with Remarque's best-selling novel *Im Westen nichts Neues* of 1929:

> Adrienne Thomas [...] hat in der *Vossischen Zeitung* ein Werk veröffentlicht, das die Leser packte **fast** [my emphasis] wie Remarque. [...] Wenn man aus solchen Zuschriften Schlüsse ziehen darf, so kann man diesem Buch einen großen Erfolg prophezeien![11]

Advertising in periodicals and newspapers reaching a wider public differed only slightly from that in the *Börsenblatt für den deutschen Buchhandel*. The *Vossische Zeitung* of 16 November 1930 was content to carry the simple notice that *Die Katrin wird Soldat* had just appeared and was available in every bookshop. *Der Querschnitt* 10, no. 12 (1930) reproduced the headline of the first announcement in the *Börsenblatt* and cleverly exploited the contrast between reality and fiction by claiming that Adrienne Thomas's diary notes in the *Vossische Zeitung* gripped readers almost as much as Remarque. Although it went on to describe it as a love story, much was made of the fact that it was based on real life: 'Mit ergreifender Einfachheit ist dieses Buch, das man auch ein Kriegsbuch nennen kann, geschrieben: ein starkes persönliches Schicksal wird auf dem Hintergrund übergroßer Ereignisse dargestellt.'

Adrienne Thomas was featured (with her photograph) in the *Vossische Zeitung* of 14 December 1930 in the company of prominent men and women writers such as Ernst Weiß, Ödön von Horváth, Georg Hermann, Vicki Baum, Gina Kaus, Rahel Sanzara and Clara Viebig, all under the heading 'Romane zum Lesen und Verschenken'. In addition, a review was quoted from the *Rigaischer Rundschau*: 'An diesem Buch, [...] von dem über kurz oder lang die ganze Kulturwelt sprechen wird, muß man haltmachen.' It is revealing that these notices all emphasize personal fate and stress the simplicity and naturalness of the diary form as a means of female expression, direct and non-reflective. For instance, in the *Berliner Illustrirte Zeitung* of 25 December 1930, we are urged to read this first novel by a new author because it is so 'ergreifend' in its simplicity. On 15 February 1931 the same magazine uses readers' letters and statements by prominent writers for publicity purposes: 'Werke von solcher Echtheit und Tiefe werden uns selten beschert, und deshalb meine ich, könnten wir nichts Besseres tun, als der Autorin dafür danken,' wrote a satisfied reader from Berlin. Waldemar Bonsels was of the opinion that 'Die Anklage erstirbt in der Klage, nicht flammt hier und da der Zorn des Widerspruchs auf, in den Orkanen des Kriegs verweht das Herz dieses kleinen tapferen Soldaten der Pietà. Aber ihr Denkmal wird bleiben.' In Ernst Penzoldt's view, 'Es ist die reine Barmherzigkeit des Buchs, die uns ergreift, seine Menschlichkeit, seine kindliche Wahrheitsliebe', while Clara Viebig enthused, 'Von einer unheimlichen Echtheit, von einer sittlichen Wahrhaftigkeit, die unsre Frauen-, unsre Mutterseele mit beiden Händen ergreift... Ja, das müssen wir lesen [...]' Walther von Hollander remained calm and realistic: 'Adrienne Thomas hat eine leichte Hand und ein schweres Herz. Was aus ihr werden wird, läßt sich nach diesem sehr persönlichen Buch nicht sagen. Was aus ihrem Buch werden wird, ist leicht zu prophezeien: Erfolg.'

In its April number *Der Querschnitt* announced with pleasure that four months after its first appearance 90,000 copies had already been printed.

Taking its cue from critical comments and readers' letters, the publishers also promoted the book as a 'war novel'. This can be seen in two fliers printed specially for it: the first one appeared in mid-January 1931, some eight weeks after the book was first put on sale. Waldemar Bonsels was more expansive here:

> Man kann dieses merkwürdige und sehr ernste Buch einer Krankenschwester ein Kriegsbuch nennen, wenn man will, aber es unterscheidet sich von denen, die wir gelesen haben, durch eine gesonderte Schau auf die Lebens- und Todesdinge, die vom Frieden zum Krieg führen und aus ihm in den Tod.

The publishers also quoted from reviews in the daily press that praised the novel as a war book: according to the *Essener Volkszeitung* it was the best and most gripping book about the young generation of women in the war; the *Prager Presse* called it one of the most humane books on peace despite its military title; the *Berliner Börsen-Courier* went so far as to say: 'Vielleicht käme Müttern, Geliebten, Gattinnen, Bräuten, Schwestern, Töchtern zum Bewußtsein, daß die Kriege immer nur gegen sie geführt werden.'

In the second flier, which came out in about March/April 1931, a similar emphasis is evident in the reported press reviews; in addition it provided the detailed report by Adrienne Thomas on the genesis of her novel.

Critical Reactions

The early reviews written in German which I have traced differ in their judgement of the novel. Alice Berend writes in the *Vossische Zeitung* of 23 November 1930:

> Ihre [Katrins] letzten Worte fragen, wofür sie sich rein gehalten hat? Diese Unberührtheit aber ist das Siegende, das Religiöse, Hoffnungsgebende, das in lichte Weite Weisende dieser Aufzeichnungen. Darum sollte der Wert des Buches, trotzdem es eine Fülle von Momenten aus historischen Tagen bringt, nicht im Politischen gesucht werden, sondern im Menschlichen.

Katrin's final words, 'O Lucien, ich war so dumm. Worauf wollte ich denn noch warten, wozu mich aufbewahren? Vielleicht nur für eine Fliegerbombe?', could perhaps be interpreted in this way. Like Alice Berend, a reviewer writing in the *Hamburger Fremdenblatt* on 20 December 1930 and signing himself H. H. emphasizes the narrative qualities alongside the human aspect: 'Der Roman, der dieses Schicksal gestaltet, tut es fein und innerlich. Kein falscher Ton stört seinen lebendigen Fluß. Ein reiches Leben wird fesselnd in die übergroße Zeit hineingestellt, anschaulich, voll scharfer Beobachtung, ehrlich und mit Geschmack.' The review by F. B. in the *Berliner Börsen-Courier* (7 December 1930) used by the publishers for their publicity stresses the novel's educational character. A review that does justice to the different levels of the novel is that by Axel Eggebrecht in *Die literarische Welt* (Jahrgang 7, Heft 1, dated 2 January 1931). Here he emphasizes how the material has been reformed in an innovative way as literature:

> Adrienne Thomas hat zwei Seiten des Kriegserlebnisses zum ersten Male erschütternd gestaltet: Das Schicksal der Grenzbevölkerung und die Rolle der helfenden Frauen. [...] In der unübersehbar gewordenen Literatur des Krieges wird dies eigenwillige und aufrichtige Buch bestehen bleiben als eins der wichtigsten Dokumente: Durch seine Ehrlichkeit und durch seine innige Einfachheit.
>
> (p. 5)

Eggebrecht realizes that the first part of the novel is not merely the simple portrayal of a schoolgirl's life; he notices that it contains some sharp observations about the interplay of social and political attitudes in the border fortress town of Metz, such as its comments about tribal differences between the inhabitants of Lorraine, the Jewish community and the Prussian officer class and civil service. Maria Prigge in 'Die Literatur' [*Das literarische Echo*], 34 (1931/32), p. 91) presents a different view: 'Das erste Drittel des Buches [...] enthält die selbstgefällig geschilderten belanglosen Erlebnisse eines hübschen, umschwärmten und begabten Backfisches.' Her overall impression is negative:

> [...] der Roman [ist] flach und oberflächlich; denn er gibt den Krieg so wieder, wie ahnungsvolle Romantiker sich ihn vor dem Kriege vorstellten. Dabei kennt Adrienne Thomas nicht einmal die Abenteuerlust oder das Kameradschaftsgefühl des Mannes. Es ist beschämend,

> daß dieser Kriegsroman von einer Deutschen verfaßt
> worden ist, nachdem die Engländerin Helen Zenna
> Smith eines der erschütterndsten Bücher (*Mrs. Biest
> pfeift*) über den Krieg geschrieben hat.

Axel Eggebrecht also refers to this English novel – '*Not So Quiet...*' *Step-daughters of War* – which appeared in London and New York: A. E. Marriott in 1930 and in German translation the same year (Berlin: S. Fischer). But he comes to the opposite conclusion: 'Erschütternd ist der Gegensatz der kleinen Catherine etwa zu der brutalen, männlichen Mrs. Biest in dem englischen Buch.' On 20 May 1931 an article by E. K. (Eduard Korrodi) appeared on the front page of the *Neue Zürcher Zeitung* which corroborates Eggebrecht's view:

> Wer so sein Tagebuch schmettert, so wahr, so keck und
> pfiffig, hat im kleinen Finger mehr Talent als hundert
> Leimsieder, die ihren Stil päppeln. [...] Dies ist kein
> Roman! Dies ist ein Dokument. Einmal wird man auch
> diese furchtbaren 'Quellen' in die Historie eingehen
> lassen, wenn auch die Frau den Schrei ihres Herzens in
> die Waagschale der Geschichte werfen darf.

Success in non-German-speaking countries soon followed. The speed with which translations appeared indicates that foreign publishers were equally confident of the book's success. The cover of the 1987 Fischer paperback edition tells us that *Die Katrin wird Soldat* was translated into fifteen languages. We have succeeded in tracing the following: *Cathérine joins up* (London: Mathews and Marrot, 1931), which was followed by an American (Boston) edition of the same translation under the title *Katrin becomes a soldier*. In the same year Mondadori of Milan produced *Catarina va alla guerra*. In 1931 a Dutch translation, *Katrien wordt soldaat*, was published by Bijleveld in Utrecht. The publishing house Librairie Stock, Paris, which had also brought out the French translation of Remarque's *Im Westen nichts Neues*, published the novel in 1933 with the title *Catherine soldat*. There followed versions in Hebrew (*Katrin haltah le-ish tsava*, Tel-Aviv, 1934) and Czech (*Katrin vojákem*, Prague, 1934).

The Reading Public's Response

Many readers took the novel to be a true historical account. The description of the visit of the Empress Auguste Viktoria to the hospitals in

Metz produced a particularly lively response. A Dr W. Fink wrote under the
headline 'Kathrin [sic] übertreibt': 'Aber ihr Gedächtnis hat sie bei dem
nachträglichen Niederschreiben ihres Tagebuchs arg im Stich gelassen.'
(*Vossische Zeitung*, 226, 21 September 1930). Adrienne Thomas replied on 28
September 1930 in no. 232 with a laconic 'Nein, das hat sie nicht' and added
with some irony:

> Ich habe mit voller Absicht alle wahren, halbwahren und
> falschen Gerüchte aus meinen keineswegs nachträglich
> konstruierten Kriegsaufzeichnungen übernommen.
> Gerade das unwahre Gerücht ist eine plastische
> Illustration dieser Zeit. Ich bin glücklich, daß ich aller
> Besserwisserei eine Gelegenheit zu langersehnter
> Betätigung gegeben habe.

Several readers read the novel as an appeal, while they neglected questions of
historical authenticity and the book as a love story:

> Es kommt ja nicht auf Kathrin Lenz [sic] und Lucien
> Quirin an! Es kommt überhaupt nicht mehr auf deren
> unglückliche Generation an. [...] Nicht müde sollten sie
> [die Überlebenden] werden, der neuen Jugend von dem
> Unheimlichen zu berichten, daß sie ein Grauen erfaßt –
> wie notwendig es ist, damit nie wieder der Gedanke an
> die Möglichkeit eines neuen Krieges auch nur in eines
> ihrer Köpfe komme! Dieses Grauen des Krieges hat die
> Kathrin erlebt – sie hat es meisterlich gezeigt. [...] Dank
> für dieses weibliche *Im Westen nichts Neues*!
>   (Dr. jur. Wera Basse in the *Vossische Zeitung*, 28
>   September 1930)

In another letter to the *Vossische Zeitung* (238, 5 October 1930) Frau Liese
Riesebeck wrote:

> Ich verstehe es nicht, wie man nach der Lektüre [...]
> Erwägungen darüber anstellen kann, ob einzelne der
> geschilderten Vorgänge sich gerade so zugetragen
> haben. Das ist doch denkbar unwesentlich gegenüber
> der Stärke dieses Buches [...].

In this connection the *Vossische Zeitung* published a discussion of the limits of
poetic freedom in Adrienne Thomas's novel in which Dr Ernst Emil
Schweitzer, a lawyer, warned:

> [...] denn wenn auch durch solche Einzelheiten der
> literarische Wert des Ganzen nicht beeinträchtigt wird,
> so setzt sich Frau Thomas durch einen Fehlgriff
> Mißdeutungen aus, und es bestünde die Gefahr, daß die

Aufnahme des Werks in der Öffentlichkeit von
politischen Parteiströmungen beeinflußt wird.
(12 October 1930)

In order to prevent misinterpretation and political speculation, a clear
'avertissement des éditeurs' was printed at the beginning of the French
edition:

> A certains dates de ce journal figurent des appréciations
> sur les origines et la conduite de la guerre, qui reflètent
> naivement l'opinion politique propagée officiellement
> dans l'ancien pays d'empire. Elles n'ont que la valeur de
> notations exactes et on ne peut en aucune façon y
> trouver la manière de voir de l'auteur. Les Editeurs,
> d'accord avec Madame Adrienne Thomas, tiennent à
> éviter cette méprise au lecteur. Ce livre est aussi loin
> que possible de toute préoccupation politique ou
> nationale.
>
> (*Catherine soldat* (Paris, 1933), p. vi)

The Novel as a Political Statement

Adrienne Thomas wrote her novel not only in order to come to terms
with her war experiences but also as a political warning and indictment, for,
during the time that the book was being written (1929-30) signs of nationalism
and militarism were again making their appearance: 'Schon marschierte man
wieder durch die Straßen Berlins. Schon gab es wieder militärische Feiern
und Paraden, schon schlug man sich.' (*Reisen Sie ab, Mademoiselle!*, p. 5)

The first two parts of the novel, which deal with the period between
1911 and 1914, are not an innocent overture to the shattering fate of a young
woman in Lorraine; the description of everyday events mirrors the
increasingly tense atmosphere in Metz just before the war. In keeping with
the diarist's youth, political pronouncements are rare but clear: 'Es ist schon
schrecklich genug, daß in Deutschland auch die Gedanken in Uniform und
Parademarsch gehen [...].' (p. 40) The problematical relationship between the
inhabitants of Lorraine and the imperial German authorities is also reflected:

> Ich lasse mir bloß von den Preußinnen nichts gefallen,
> die uns erstens beibringen wollen, wie deutsch
> Lothringen eigentlich ist – wie französisch es ist, können
> sie natürlich nicht wissen, weil sie dazu erst französisch
> sprechen können müßten –, und zweitens sich

aufspielen, als wären sie unsere Vorgesetzten.
(*Die Katrin wird Soldat*, p. 22)

As both a Jewess and a Lorrainer, Katrin is wounded by the comments of daughters of Prussian administrative families. When, later, soldiers of Jewish extraction 'das alte, böswillige Vorurteil beseitigen [sollen], das des Juden Treue und Hingabe an sein Vaterland nicht wahrhaben [will]' (p. 203), she realizes that in showing such patriotic enthusiasm 'die Metzer Gemeinde genoß – weil sie dumm ist – die Sensation, unter ihren Andächtigen das erstemal Juden in Offiziersuniform zu haben.'

When, in the second part, the heroine falls in love with her school-friend Lucien Quirin, whose mother is French by birth, there is further opportunity to express conflicts of nationality. This polarization is very much to the fore in the conversations of schoolfriends noted down by Katrin (e.g. 'Na, hoffentlich verschwindet im neuen Jahr von dem deutschen Rathaus einer deutschen Stadt das Schild mit der Inschrift "Hôtel de ville"', p. 88). After the assassination of the Austrian heir to the throne in Sarajevo, the schoolchildren discuss the question of taking part in the war and the mobilization of Germany. Lucien reproaches Katrin, saying: 'Das Vaterland ist in Gefahr – da ist es Pflicht eines jeden Deutschen, es bis auf den letzten Blutstropfen zu verteidigen. Siehst du das denn nicht ein?!' But she proves herself to be impervious to patriotic fervour; on the contrary: 'Nein, ich sehe es nicht ein – aber was nützt es, das zu sagen? Einer im Pennal ist von der Tollwut befallen worden und hat die anderen alle angesteckt.' (p. 129) Attentively she registers the growing war fever in the country and the demagogic effect of the press, which even makes Lucien speak like the newspapers.

In the third part, confronted by the reality of war, Katrin can no longer hold back from taking up a position, and develops into a pacifist. After the French socialist leader and pacifist Jean Jaurès is shot by an assassin, officially described as 'deranged' on 31 July 1914 and all hope of a Franco-German rapprochement collapses, Katrin is left to speculate sadly: 'Wer weiß, ob er nicht eine Weigerung der französischen Sozialisten, in den Krieg zu ziehen, durchgesetzt hätte, und wer weiß, wie sich dann seine Parteigenossen auf der ganzen Welt verhalten haben würden.' (p. 145) The first aerial combat near Metz, which Katrin watches through binoculars, makes her doubt the blessings of technological progress: 'Der uralte Traum der Menschheit, wie die Vögel im blauen Äther zu fliegen, ist in Erfüllung gegangen. Und wozu nützt es der Mensch?' (p. 156). Faced with this proof of war their inner struggles are sharpened: 'Ich weiß, daß ich in diesem Moment die miserabelste Deutsche bin, aber ich muß laut vor mich hin sagen: "Lieber Gott, unsere dürfen, dürfen nicht getroffen werden, aber laß die Franzosen heil entkommen!"' (p. 157)

On 16 August 1914 she becomes a Red Cross auxiliary at the refreshment stall at the main station. Suddenly the well-brought-up girl finds herself confronted by the misery of the civilian population from the poor districts of Metz who on 20 August 1914 begin to be evacuated to Germany:

> Warum kommt wohl niemand auf den Gedanken, einen Feldzug gegen die Armut zu rüsten? Mein Gott, wer möchte sich in einen Krieg einlassen, in dem nichts zu gewinnen ist, keine Hochöfen, keine stolzen Festungen, kein Geld und kein Land?
>
> (p. 166)

The broader relevance of her experiences is stressed by Eduard Korrodi:

> Die Bilder, die sie von dem Wahnsinn und Elend beschreibt, wird man ihr glauben — denn so möchte man fast paradox sagen —, sie ist ja nicht nur an einem Segment der Front gewesen, sie hat der Menschheit ganzen Jammer tag-, tag-, jahrlang im Bahnhofdienst von Metz mitangesehen.
>
> (*Neue Zürcher Zeitung*, 20 May 1931)

The clever choice of a railway station as the main setting for the events provides scope for an especially rich variety of descriptive contrasts:

> Immer dasselbe doppelseitige Bild: Oben auf dem Bahnsteig ausziehende, singende, nichtsahnende junge Menschen — unten in der Baracke die Zurückgekehrten mit blutleeren Gesichtern, zerschmetterten Gliedern.
>
> (p. 202)

Apart from hard work, the sight of so much misery and her anxiety about friends, the heroine also has to put up with the contradictions of politically slanted information: bound by an oath of secrecy, she learns about events that are hushed up in the newspapers. Metz station is given a key role in the structural development of the novel, for it is here that information from the front is brought up against what is being disseminated at home.

The diary form of the novel allows the writer to combine the inner and outer contradictions she experiences so traumatically with a radical critique of the prevailing political situation. Adrienne Thomas reinforced her earlier comments in a conversation with Gabriele Kreis on 6 March 1980:

> Die Katrin...ja, das war ich. Das heißt, ich war es insofern, als Punkt für Punkt die politischen Ereignisse stimmten; so habe ich sie erlebt. Aber um einen Menschen zu schildern, muß man zehn kennen.
> (Postscript to *Reisen Sie ab, Mademoiselle!* (Hamburg, 1982), p. 383)

Jean Giraudoux, in his foreword to the 1933 French translation, picks out Adrienne Thomas's novel from the mass of war books that appeared in Germany around 1930 because 'La vérité et l'émotion du roman de Madame Adrienne Thomas existent en fonction de son talent: elles agissent discrètement, modestement, et elles sont éclatantes' (*Catherine soldat*, p. x). Giraudoux deals critically with the then fashionable theory that the First World War could be explained in terms of the German national character: '[...] En dépit de toute légende et de toute théorie, il y a une contradiction entre le bonheur allemand et la guerre' (pp. viii-ix). Adrienne Thomas's novel had the merit of arguing against the accepted glorification of war:

> Il [le bonheur allemand] se fracasse contre la vraie guerre, c'est-à-dire contre la famine, le réserviste, la défaite. [...] La guerre qu'elle [la nation allemande] mena alors est le plus grand combat que l'imagination ait livré à la réalité. Elle s'efforça de lui conserver aussi longtemps qu'elle put son caractère d'idylle.
> (p. ix)

Giraudoux goes on to say that one of the novel's merits was to show that such attempts to ignore the truth about the war could not persist for long, as any reader of it would soon gather:

> Tel est l'ordre de vérités qu'avive la lecture de *Catherine soldat*, sans qu'il soit question d'en tirer la moindre conclusion sur l'origine des guerres passées ou la prévision des guerres futures.
> (p. ix)

On the author's seventy-fifth birthday Hermann Kesten published a sensitive appraisal in the *Süddeutsche Zeitung* of 24 June 1972:

> Adrienne Thomas erweist sich in diesem wie in allen ihren Romanen als scharfsinnige und unerbittliche

> Beobachterin von Menschen und Ereignissen, bewahrt
> aber ein kindliches Gemüt. [...] sie hat zugleich auch den
> durchdringenden unerbittlich kritischen Blick des
> genauen Beobachters und obendrein den Witz des
> Grenzbewohners, der automatisch das Divergente und
> im Vergleich Absurde zweier Völker auffaßt, ebenso wie
> ihre Vorzüge und Meriten.

What Kesten said about her personal attitudes and her resilience in exile
applies equally well to her novels, and especially to *Die Katrin wird Soldat*:

> [...] sie erwies sich [...] als so geschickt und weltklug, daß
> man den Verdacht faßte, als sei ihre Naivität zwar nicht
> gespielt, aber ein Teil ihrer epischen Qualitäten und im
> Handumdrehen eine Art Scharfsinn.

NOTES

[1] *Börsenblatt für den deutschen Buchhandel*, 276, 28 November 1930.

[2] *Die Literatur* 33 (1930/31), p. 603.

[3] See Thomas, 'Exilerinnerungen', in *Österreicher im Exil 1934 bis 1945*, ed. by H. Maimann and H. Lunzer (Vienna: Österreichischer Bundesverlag für Unterricht, Wissen und Kunst, 1977), pp. 509-14.

[4] See *Deutsche Nationalbiographie, Ergänzung 1: Verzeichnis der Schriften, die 1933-45 nicht angezeigt werden durften* (Leipzig: Verlag des Börsenvereins der deutschen Buchhändler, 1949), p. 302.

[5] Reprint (Vaduz: Topos, 1979).

[6] See 'Exilerinnerungen', pp. 509-14, and especially the article by E. E. Theobald, 'Adrienne Thomas', in *Deutschsprachige Literatur seit 1933* (New York and Berne, 1989), pp. 905-13, which contains much otherwise unobtainable information mentioned here. Biographical details may also be found in Gabriele Kreis, *Frauen im Exil* (Düsseldorf: Claasen, 1984), pp. 211-21. See also 'Adrienne Thomas: Eine Lebensrettung dank der stillen Résistance des französischen Volkes', in *Sie flohen vor dem Hakenkreuz*, ed. by Walter Zadek (Reinbek: Rowohlt, 1981), pp. 101-105.

[7] Theobald, op. cit., p. 910.

[8] *Börsenblatt*, 251, 28 October 1930.

[9] *Börsenblatt*, 280, 3 December 1930.

[10] *Börsenblatt*, 295, 20 December 1930.

[11] *Börsenblatt*, 251, 28 November 1930.

Emmy Ball-Hennings

8

Emmy Hennings: A Woman Writer of Prison Literature

Sabine Werner-Birkenbach

I

Emmy Hennings once wrote: 'Die Welt ist in Wirklichkeit nicht so schön, als man sie träumen kann. Darum spielte ich sie.. Spielte, was ich mir ersehnte.. Spielte mir mein Ideal.. spielte so lange und alles wurde mir Wahrheit...'[1] Writing about Emmy Hennings presents a constant temptation to dream her dreams all over again and − drifting between one's wishes, her wishes and reality − to carry on with her games. Anna Rheinsberg, who has written a good deal about Hennings,[2] is a case in point. She makes no pretensions to literary criticism; for her Emmy Hennings is 'ein blonder Hunger, welt-umarmend', always on the go, forever on the move: 'früh schon ist sie ein Lauf. Unterwegs! Sie hält immer nur kurz an, eine Atempause lang, und ist gerade fort, wenn etwas herumdreht, woran sie rührt.' (*Kriegs/Läufe*, p. 8) The poetic language brings Rheinsberg and her subject so close together that they become almost indistinguishable for the reader. In this lies both the strength and the weakness of this approach. The qualities that Rheinsberg adduces as characteristic of Hennings come across particularly vividly, yet her characterization includes judgements that could well be false: who can decide in the case of an author who played until everything became real? Her later autobiography carries the title 'Das flüchtige Spiel',[3] and, as she herself said, memory, on which all autobiography depends, is for her a 'Dichterin' and 'Täuscherin':

> Das Schöne fällt uns ein, das weder Anfang noch Ende haben darf, und alles Zufällige, Zeitliche lassen wir beiseite, es fällt von uns ab. Die Erinnerung ist insofern eine Täuscherin, eine Schleiermacherin, indem sie uns vor allem das Kostbarste vor Augen führt, sie ist eine rührende Dichterin, die alles Nebensächliche, Trübe möglichst unberührt läßt. Die Erinnerung hat recht, so vorzugehen...[4]

Writing about Emmy Hennings demands of the literary scholar a commitment to biographical accuracy. It is difficult to do justice to this requirement, however, as the autobiographical works − *Das Brandmal. Ein Tagebuch* (Berlin: Reiß, 1920), *Blume und Flamme. Geschichte einer Jugend* (Einsiedeln and Cologne: Benziger, 1938 and Frankfurt/M.: Suhrkamp, 1987), *Das flüchtige Spiel* (Einsiedeln: Benziger, 1940), as well as the partly biographical, partly autobiographical *Hugo Ball. Sein Leben in Briefen und Gedichten* (Berlin: S. Fischer, 1930), *Hugo Balls Weg zu Gott. Ein Buch der Erinnerung* (Munich: Kösel & Pustet, 1931) and *Ruf und Echo* (Einsiedeln: Benziger, 1953) − contain significant discrepancies, as for example in the descriptions of the circumstances leading to her arrest, or of her emigration to Switzerland at the outbreak of war, where fact and fiction seem to merge. Thus it is not surprising that Emmy Hennings has not yet been the subject of a biography or of a monograph and that there has not even been a reliable chronology of her life (however, see the 'Outline of her Life' at the end of this essay). It is therefore especially important in her case to discover which themes produced contradictions in her autobiographical writings and to remember that her factual statements are not always reliable, which makes it necessary to compare them wherever possible with other sources such as letters and the reminiscences of her contemporaries. This is particularly important when considering the theme of imprisonment in her work. Her autobiography cannot be dismissed as entirely unreliable; after all, as Luise Rinser points out: 'Über das Leben im Gefängnis kann nur jemand schreiben, die/der Gefangene/r war.'[5] The secondary literature on Emmy Hennings offers no help concerning the background to her arrest. The only scholarly work on her arrest and imprisonment is Heinz Ohff's postscript to the Frankfurt/M.: Ullstein, 1985 edition of *Gefängnis* (Berlin, 1920), where we read:

> Was geschehen ist, wissen wir nicht. Daß es sich um einen – bei dem geringen Strafmaß vermutlich nur geringfügigen – Diebstahl, wahrscheinlich um Mundraub, handelt, erfährt auch der Leser erst relativ spät. Irgendwann in der Münchner Zeit, als sie mal wieder als Hausiererin das Notwendigste zu verdienen suchte, muß die Versuchung für Emmy Hennings zu groß gewesen sein. Sie selbst läßt keinen Zweifel daran, daß sie tatsächlich gestohlen hat.
>
> (p. 144)

Ohff does not make clear to which of her biographical statements he is referring, and Hermann Burger, reviewing the new edition in the *Frankfurter Allgemeine Zeitung*, simply paraphrases his statement when he writes:

> In kritischen Zeiten schlug sie sich als Hausiererin mit einem Bauchladen durch, und da wird sie auch mal kleinere Diebstähle verübt haben. Deshalb kommt es zur geschilderten Doppelhaft...[6]

The circumstances of Emmy Hennings's arrest had in fact been explained in 1984 by her daughter Annemarie Schütt-Hennings in the *Hugo-Ball-Almanach* published to mark the centenary of her birth. In an introductory survey of her mother's life and work, written in collaboration with the Ball scholar Franz L. Pelgen, we find the following account of the events:

> Gelegentlich ist zu lesen, sie sei wegen Paßfälschung verhaftet und ins Gefängnis gesteckt worden. In Wirklichkeit wollte Emmy Hennings einer fremden Frau, die sie traurig in München auf der Straße getroffen hatte, helfen. Wegen Unklarheiten im Nachweis der Identität wurden beide verhaftet, – weil der Mann der Frau ein Deserteur war. Emmy Hennings war unschuldig und wurde völlig grundlos mehrere Wochen im Gefängnis festgehalten.[7]

Annemarie Schütt-Hennings was only eight years old at the time and living at her grandmother's in Flensburg; her statement (and it is the only evidence we have for this explanation) is therefore not necessarily reliable. The exact circumstances may have been withheld from the little girl, so that she became an unintentional transmitter of inaccurate information. In the same issue of the *Hugo-Ball-Almanach* we find the following comment on a letter, which conflicts with her statement: 'Wegen einer Paßangelegenheit wurde Emmy Hennings verhaftet und mußte mehrere Wochen im Gefängnis verbringen.[8] This is probably based on a passage from *Ruf und Echo* (pp. 47-48), although no source is given and there is no mention of the fact that her autobiographical writings differ widely at this point. The situation is indeed confused, as Anna Rheinsberg clearly stated in a 1988 radio talk:

> Emmy Hennings gerät unversehens unter die Gespenster – sie gerät ins Gefängnis. Warum ist nie ganz geklärt worden. Sie selbst hat später die Heiligen und alle (un)möglichen Ausreden bemüht. Ihre Tochter, Annemarie Schütt-Hennings, spricht von einem Versehen; warum, es ist ja auch egal.[9]

We shall now examine the problem from two different angles. On the one hand we shall attempt to reconstruct the sequence of events as accurately as possible on the evidence of letters and police reports. On the other, the divergencies in Hennings's autobiographical writings will be collated in order to demonstrate that, when understood as characteristic of her creative approach, they can in fact shed valuable light on the relationship between real events and their transformation into literature.

In writing about Emmy Hennings, the literary scholar should always bear in mind that her creative work is ultimately of greater consequence than biographical exactitude. Hermann Burger's review of *Gefängnis* shows us what happens if the writer is regarded as more interesting than her work. He begins by stating 'an diesem Gefängnistagebuch, das 1916 begonnen wurde und 1919 erschien, ist das Schicksal der Autorin bei weitem interessanter als der Text'.[10] He goes on to call her a weak personality, which is an underestimation: 'Die Chansonette ist der existentiellen Bedrohung einer Einkerkerung nicht gewachsen...' This in Burger's eyes accounts for the alleged mediocrity of her work: '[...] darum wirken die Szenen mit den Mitgefangenen, mit der Hafner, die einen Grafen zu Tode gepflegt hat, und der siebzigjährigen Blinden, die als "Mutterle" angesprochen wird, wie Ausschnitte aus einem schlechten Edgar-Wallace-Film.' By the end of his review he has come to the conclusion that *Gefängnis* has nothing to contribute to our understanding of its author, as if the story of her life were the main aim of her literary activity: 'Nein, die vielbegabte Gefährtin Hugo Balls wird, wenn überhaupt, eine Legende bleiben, zu der dieses verwurstelte Buch wenig beiträgt.'

(Burger, op. cit., see note 6). Such an approach must be rejected, for it leads to a blanket condemnation of a book which is of central importance to Emmy Hennings's treatment of the theme of imprisonment. In our exploration of this subject, a careful distinction will have to be made between works of fiction based exclusively on the experience of prison, such as *Gefängnis*, the 1929-30 version of *Das Haus im Schatten* and the three prison poems on the one hand,[11] and the semi-fictional, semi-documentary passages in Hennings's autobiographies, including the 'double biographies' of herself and Hugo Ball and her literary diary *Das Brandmal* of 1920 on the other hand.

II

She is Emmy Hennings, née Emma Maria Cordsen, married name Emmy Ball or Emmy Ball-Hennings. But she is also Editha von Münchhausen[12] and '...Maria Lund, genannt Liane Zumsteg oder Nachtvogel, in Gelsenkirchen auch als weiblicher Humorist unter dem Namen Charmette genannt und bekannt' (*Schatten*, p. 2). And sometimes she is Jessy (in *Das Brandmal*, p. 27), Helga (see *Blume und Flamme*; cf. *Das flüchtige Spiel*) or Finny.[13] As she put it in *Schatten*:

> Alle vierzehn Tage wechsle ich meinen Namen.
> Vielleicht, daß irgend ein Name besseren Anklang
> findet, als ich, die Trägerin. Da mir vieles unsicher
> geworden ist, ich mein eigenes Wesen in mir verändert,
> schwankend fühle, warum sollte ich den immer gleichen
> Namen tragen, der auf meinem Geburtschein steht? Es
> ist nur ein Schein und darauf will man mich festlegen.
> Meine Ehrlichkeit lehnt sich dagegen auf.
>
> (p. 2)

Attempts to pin her down to specific names, dates and places have only been partly successful.[14] In other words, she presents much the same problem as her friend, the better-known writer Else Lasker-Schüler, of whom it has been said that she disappeared behind the legend she had herself helped to create in her writings:

> Else Lasker-Schüler ist hinter der Legende
> verschwunden, die sie selbst zu schreiben begonnen
> hatte. Schon ihre autobiographischen Mitteilungen
> tragen Legendenscharakter, und ahnungslose Gut-
> gläubigkeit hat sich allzu lang an die verklärten

Tatsachen und rundweg falschen Daten gehalten, die sie
bekanntgegeben hat.[15]

Emmy Hennings played various roles in private life, on the stage and in
her works, and different facets of her personality are forever contradicting one
another so that it is virtually impossible to reconcile them into one coherent
image. Each self-portrayal is only of brief duration. Then she moves on to a
new scene and a new public, to whom she presents herself in a new guise and
by whom she is reflected in a new way. Before starting any discussion, we
must therefore be aware that her life and work are not related in linear
fashion, but that they affect one another in all kinds of ways. Real life is not
just fragmented and pieced together again in the literary text; artistic elements
affect the patterning of her everyday existence, whether in Berlin's
Romanisches Café or on the stage of Simplicissimus in Schwabing, in
Munich's Café Stephanie or Dada soirées in the Cabaret Voltaire.

In her autobiographical writings she introduces her life to her readers
in a variety of ways. In *Ruf und Echo* she sketches a thoroughly naïve Emmy
Hennings, probably vanishing yet again behind the role she has sketched:

> Hugo [Ball] hatte sich zum Militär stellen müssen, war
> indessen wieder zurückgestellt worden, während man
> mich einfach von der Straße weg verhaftete und ins
> Polizeipräsidium, ins Untersuchungsgefängnis gebracht
> hatte. Warum, das weiß ich heute noch nicht genau.
> Verhaftungen waren jedoch in der ersten Kriegszeit
> nichts Besonderes, da man in manchen Personen Spione
> vermutete. Von mir nahm an, ich wisse um eine
> falsche Paßfabrik Bescheid. [...] Bisweilen hatte ich fast
> Mitleid mit den Beamten, die ich mit meiner
> Unwissenheit auf dem Gebiet der Falschmünzerei zur
> Verzweiflung brachte. Man fragte mich, ob ich wirklich
> so dumm sei oder mich nur so anstelle. Die Anstellerei
> wäre mir bei den vielen Kreuzverhören viel zu
> anstrengend gewesen, und von den Deserteuren, die so
> eifrig gesucht wurden, meinte ich beruhigend, sie kämen
> gewiß gelegentlich von selbst wieder. Sicherlich wäre ich
> im Verlauf von sechs Wochen nicht so mürbe geworden,
> wenn ich einen reellen Bankeinbruch verübt hätte, aber
> gerade meine hoffnungslose Unschuld in dieser Sache, in
> der man mich beschuldigte oder verdächtigte, ging mir
> auf die Nerven. Warum man mich von einer Stunde auf
> die andere entließ, weiß ich nicht.

(*Ruf und Echo*, pp. 47-48)

In her literary diary *Das Brandmal* she contradicts this version and implies that she was arrested for streetwalking:[16]

> Ein Schutzmann könnte mich so leicht in Polizei-
> gewahrsam bringen. Mir träumte einmal, das sei der
> Straßenmädchenhimmel. Die Sittenpolizei hat mich
> noch nicht beobachtet, obgleich ich nicht behaupten
> kann, ich sei ihr gar so sehr aus dem Wege gegangen.
> *(Das Brandmal*, p. 185)

Prostitution and theft are merged in *Das flüchtige Spiel* in the offence known as 'customer robbery':

> Es stellte sich heraus, daß Finny auch eine Zeitlang
> hausieren gegangen war, aber nicht grad mit Motten-
> pulver. Es gibt ja noch manches andere, was sich
> anbieten läßt. [...] Sie hatte bei einem ihrer Freunde eine
> goldene Herrenuhr mitgenommen...
> *(Das flüchtige Spiel*, pp. 151-152)

The protagonist here, Helga Londelius, goes to prison for her friend Finny Andres: 'Es handelte sich um eine Rolle, die ich zu Ende zu spielen hatte, um nichts anderes.' (p. 155). Finny Andres in prison is therefore a role played by Helga Londelius, just as the life of Helga Londelius is one of the roles of Emmy Hennings, which goes to show that reality only found its way into the literary text after it had undergone a series of fragmentations, making evident the creative will of the author as well as her delight in playing games, even when it is a question of reworking the existential experience of being in prison. Whether she was as successful in playing with this searing experience in real life is more doubtful precisely because the prison theme recurs so frequently in her work. Yet this is what she wants us to believe, to judge by a letter she included in her first 'double biography', *Hugo Ball. Sein Leben in Briefen und Gedichten*, in which she tells him:

> Ich bin derart unschuldig hineingeraten in das
> Gefängnis, daß es beschämend ist, davon zu sagen. Für
> mich und für alle andern. Es war ein kleines Kunststück,
> meine Unschuld zu verbergen, denn, Hugo, es gibt eine
> bewußte Unschuld. Es gibt einen Willen zur Unschuld,
> davon sich nicht leicht sagen läßt. Die größte Mühe
> habe ich mir gegeben, diese Unschuld zu verbergen. Es
> ist mir gelungen! Ich hatte den Triumph, daß man mich
> mehr verdächtigte, als ich erwarten konnte. Va bene...
> Das Leben ist ein Spiel... Und mir kann man nichts
> wollen.[17]

'Und mir kann man nichts wollen...' This phrase, written in about 1919, and in a letter to Hugo Ball, could also have something to do with the enquiries being carried out at that time by the Swiss police in Zurich and Berne about Ball and Hennings. As the police records show, she managed to preserve a low profile during these investigations.[18] The police found it just as difficult to get an exact idea of her real-life circumstances then as we do today when examining the extant documents and personal statements of the author. Although a detective was commissioned to carry out a search by the examining magistrate in Berne and the criminal commissariat in Zurich had been pressing for their extradition ('Ball u. die Hennings dürften sich i. Bern aufhalten u. gehören ohne Aufschub ausgewiesen'), the police could find no proof for their suspicion that Ball and Hennings were anarchists propagating 'revolutionary ideas'.[19] The police records of their 1919 investigations are in fact of less documentary value than one might expect. They contain crass errors of judgement and factual errors: at one point Copenhagen is wrongly indicated as Emmy Hennings's place of birth instead of Flensburg.[20] Hugo Ball is described as going under the anarchist name 'Ha Hu Baley', which was in fact an amalgam of the names Ha(ns), Hu(go), Bal(l) and Ley(bold): both writers had signed poems in this way which were their joint work.[21] The police reports also contain statements by unreliable witnesses – innkeepers, concierges and neighbours – voicing their speculations concerning the relationship between Ball and Hennings. It is against this background that we should understand the detective's written statement to the examining magistrate on the subject of Emmy Hennings's period in custody: 'Sie soll s[einer] Z[eit] in München wegen anarchistischer Propaganda in Haft gewesen sein.'[22] The mention of Munich accords with the description in *Ruf und Echo* (pp. 47-48) and with the town 'M.' in the story *Gefängnis* (p. 7), but there is no other evidence to corroborate anarchistic propaganda as the reason for the arrest. It is probably more easily understood in the context of the Swiss authorities' pursuit of Emmy Hennings as a 'dangerous alien'.[23] It is improbable that she would have concealed the political motivation for her arrest in her accounts of her imprisonment, but there is also another argument that casts doubt on the theory of political harassment. 7 March 1915 is given in a letter from Hugo Ball to his sister as the date of her release from prison, but it is in fact impossible to say precisely how long the imprisonment lasted.[24] The letters exchanged between Hennings and Ball at the time are both undated.[25] The war archives of the Hauptstaatsarchiv in Munich house the records of court proceedings for the period before 7 March and therefore of course all cases of political prosecution, yet there is no mention of Hennings. For their part the Swiss records shed no light on whether she spent six weeks in detention there awaiting charges, as she states in *Ruf und Echo* (p. 48) or whether she was sentenced to four weeks' detention without bail followed by four weeks' imprisonment as described in *Gefängnis* and *Das Haus im Schatten*.

If we re-examine the police records along with the autobiographical writings, it becomes clear that the author takes up the various charges made in them against herself and Ball. The accusations of the Swiss police must have been known to her from her interrogation by the detective in Berne.[26] In fact all the charges ever raised against her and Ball reappear somewhere or other in her autobiographical writings. An example is the report about Ball's forged passport. According to the report of the Zurich city police he had stuck his own photograph into the passport of the painter John Höchster and had used it to travel from Germany to Switzerland; this corresponds with *Ruf und Echo*, where Hennings writes, she was arrested for forging a passport (pp. 47-48).[27] The street-walking charge is also given several treatments; that in *Das flüchtige Spiel* (p. 152) has already been quoted. According to police records she possessed no identification papers, and Annemarie Schütt-Hennings mentions this as one reason for her incarceration.[28] It is as if on the literary level Emmy Hennings was taken into custody for every charge levelled against her or Hugo Ball (with whom she identified herself), and that she was set free again through the process of writing.

In her late literary re-working of the prison theme, *Das flüchtige Spiel*, Hennings summarizes the connection between the problem of identity and the experience of imprisonment and in so doing speaks about the psychological background to her frequent changes of name and role:

> Warum nur war es gerade im Gefängnis so schwer
> erträglich, sich mit einem fremden Namen angesprochen
> zu hören? Warum hatte es mir in der Freiheit, da es mir
> gut ging, so wenig bedeutet, ob ich mich so oder anders
> nannte? Es war allerdings stets ein fingierter Name

gewesen, hinter dem keine andere Person als ich steckte,
aber das Betrügerische, das Verlogene kam mir erst hier
recht zum Bewußtsein. Ich begann nach den Gründen
meines Spieltriebes zu forschen und kam dahinter, daß
mein Wesen sich von den Gestalten, die ich darstellte,
zum Teil genährt und gebildet hatte, und hinter all
diesem Erspielten witterte ich einen anderen Menschen
in mir.

(*Das flüchtige Spiel*, p. 163)

In a poem of 1922 Emmy Hennings gives us a self-portrait:

Ich bin so vielfach in den Nächten.
Ich steige aus den dunklen Schächten.
Wie bunt entfaltet sich mein Anderssein.[29]

Her many faces are in fact her roles in everyday life as well as in autobiography and fiction: even here the frontiers are fluid. In this respect she can
most easily be compared to Else Lasker-Schüler[30] – her appearances as
'Prinz Jussuf von Theben' come to mind – or to Claire Goll, who seems to
change as she mirrors herself through her current lover. By introducing the
poem into her unpublished novel *Das Haus im Schatten* (1929/30) she makes a
clear connection between her stay in prison and problems of identity and
thereby confirms her prison experience as the existential crisis she had already
described in 1919 in *Gefängnis*, her earliest story on the theme: 'Mir ist als
hätte ich für immer einen Schock bekommen, einen Knacks, der sich nicht
rückgängig machen läßt.' (p. 74)   The traumatic experience conceals one
fragment of her identity, an unchangeable facet of the personality of an author
who was to reexamine herself in the light of the theme of imprisonment for
the remainder of her life – the earliest relevant publication being her poem
'Gefängnis' of 1915[31] and the latest the chapter 'Das Gefängnis' in *Das
flüchtige Spiel* (pp. 154-170). In the course of writing she uncovers her identity
step by step.   In the course of this process the conflict between her
unconventional behaviour and the society that is represented by the judicial
system stands out ever more clearly.   In her later book on prison life, *Das
Haus im Schatten*, she defined it thus:

Stets habe ich gern ein Wesen hingestellt, das nicht
wesentlich war und mit diesem Unwesentlichen war man
ungemein zufrieden.   Nun aber, da ich mich einmal
getrieben fühlte eine kleine Spur meines wahren Wesens
zu zeigen, ist man geneigt mich zu köpfen.

(*Schatten*, p. 4)

III

The following dialogue between Emmy and her cell-mate Anna takes place in the earlier story:

> '...Weswegen sind Sie denn da?' Ja, das ist es ja gerade...
> Und die erste Qual kommt wieder. Warum rührt sie
> daran? Und ich bekomme sofort wieder drückende
> Herzschmerzen. [...] 'Wegen Fluchtverdacht.' Und fühle
> wieder: das kann nicht stimmen. Fühle, wie ich die
> Farbe wechsle. Bin verlegen, sehr verlegen, möchte eine
> Entschuldigung sagen. Aber ich kann mich nicht
> entschuldigen. Ich weiß, ich bin nicht zu entschuldigen.
> Ich denke über Vergangenes nach. Anna stützt mit dem
> Ellbogen ihren Kopf und sieht mich forschend an. Dann
> sagt sie: 'Wegen Fluchtverdacht? Das ist doch kein
> Delikt! Weshalb sind Sie geflohen? Da muß man doch
> vorher...' Ich falle ihr ins Wort. 'Doch, doch. Flucht ist
> gesetzwidrig. Ich wollte fliehen. Ganz einfach fliehen.
> Sonst nichts. Für mich hatte ich keinen Grund zu
> fliehen. Ich habe wohl Angst bekommen, sonst wäre ich
> wohl nicht geflohen. Hätte wohl nicht versucht, zu
> fliehen. Es ist mir ja nicht geglückt... Mir selbst ist gar
> nicht klar geworden, daß ich fliehen wollte...'
>
> (*Gefängnis*, pp. 48-49)

In the first part of this story, which describes the remand period, there is an account of the circumstances which led to Emmy's arrest. In the run-up to the hearing in the court of inquiry she had declared in a letter her intention to travel to Paris, and this was interpreted as an attempt to escape:

> 'Ich bin doch nicht fluchtverdächtig!', versuchte Emmy
> dem Untersuchungsrichter zu erklären und die Verhaf-
> tung abzuwenden, 'Weiß Gott, Sie tun mir Unrecht! Wie
> kann man nur so etwas sagen? Es tut mir leid, aber das
> muß ich doch sagen; ich habe Ihnen doch meine Absicht
> mitgeteilt. Wie kann ich nur verdächtig sein? Ich bin
> freiwillig zu Ihnen gekommen, um eine Antwort
> abzuholen, und Sie verhaften mich? Sie tun mir
> Unrecht!'
>
> (*Gefängnis*, pp. 15-16)

When she has exhausted every argument − the examining magistrate does not address a single word to her and the police officer is about to lead her away − Emmy, seized by a sudden panic, does in fact try to escape. Thus the paradoxical situation arises that the accusation of trying to escape actually provokes an attempt to do so, and the magistrate's decision is thus vindicated

by the subsequent event. In *Das Haus im Schatten* Hennings develops lines of
thought merely hinted at in the earlier story. The link between the two
becomes clear in the letter to Hermann Hesse written on 24 November 1929:
'Mein Gefängnis wollte ich auf einen Wunsch hin "bearbeiten" und sehe auch
hinein, kann aber nie und nimmer die selben Worte schreiben und aus den
frühen Worten lese ich ganz andere, neue und fremde heraus. Wie von
selbst.'[32] The ways in which the protagonist of *Gefängnis* reacts are typical of
its central character, Liane Zumsteg: 'Kommt mir einer mißtrauisch, kann ich
auf die Dauer sein Mißtrauen nicht enttäuschen. Nur der wird bestohlen, der
bestohlen werden will...' (p. 76) Thus she questions the roles of perpetrator
and victim, and undermines the categories of guilty and not guilty:

> Vor Gericht hätte ich behaupten wollen: 'ich bin
> unschuldig' – es wäre ebenso anmaßend gewesen, als
> wenn ich behauptet hätte: 'ich bin schuldig'; denn ich bin
> nicht allein schuldig geworden. Hätte mein Kläger nicht
> auch zur Rechenschaft gezogen werden müssen? Aber
> mein Kläger war gar nicht da.   Er ließ sich
> entschuldigen...
>
> (*Gefängnis*, p. 104)

In the story *Gefängnis* the question of the crime on which the legal
proceedings rest is taken up again much later, at the beginning of the second
part, where the four-week penal confinement is described. This accords with
the logic and structure of the book. The fact that she is accused of an attempt
to escape is enough to justify the earlier description of the period of detention.
The court proceedings themselves are not dealt with: they fall into the period
not described between remand custody and prison sentence. When she is
remanded, a prison warder asks the dreaded question, 'What are you in for?'
and Emmy cannot avoid answering, 'Theft'.

> 'Wegen Diebstahls', sage ich nebenbei und so
> gleichgültig wie möglich. [...] Ich denke, es kommt auf die
> Umstände an. Doch das sage ich nicht. Denn es würde
> nur ein Durcheinander geben. Ich würde mich nur
> aufregen: ich bin nämlich der Ansicht, daß ich nicht
> gestohlen habe.
>
> (*Gefängnis*, p. 92)

The contrast between the court's verdict and the protagonist's view that she
had not committed theft is not resolved in *Gefängnis* and only partially in *Das*

Haus im Schatten, where the situation which led to the theft is explained as follows:

> Warum ich eigentlich das Geld genommen habe?
> Genau weiß ich es nicht. Mein Freund hatte es mir
> übrigens versprochen und noch mehr. Das ist allerdings
> kein Grund etwas zu nehmen, das sehe ich ein. Er hat
> aber zuviel Geld gehabt, das tat ihm nicht gut. Ich hab
> ihm nicht gründlich helfen können. 'Er hat sich nur
> geärgert, daß ich nicht bei ihm geblieben bin, darum hat
> er mich angezeigt.' [...] 'Bei mir hat man nicht zu
> schlafen, das hat mich gekränkt und ich habe ihm vorher
> gesagt, wenn er mir das Reisegeld nicht gibt, daß ich von
> ihm wegfahren [kann], nehme ich es mir. Ich habs doch
> verdient.'
>
> *(Schatten,* pp. 113-114)

The fragmentary description of what actually happened offers no clear account of the events and leads one to suppose that Liane Zumsteg, like Finny Andres in *Das flüchtige Spiel* (p. 152), perpetrated the act of customer theft, especially as she claims she has 'earned' the money. This interpretation becomes even more probable if one takes into consideration the passages where the legal situation of prostitutes and their clients is discussed (*Schatten,* p. 14, pp. 170-171). A similar passage also occurs in *Gefängnis*:

> Würde ich mich befassen mit solch zwecklosen Dingen
> als da sind: Sünder bestrafen und Buße verschreiben, ich
> wäre gründlicher gewesen bei Abfassung der Gesetze.
> Man nehme das schutzloseste Geschöpf, ein Straßen-
> mädchen. Wenn es verboten ist, sich Liebesstunden
> bezahlen zu lassen, muß es verboten werden, sich
> Liebesstunden zu kaufen. Aber die Erfahrung lehrt, daß
> der Mensch ohne Liebesstunden nicht leben kann. Also
> müßte die Liebe anders organisiert werden. Aber
> 'organisierte Liebe' klingt so peinlich. Dennoch kommt
> man darüber nicht hinweg.
>
> *(Gefängnis,* pp. 104-105)

Emmy Hennings regarded *Das Haus im Schatten* as an adaptation of *Gefängnis*,[33] and the close relationship between the two stories is confirmed by a large number of identical passages. One may therefore conclude that in both cases she regarded customer theft as the crime in question, though the connection between theft and prostitution is no more than hinted at. This means that the question of relative guilt or innocence is not just raised by a concrete example, but is treated as a point of reference for an abstract

discussion about the relationship between an individual woman and the
overall social conditions of her life, in both stories interest being focused
exclusively on women in custody. In *Gefängnis* she complains:

> Der Gerichtshof besteht aus Männern, und es erfordert
> weniger Kraftaufwand, das schwache Geschlecht zu
> bestrafen, als Männer zur Rechenschaft zu ziehen, die
> ihre stärksten Neigungen geheim zu halten wünschen.
>
> (*Gefängnis*, p. 105)

Here she makes it clear that a male-dominated system defines its own
understanding of female criminality and then acts on it by means of the
judicial system. How intensely she deals with the significance of gender roles
in social development can be seen in her feminist manifesto, 'Das neue Recht
der Frau', which appeared at the same time as *Gefängnis*. In it she declares
men to be responsible for the collapse of Central European culture in the
First World War:

> Die unter der Herrschaft des Mannes in den letzten
> neunzehnhundert Jahren entwickelte. europäische
> Kultur hat mit ihrem Streben in diesem Weltkrieg
> bankerott gemacht. [...] Mithin erscheint, da der Mann
> sich als unfähig erwiesen hat, die europäische Kultur und
> Zivilisation in steigender Entwicklung zur Höhe empor
> zu führen, die Frage berechtigt, ob nicht vielmehr die
> bislang unterdrückt gewesene Frau mit ihrem Reichtum
> unverbrauchter und bisher unerschlossener Kräfte dazu
> berufen ist, diesen Bankerott zu liquidieren, um aus ihm
> zu retten, was zu retten ist und mit Hilfe ihrer frischen
> Fähigkeiten aus den auseinandergefallenen Bestand-
> teilen und der alten Kultur eine neue aufzurichten.[34]

In order to carry out these aims she claims new legal means for women – she
calls them "Gewaltmittel":

> Diese Gewaltmittel in Form von verfassungsmäßigen
> Sicherheiten und gesetzlichen Verordnungen fordert
> nunmehr die Frau als ihr neues Recht, als das neue
> Recht der Frau. Nicht um ihrer selbst und ihrer Kinder
> willen, sondern zur Rettung der europäischen
> Menschheit.
>
> (Ibid., p. 23)

IV

> Der beste Menschenkenner, der feinfühlendste Dichter
> vermag keinen Gefangenen zu begreifen, wie es diesem
> zu Mut ist, dem man die Freiheit gedrosselt hat. Vieles,
> alles mag ein Psychologe verstehen, nicht aber was die
> zwangsmäßige Haft für Wirkungen mit sich bringt.
> *(Schatten*, p. 94)

In the early story *Gefängnis* and in the later *Das Haus im Schatten*, Emmy
Hennings describes in depth the physical and psychological effects of the
withdrawal of freedom.   They are in two parts, 'Remand' and 'Penal
Confinement', in both of which the protagonist Emmy or Liane Zumsteg, as
the case may be, is first placed in solitary confinement.   This is quickly
described:

> Sechs kleine Schritte kann ich gehen, sechs Schritte auf,
> sechs Schritte ab. [...] Seitlich kann ich nicht gehen.
> Breite ich meine Arme aus, kann ich beinahe mit den
> Fingerspitzen die Wände berühren.
> *(Schatten*, p. 58)

The door is of iron and provided with a spy-hole, the window high up and
barred.   The furnishings consist of an iron bedstead, folded up against the wall
during the day, and a board that serves as something to sit on:

> Die Zellentür wird geschlossen, und ich bin allein. Ich
> suche gierig nach einem bunten Gegenstand, einiger
> Unordnung, die mich anregen könnte. Aber es ist alles
> peinlich sauber und grau.   Ich konstatiere diese
> Korrektheit leider nur zu schnell.
> *(Gefängnis*, p. 35)

To be confined in such a space means to be isolated in a state of total inner
turmoil and left entirely to one's own devices, with no diversions and no
opportunity for physical movement to work off one's frustration.   In addition
there is the awareness of being at the mercy of an institution that robs every
prisoner of her right to make her own decisions by keeping her dependent and
reducing her at predetermined times to her minimal needs – eating and
sleeping.   In *Gefängnis* Emmy reacts to these restrictions with a series of
particularly violent and psychological symptoms.   She lives through the stages
of aggression, anxiety, auto-aggression and change of perception, to the point
where consciousness is lost.   Anger is the immediate reaction to the

experience of powerlessness and is psychologically necessary in order to protect the personality against the inhumanity of the prison system. Thus Emmy's feelings well up almost as soon as she is left alone in her cell:

> Oh mein Gott, laß mich nicht "natürlich" bleiben; denn dann tobe ich. Bleibe ich ruhig in diesem Käfig, bin ich mir untreu geworden. Das ist das Allerschlimmste. Ich darf mich nicht beschwichtigen. Ich darf mich nicht hinwegtäuschen, über mich selbst hinweg.
>
> (*Gefängnis*, p. 36)

Her anger can find no concrete object on which to vent itself in the hope of changing the situation; it rushes into a void and brings home to her how helpless she is:

> Werde ich mich über Eisengitter hinwegsetzen können? Mauern stürzen lassen? Türen brechen, wenn ich immer vor mir sehe eine verschlossene Tür? Wo werde ich die Kraft hernehmen? Und eine Verzagtheit überfällt mich. Der Schweiß bricht mir aus der Stirne. Ich presse mein Gesicht an die Eisentür. Besinnung, verlaß mich nicht! Ich fürchte mich.
>
> (*Gefängnis*, p. 37)

Her anxiety is reinforced by a feeling of being under constant supervision, expressing itself initially in physical restlessness:

> Ein Auge sieht mich wohl von draußen. Des Wärters Auge. Schwarzes Verräterauge sieht auf mich. Falsch bist du. Ich wende mich ab und beginne eine monotone Wanderung. Sechs Schritte auf, sechs Schritte ab, und immer wieder von neuem.
>
> (*Gefängnis*, p. 37)

In a state of isolation and limited freedom of movement there is no adequate means to express fear and anger; this is why aggression tips over into auto-aggression and the body expresses the pain being suffered by the mind:

> Ich habe fortwährend Brechreiz. Fühle mich so schwach, daß ich mich nicht auf den Beinen halten kann. Ich muß mich auf den Boden legen. Habe Leibschmerzen, hauche immer auf meine Hände, lege sie dann auf den Leib, damit die Wärme in mich dringt. Jeden Augenblick muß ich aufspringen, weil mir übel wird. Der Toiletteneimer steht an der Tür. Er ist desinfiziert mit einer teerartigen Flüssigkeit, die mir noch heftigere Übelkeit verursacht. Wenn ich mich erhebe, wird mir schwindelig. Nach kurzer Zeit bin ich so schwach, daß ich nicht mehr aufstehen kann. Ich weiß mir nicht mehr zu helfen. Muß es also aufgeben, und

kann mich nicht mehr um mich kümmern. [...] Aber ach,
die Schmerzen! Ist das Magengegend? Ist das die
Seele? Ist alles dasselbe. Geht in einem hin.
                                        (*Gefängnis*, pp. 40-41)

Hennings points clearly to the connection between 'Magen' and 'Seele'. In
psychosomatic terms the condition that leads to the symptoms she describes
may be formulated thus:

> Da Körper und Seele voneinander abhängig sind und
> ständig aufeinander einwirken, rufen starke Gefühls-
> bewegungen deshalb immer Reaktionen in bestimmten
> Organen hervor. [...] Der Magen reagiert nun vor allem
> auf zwei Arten von starken Gefühlsbewegungen: – Auf
> den dringenden (unerfüllten) Wunsch nach Anlehnung,
> Hilfe, Versorgtheit, – auf ständig unterdrückten
> Ärger.[35]

Recent scientific research has shown that nausea and vomiting are a normal
reaction to solitary confinement, which makes every kind of human contact
impossible, but may also be an expression of the need to fight down anger
against the judicial system and the punishment it prescribes. Hennings's
description of the symptoms is in no way exaggerated: it fits the situation.

Images from her memory surface in rapid succession as she grows
weaker, as they do in high fever or under the influence of drugs. In a
sequence of fragmented thoughts and sentences she makes us feel the
breathlessness of this process as image chases image:

> Es riecht nach Sommer, Bodenkammer, alten Äpfeln
> und überwinterten Kartoffeln und Teer. Und diese
> Eisentür immer sehen müssen... Es ist schrecklich heiß.
> So heiß war es noch nie. Und dieser Teergeruch! Wann
> roch es doch nach Teer? Als Kind lesend auf der
> Bodenkammer. Die Dachluke war geöffnet, das
> Schieferdach geteert. Die Liebesbriefe meiner Mutter
> waren sehr schön, so vergilbte Briefe... Lavendel, Myrth'
> und Thymian... Sind wir schon Ende Juli? Aber das ist
> ja ganz... Oh, ist mir übel!
>
>   (*Gefängnis*, p. 41)

The flood of images produced by her imagination and her memories indicates
that her perception of the outer world is also disturbed. Instead of the grey
walls she sees colours, and she can no longer relate to time and place:

> Mir wird bunt vor den Augen. Noch regenbogen-
> farbener. Die Zelle zerfällt in Würfel. Wenn die nur
> nicht auseinanderfallen. Nachher hab' ich wieder die

Schuld. Wenn die Zelle auseinanderfällt, hält die Decke
auch nicht lange; denn alles hängt zusammen, alles hat
seinen Grund, oder alles ist Luft.

(*Gefängnis*, p. 41)

These changes of perception should not be understood as symptoms of
weakness or feverishness; they are a consequence of the withdrawal of all
forms of stimulus. In the 1950s volunteers exposed to experiments of stimulus
withdrawal or to a mono-stimulus situation, such as doubtless happens in a
prison cell, experienced very similar limitations in their perceptions: 'Die
Wände bewegten sich, Ecken und Flächen waren verborgen, eigene Kopf-
bewegungen wurden als Bewegung der Umgebung erlebt, intensive Farb- und
Kontrasterlebnisse traten auf.'[36] A few hours in an unchanging stimulus
situation are sufficient to alter perceptions. As concentration diminishes,
thoughts begin to drift, then perceptions become distorted until actual
hallucinations occur and the subject of the experiment can no longer
distinguish between fantasy and reality (ibid., p. 49). The circumstances and
effects of stimulus deprivation have led in recent discussions about prison
conditions to the definition of solitary confinement as torture by isolation
('Isolationsfolter'). Against this background, which makes clear the degree of
terror caused even by short-term imprisonment, which for those not involved
seems so harmless, we can understand how Hennings can almost equate the
withdrawal of freedom with execution: 'Beim Verhör habe ich schon den
Vorschlag gemacht, man möge mich doch aufhängen, das sei etwas exaktes,
aber man hat es abgelehnt.' (*Schatten*, p. 2a) In *Gefängnis* the author makes it
clearer still that she sees imprisonment as an act of murder perpetrated on the
soul: 'Es handelt sich um mehr als um eine vorübergehende Freiheits-
beraubung. Etwas in mir wird hingerichtet.' (p. 104)

Emmy loses consciousness in her cell. The following morning she is
found by a prison warder in a state of collapse and is transferred to the sick
bay. The hours or days of solitary confinement are over, and her initial shock
slowly gives way to the daily routine of prison life. In the second stanza of the
poem 'Gefängnis', which the author later inserted with a different second line
into *Das Haus im Schatten* (pp. 177-178), nature images are inspired by the
colours of her handkerchief:

> Mein Taschentuch hat grünen Saum
> Ein gelbes Feld ist in der Mitte
> [Ein Blumenfeld träumt in der Mitte]
> Und auf und ab sechs kleine Schritte
> Mein Taschentuch, mein grüner Baum.

In the grey cell the yellow and green provide an impulse which Emmy transforms into images of trees and flowers. Sigrid Weigel sees references to nature in the prison writing of Wera Figner and Rosa Luxemburg as signs of longing for life.[37] In Hennings's case the green tree also signifies the return of vital energy, an energy no longer exhausted by restless pacing up and down but which becomes even more intense as she imagines herself strolling through a flowery meadow. As her physical and mental state improves, her interest in her fellow prisoners increases. Her first observations contradict her expectations. They give her the impression of victims: 'unansehnliche Mädchen, sehr viele von ihnen sehen aus, als seien sie die Betrogenen, die Übervorteilten. Sie erscheinen mir geprellt. Etwas stimmt nicht. Ich muß dahinter kommen.' (Gefängnis, p. 63). As the days go by, the author and her reader discover much about the other women's life stories, starting with the circumstances that led to their arrest. In the 1919 story we are already given such details; in Das Haus im Schatten more are added. Some of the women are simply referred to by the name of the crime of which they are accused, for instance 'Wegen Blutschande' and 'Wegen Kindesmißhandlung'. They are divided into two groups according to the offences they are said to have committed. To the first group belong petty acts of theft and embezzlement, misdemeanours rather than crimes, usually motivated by the woman's social condition. To this group belong Anna, who is doing her time 'wegen fünfzig Pfennig Schokolade' (Gefängnis, p. 50), Marie, who is accused of having misappropriated the 'Knochenkasse' in a hotel kitchen (ibid., p. 114), the faith healer who accepted money for her services but only 'das Geringe, was ich zum Leben brauchte. Ich habe eine große Familie' (ibid., pp. 65-67 and Schatten, p. 109), and the blind woman of whom it is said:

> Die Blinde ist von Beruf wohl Bettlerin, hat es aber
> einmal ausnahmsweise 'mit der Musik versuchen wollen'.
> Ein kranker Leierkastenmann hatte ihr für einige Tage
> seine Orgel überlassen, aber ohne polizeiliche Erlaubnis
> dürfe man nicht spielen.
>
> (Schatten, p. 183)

Material need is always the reason for the petty offences described in Emmy
Hennings's prison texts, and in *Das Haus im Schatten* she makes this even
clearer than in *Gefängnis*:

> Von oben bis unten anständig und fromm bleiben, das ist
> ein Luxus, den sich reiche Leute leisten können und ich
> will darum Niemand beneiden. Die aber immer
> genügend haben, müßten es einmal ausprobieren, wie es
> ist, nichts zu haben, und sie würden anders, milder
> darüber urteilen, wenn von Armen ihnen einmal ein
> wenig abgenommen wird. Betteln ist doch verboten.
> Wie aber soll die soziale Not aufhören, wenn nicht
> einmal mehr gebettelt werden darf?
>
> (*Schatten*, p. 115)

The second group of offences which Hennings describes in greater
detail in *Das Haus im Schatten* than in 'Gefängnis' have their origin not only in
the penury of their perpetrators but in their social standing as women. There
is 'Hafner' for example. She has 'cared for' a Count, first as his mistress, and
later reduced to the function of housekeeper. With the help of an apparently
forged will, she attempted to procure at least some financial compensation
after his death for her years of sacrifice, during which security and social
acceptance were denied her. Anna, who is housed with Emmy and 'Hafner' in
the sick bay, brings the problem to a head by accusing 'Hafner' of having been
the Count's whore for twenty-three years. The combination of sexual
exploitation and economic dependence forms the basis for all the offences in
this second group, including illegal prostitution (*Schatten*, pp. 160-161),
abortion (ibid., p. 21; the passage is crossed out in the typescript), father-
daughter incest, for which at that time the daughter was punished for being
partly responsible (*Gefängnis*, pp. 127-128) and infanticide. Stella in *Das Haus
im Schatten* killed her new-born child. She tries to get across to her cell-mates
what made her do it: 'Ich habe das Kind nur umgebracht, weil ich den Vater
nicht mehr... nicht mehr... ach, ich mag nicht mehr.' (p. 92) Her act was
clearly a desperate attempt to escape from dependence on the baby's father
and seemed the only way out, for, as she goes on to explain, 'Man tut nichts,
was nicht nötig ist. Es muß alles sein, wie es ist. Jede Tat ist notwendig. Das
ist ja das Schreckliche.' (*Schatten*, p. 92)

In both books confrontation with the life-stories of their fellow-
prisoners leads the protagonists to identify closely with them. As Liane

Zumsteg says, 'Vielleicht aber hat es ein Gutes, daß ich hier bin: ich achte weniger auf mich selbst, als auf andere und wenn ich auf mich selbst achte, meine ich nur die Andern damit.' (*Schatten*, p. 100) In *Gefängnis* this strong bond is limited to the period of Emmy's detention; when she is released, she feels it a betrayal not to take the others with her (p. 82). She herself feels liberated: 'Je länger ich gehe, desto freier fühle ich mich. [...] Ich breite meine Arme aus vor Glück.' (p. 133) After the experience of prison had troubled her for many years, Hennings knows that the withdrawal of freedom, even if only for a limited time, will continue to affect her all her life:

> Bis an meinen Tod werde ich mich belastet fühlen, denn damit, daß ich frei bin, frei sein werde, ist mir nicht geholfen, weil ich zu genau wissen werde, wieviele gefangen sind. Nie werde ich mich ganz frei fühlen dürfen, immer wieder wird es mich wie ein Schatten überfallen.
>
> (*Schatten*, p. 124)

V

Emmy Hennings and Erich Mühsam have much in common. Both writers belonged to anarchist circles in the years before the First World War – he as a central figure, she more on the fringe – and shared comparable political attitudes. She even wrote for his periodical *Der Revoluzzer*.[38] Common to both is the experience of being in prison. On 29 October 1909 Mühsam was placed under arrest in Berlin for political reasons and remanded in custody in Charlottenburg. After eleven days of detention he was set free, and was never convicted. While in prison he wrote his *Tagebuch aus dem Gefängnis*, which he published in 1911 with a number of name changes and omissions but without any other alterations.[39] At the time he was involved in a relationship with Emmy Hennings, as we can see from the entry of 22 May 1911 in his diary.[40] Mühsam's *Tagebuch aus dem Gefängnis* and the prison stories of Emmy Hennings are similar in many respects. For example, when interrogated by the police Mühsam is on the point of leaving for Zurich (*Kain* 1, p. 9); the protagonist of *Gefängnis* is also getting ready for a journey, to Paris, when the official enters her room (p. 8). The drive from the police station to remand prison is described in very similar terms.[41] Whether such parallels permit the conclusion that Hennings made use of Mühsam's diary as a source, or whether they simply result from the similarity of events, cannot be ascertained here. As far as the analysis of their texts on the basis of gender roles is concerned, what is particularly interesting are the differences in their experience of imprisonment. Mühsam and Hennings are particularly well suited for such comparison because of their similar social and political environment as well as the fact that their arrests took place within a short time of each other.[42]

Right from the moment they enter the police station, Hennings's protagonists differ clearly from Mühsam: his account is of course wholly auto-biographical. His growing sense of uncertainty, caused by a situation beyond his control, is concealed behind dismissive descriptions of the premises and people:

> Man kann mich totschlagen: Ich weiß nicht mehr, ob ich dort Treppen steigen mußte, ob ich in Hinterhäuser geführt wurde oder wie die Baulichkeit beschaffen war. Diese nüchternen Büro- und Quälhäuser haben genau wie Polizeibeamte Visagen von stereotyper Ähnlichkeit, für deren Einzelheiten man sich nicht im geringsten interessiert. Es war mir zunächst ganz gleichgiltig, was man mich fragte; ich war nur etwas traurig.
>
> (*Kain* 2, p. 22)

By contrast Liane Zumsteg becomes afraid as soon as she enters the police station. She feels that the building is a place in which power is exercised: 'Mir ist, als bestünde die Welt aus lauter Beamten. [...] Meine Gegner haben die Gewalt, die Macht.' (*Schatten*, p. 1) In her view there is a close association between power, the authority of the state, physical violence and sexual violence. This leads to her fear of becoming a victim of state violence, as represented by the police, and is expressed in terms of a fear of rape:

> Es ist merkwürdig still hier und hier auf dieser Etage ist ja überhaupt kein Mensch zu sehn. Als wär's gar nicht bewohnt. Wer weiß,... Wer weiß, wozu mich die beiden Männer [gemeint sind die Beamten, die die Vorladung überbracht hatten] eingeladen haben. [...] Würde mir aber einer zu nahe treten und mir zumuten, was mir nicht paßt und ich wäre in Notwehr, könnte nicht weglaufen, oho, dann sollte es mir nicht darauf ankommen... Wo die Leute die sogenannten Herzen sitzen haben, das weiß ich auch. Ach Gott, meines wird ganz blaß bei dem Gedanken und wir sind in den

Nummern um 140 herum und ich muß ganz schnell eine
halbe Cigarette rauchen, um mich zu beruhigen. In
Nummer 144 ist kein Mensch. Ich hab' durchs
Schlüsselloch geguckt. Der Schlüssel steckt von draußen
und ich könnte ja einfach abschließen, den Schlüssel
mitnehmen und mich beim Publikum auf der Straße
erkundigen, ob das mit Nummer 144 und mir seine
Richtigkeit hat, könnte mir ein paar handfeste Zeugen
mitnehmen, denn man kann von mir nicht verlangen,
daß ich mich hier womöglich soll vergewaltigen lassen.

(*Schatten*, pp. 26-27)

Both Mühsam and Liane Zumsteg are about to be charged and both become
victims of state violence; though Mühsam feels 'sad' in this situation, he
remains aloof and intellectually superior to the officials with their stereotyped
countenances. In contrast to Liane Zumsteg, he does not identify with the
role of victim meted out to him. The differences become clearer still when
Mühsam's experiences are compared with those of Hennings's protagonists
during their first night in custody. His uncontrolled and rapidly changing
thoughts are a reaction to the isolation of solitary confinement comparable to
the flood of images Emmy experiences in *Gefängnis*, even if in his case they do
not lead to a change of perception:

Ich sah mit der größten Lebendigkeit eine Unmenge
meiner Bekannten, beteiligte mich an Gesprächen über
letzte Weisheiten und Wahrheiten, führte juristische
Disputationen über den wahrscheinlichen Inhalt der
Paragraphen 128 und 129, die ich fortgesetzt verletzt
haben sollte, und von deren Bedeutung ich keine
Ahnung hatte, stand vor Gericht und überzeugte in einer
forensischen Meisterleistung das Auditorium von der
Unsinnigkeit jeglicher Justiz, rief mit Lebhaftigkeit nach
dem Kellner, um für mich einen Kaffee schwarz, für
Stella einen Cognak zu bestellen, dankte nach der
Premiere meines neuen Stückes für den Applaus, riet
den Genossen energisch ab, mit Bomben zu werfen, bat
Cläre um einen Kuß und Herrn K. um 2000 M.
Vorschuß[,] gestand Gertrud L. meine Liebe und wider-
legte H. W. seine Existenzberechtigung, kurz: ich hatte
tausend Wachträume, die mir durch die infame Kirch-
turmuhr alle Viertelstunde als Wachträume bestätigt
wurden...

(*Kain* 2, p. 25)

The rage, nausea and physical collapse so intensely portrayed by Hennings as
reactions to the withdrawal of freedom are completely absent from Mühsam's
diary. One possible explanation for this lies in the differing social conditioning

of the sexes, which makes men independent individuals but influences women towards a life of dependence. Being at the mercy of other people in prison repeats in an extremer form women's lack of power in society; for the male prisoner, on the other hand, who is accustomed to the privilege of self-determination, being locked up means a personal insult, not the intensified version of an existential conflict.

In custody Mühsam, Emmy and Liane develop different survival strategies. The two women take an interest in the life stories of their fellow prisoners, recognizing themselves in these and overcoming their own crises by seeing their own anxieties and hopes mirrored in those of others. In this way their own self-esteem is re-established:

> 'Marie, ich will Ihnen sagen, was es ist. Es ist ja das Einzige: Sie sind es. Sie sind da und, verstehen Sie mich recht: ich kann nicht untergehen. Sie lassen mich nicht versinken... Begreifen Sie? Sie sind es. Sie allein.' [...] Und dann höre ich: 'Sie sind es ja auch. Sie ja auch. Wirklich. Sie auch. Wir sind es beide...'
> (*Gefängnis*, p. 122)

How different is the survival strategy of Erich Mühsam! As a political prisoner he distances himself from his 'criminal' fellow prisoners and accepts these categories without ever thinking that any violation of human rights has its origin in the failings of the social system. In them he seeks confirmation of his own superiority: 'Ich war etwas in Verlegenheit, wie ich verständlich antworten sollte und sagte dann kurz und politisch [bündig?]: "Politisch". Der Proletarier wurde von Respekt erfüllt. Das war an dem Ton kenntlich, in dem er erwiderte...' (*Kain* 5, pp. 71-72) His disparaging description of the other inmates increases the gap: 'blaß, kränklich und wenig intelligent sahen fast alle aus, wenige robuste Kerle nur, und fast gar keine geistig beträchtlichen Physiognomien' (*Kain* 3, p. 35). During exercise periods in the yard he meets the 'bei weitem elegantesten der Häftlinge. Aber das Gesicht von ganz minderwertigem Ausdruck, blöde, reuig, interesselos'; he also encounters a young man whom he describes as 'wohl das häßlichste und abschreckendste Menschenexemplar, das ich je gesehen habe. [...] Der vollendete Typ eines psychopathischen Schwerverbrechers, unsäglich roh in Bewegungen und Gebahren.' (p. 36) The *Tagebuch* also contains comments about the offences of the others. These are based solely on observation, and say more about the author's outlook than about the persons in question. One gains the impression that he is describing life around him from the perspective of a prison warder, classifying prisoners according to such criteria as intelligent or stupid, evil or pathological, political or criminal. His viewpoint is like that of a prison governor, so it is hardly surprising that the governor becomes one of his closest associates: 'Ich kann sagen, daß ich an diesem Inspektor hier meinen besten Freund, meine zuverlässigste Stütze habe. Der Mann erleichtert mir das Leben, soviel er irgend kann...' (*Kain* 12, p. 185) In her study of prison literature, Sigrid Weigel describes Mühsam's behaviour as the 'Praxisschock des Anarchisten', and shows how his political activism as a free man is reversed in the prison environment:

> Als anarchistischer Theoretiker hatte er die These von der revolutionären Bestimmung des 'Lumpen-proletariats' vertreten. Die Arbeiter seien in ihrem Kampf gegen den Kapitalismus, in dem sie sich die Formen ihres Widerstandes von diesem aufzwingen ließen, verbürgerlicht. Das revolutionäre Potential der Zukunft sei dagegen in solchen Klassen zu suchen, die durch ihre Lebensweise in praktischer Opposition zur bürgerlichen Ordnung sich befänden.[43]

Mühsam's tendency to set himself apart from the 'Lumpenproletariat' in prison and to see himself as the equal of the governor, the highest representative of the state in a prison, comes close to a betrayal of his own political objectives, a result of being on remand which in all probability the 'friendship' of the prison governor was designed to achieve.

The relationship between Mühsam and Emmy or Liane and their fellow inmates, if considered in the light of the different socialization of the sexes, makes the differences between their survival strategies even more apparent. Mühsam's conduct can then be understood as an attempt within the social structure of a prison to uphold the self-image of male strength and power which is deeply rooted in men. His need for personal reassurance is increased when his freedom is withdrawn, making it impossible for him to analyse or criticize class relationships behind prison walls because the conscious awareness of his total dependence which such an analysis would entail would inevitably lead to the realization that he has become a victim of state violence. Hennings's women protagonists, in keeping with their social role as women, already feel inferior before they are arrested and taken to the police station, but they discover a hidden strength in the company of their fellow prisoners. Mühsam allows his position in prison society to be defined by others; Emmy, Liane, 'Hafner', the child murderess Stella, the blind barrel organ player and all the other inmates challenge the powers-that-be by their life stories as women and by their social deprivation.

The prison chapter in *Das flüchtige Spiel*, Hennings's last text on this theme, ends with a poem which she introduces with the words: 'Und dann kam der Tag, an dem ich das graue Haus verlassen durfte. Schön war es, sehr schön, sich einer neuen Freiheit zurückgeschenkt zu fühlen. Es kam nur darauf an, welchen Gebrauch ich von dieser Freiheit machte.' (*Das flüchtige Spiel*, p. 71) Writing, as represented by the stanzas that follow – leaving aside their religious content – and writing about the experience of prison in particular, is her way of making use of her regained freedom. In contrast with Mühsam's *Tagebuch aus dem Gefängnis*, her works illuminate the period of imprisonment in retrospect. A constant feature in them is her criticism of the system of justice and punishment – 'das System ist eine infame Teufelei' (*Gefängnis*, p. 64) – and her protest against it, together with her attempt to overcome the trauma of the loss of freedom, is a further motivation to write 'auf daß nicht spurlos meine Zeit verrinne...' (*Das flüchtige Spiel*, p. 171).

VI

A comparison of Erich Mühsam's *Tagebuch aus dem Gefängnis* and Emmy Hennings's literary reworkings of her prison experience suggests that socialization based on gender roles may be a significant aspect of the subject which should be taken into account when analysing prison texts by other writers. As the genre is still assumed to consist almost exclusively of works by male authors – the only women writers Sigrid Weigel mentions in her study are Rosa Luxemburg (*Briefe aus dem Gefängnis*, Berlin: Junge Garde, n.d. [1920]) and Wera Figner (*Nacht über Rußland. Lebenserinnerungen*, Berlin: Malik, 1926) – this is an aspect which has yet to be explored in the detail it may well deserve.[44] In her study of prison literature by French women authors Elissa Gelfand concludes that such works are overlooked because they do not correspond or measure up to criteria based on male prison literature. Whether this also applies to literature in German must remain unanswered until the relevant texts become available.

Emmy Hennings's poem in *Die Aktion* in 1915 initiates the evolution of the genre of German female prison literature in the twentieth century. It was followed by Rosa Luxemburg's *Briefe aus dem Gefängnis*, Elisabeth Janstein's poem 'Gefängnis', also in *Die Aktion*[45] and the memoirs of Wera Figner in the same year (1926) as Marie Luise Fleißer's play *Fegefeuer in Ingolstadt* (first performance, Berlin 1926). Immediately after the end of the Second World War, Luise Rinser's *Gefängnistagebuch* was published (Munich: Kurt Desch Zinner-Verlag, 1946); she took the theme up again in 1987 with her anthology of texts written by women in or about prison. Traude Bührmann's novel *Flüge über Moabiter Mauern* (Berlin: Orlanda, 1987) should also be mentioned. But Emmy Hennings deserves a special place because of her deep personal involvement with the theme of imprisonment over a long period of time. My list of prison texts by women writers consists entirely of chance discoveries; the relevant literature has not hitherto been systematically screened from this point of view. Yet the existence of such texts supports my view that they deserve to be taken into account in any comprehensive history of women's literature (or, to put it more accurately, of women, literature and history)[46] which is alive to the specific factors governing women's writing and its lack of overall continuity.

NOTES

[1]Emmy Hennings, *Das Haus im Schatten. Eine Erzählung aus dem Gefängnis*, Marbach, Deutsches Literaturarchiv, unpublished typescript, p. 45. The Hugo Ball collection of the Stadtbücherei in Pirmasens has a duplicate copy. The typescript was completed on 20 February 1930: see Emmy Hennings's letter to Hermann Hesse of 21 February 1930 in *Emmy Hennings. Briefe an Hermann Hesse* (new edn Frankfurt, 1985), p. 144. Later references to this typescript abbreviated to *Schatten*. Full bibliographical details of all Hennings's published works are listed at the end of this essay.

[2]Anna Rheinsberg, *KRIEGS/LÄUFE. Namen. Schrift. Über Emmy Ball-Hennings, Claire Goll, Else Rüthel* (Mannheim: Persona, 1989) and 'Emmy Hennings. "Der Kaffee ist so grau und kalt"', in *Bubikopf. Aufbruch in den Zwanzigern. Texte von Frauen*, ed. by Anna Rheinsberg (Darmstadt: Luchterhand, 1988), pp. 94-105.

[3]Emmy Hennings, *Das flüchtige Spiel. Wege und Umwege einer Frau* (Einsiedeln: Verlagsanstalt, 1940). I quote from the new edition (Frankfurt/M., 1988), here abbreviated to *Das flüchtige Spiel*.

[4]Emmy Hennings, *Ruf und Echo. Mein Leben mit Hugo Ball* (Einsiedeln: Benziger, 1953 and Frankfurt/M., 1990). My quotations are taken from the 1990 edition: here pp. 9-10.

[5]See Luise Rinser, *Laßt mich leben. Frauen im Knast* (Hagen: Padligur, 1987), preface, p. 9. Luise Rinser too had experienced prison and wrote about it in her *Gefängnistagebuch* (Munich: Desch, 1946, new edn Frankfurt/M.: Fischer, 1973).

[6]Hermann Burger, 'Innehalten zwischen Haft und Haft. Gefängnis – das Tagebuch der Emmy Hennings', *FAZ*, 217, 19 September 1985, p. 26; even Burger's title is incorrect, because Hennings's story is in no way identical with the diary.

[7]Annemarie Schütt-Hennings and Franz L. Pelgen, 'Emmy Ball-Hennings. Anmerkungen zu ihrem Werk und ihrer Person', *Hugo-Ball-Almanach*, 8 (1984), p. 14.

[8]Ernst Teubner (?), 'Kommentar zu "Emmy Ball-Hennings. Briefe an Hugo Ball"', *Hugo-Ball-Almanach*, 8, p. 133.

[9]Anna Rheinsberg, 'Wiederentdeckt: Emmy Ball-Hennings'. Radio broadcast of 28 May 1988 on Hessischer Rundfunk. The script is now in the Hugo Ball collection at Pirmasens.

[10]She had actually worked on the story earlier and sections had been published in Erich Mühsam's periodical *Der Revoluzzer*. See Emmy Hennings 'Im Gefängnis' (*Der Revoluzzer*, 12, 16 October 1919, no page number).

[11]Hennings, 'Gefängnis I, II, III', in *Helle Nacht* (Berlin: Erich Reiß, 1922). 'Gefängnis II', beginning with the line 'Im Süden rauscht des Wassers Seide', was first published in *Die Aktion* 20/21 (1915), col. 253.

[12]Editha von Münchhausen, 'Das neue Recht der Frau', *Der Revolutionär*, 10 (1919), pp. 19-23. For this pseudonym see the letter of 7 July 1919 from the examining magistrate to

a detective in Berne in the Schweizerisches Bundesarchiv, Berne. The other names occur in *Schatten*, p. 2.

[13]See Hennings, *Blume und Flamme* and 'Gefängnis' in *Das flüchtige Spiel*, pp. 154-180.

[14]For this reason no short biography is offered here. The essential details can be found in the special number of the *Hugo-Ball-Almanach* 8, 1984, in the chapter entitled 'Biographische Daten' in Rheinsberg, Mannheim: Persona, pp. 36-41, and in the chronicle of Hennings's life at the end of this essay.

[15]See Sigrid Bauschinger, *Else Lasker-Schüler. Ihr Werk und ihre Zeit* (Heidelberg: Lothar Stiehn, 1980), p. 21.

[16]Such arrests, carried out in accordance with paragraph 361/6 of the *Reichsstrafgesetzbuch*, were frequent until the passing of the law of 18 February 1927 to combat venereal diseases. From a note by Erich Mühsam one learns that the Munich police in 1913 even employed informers to check women who were out walking after dark without male escort. See Mühsam, 'Lockspitzel', in *Kain. Zeitschrift für Menschlichkeit*, 3 (1913/14), pp. 30-31.

[17]Undated letter to Hugo Ball, reproduced in *Hugo Ball. Sein Leben in Briefen und Gedichten*, p. 105. The context suggests it was written when Ball was writing *Die Kritik der deutschen Intelligenz* (Berne, 1919).

[18]The relevant police file is held in the Schweizerisches Bundesarchiv in Berne.

[19]See manuscript note on a letter of the Zurich city police dated 2 July 1919 concerning 'dangerous foreigners', and the letter of the examining magistrate in Berne to a detective dated 7 September 1919.

[20]Report from the detective to the examining magistrate in Berne, dated 15 July 1919.

[21]Letter from the Zurich city police to the Zurich criminal commissariat dated 2 July 1919.

[22]Report from the detective to the examining magistrate in Berne dated 15 July 1919.

[23]See note 21.

[24]Letter to Marie Hildebrand-Ball dated 8 March (1915), in Hugo Ball, *Briefe 1911-1927* (Einsiedeln: Benziger, 1957), p. 39. The date is wrongly given as 'probably 1916': as in it Ball announces the publication of his 'Leybold-Rede' in the next number of *Die Weißen Blätter*, 1915 must be the correct date. His 'Totenrede' appeared in no. 11/4 (April 1915), pp. 525-27.

[25]Hennings, letter to Hugo Ball in *Hugo-Ball-Almanach* 8, pp. 133-134. Ball, letter to Emmy Hennings, in *Briefe 1911-1927*, pp. 36-37.

[26]See note 22.

[27]See note 21; this mentions the report in the *Zürcher Polizeianzeiger* 1915, article 6845.

[28]*Hugo-Ball-Almanach* 8, 1984, p. 14.

[29]'Traum 2', in *Helle Nacht* (Berlin: Erich Reiß, 1922), p. 45. Later reprinted as 'Ich bin so vielfach' in *Die literarische Welt*, 21/22 (1926), p. 3.

[30]See Susanne Mittag, 'Else Lasker-Schüler. Der Entwurf einer rücksichtslos poetischen Existenz', in *Die Rolle des Autors. Analysen und Gespräche*, ed. by Irmela Schneider (Stuttgart: Klett, 1981), pp. 64-70.

[31]'Gefängnis', in *Die Aktion*, 20/21 (1915), col. 253.

[32]*Briefe an Hermann Hesse* (Frankfurt/M.: Suhrkamp, 1985), p. 130.

[33]Ibid., p. 130.

[34]Editha von Münchhausen (= Emmy Hennings), 'Das neue Recht der Frau' in *Der Revolutionär* 10 (1919), 19-23 (pp. 22-23).

[35]Reinhart Stalmann, *Psychosomatik. Wenn die Seele leidet, wird der Körper krank* (Frankfurt/M.: Fischer, 1991), p. 54.

[36]Heiner Legewie and Wolfgang Ehrlers, *Knaurs Moderne Psychologie* (Munich: Knaur, 1978), p. 50.

[37]Sigrid Weigel, 'Und selbst im Kerker frei...!' *Schreiben im Gefängnis. Zur Theorie und Gattungsgeschichte der Gefängnisliteratur (1750-1933)* (Marburg: Gutlandin & Hoppe, 1982), p. 86.

[38]'Gedicht', *Der Revoluzzer* 8 (July 1915); 'Hinrichtung', *Der Revoluzzer* 9 (19 July 1915); 'Im Gefängnis', *Der Revoluzzer* 12 (16 October 1915).

[39]Erich Mühsam, *Tagebuch aus dem Gefängnis*, in *Kain, Zeitschrift für Menschlichkeit*, 1 (1911), p. 9.

[40]Erich Mühsam, 'Tagebuch vom 27. Mai 1911', in Chris Hirte, *Erich Mühsam. 'Ihr seht mich nicht feige'* (Berlin: Neues Leben, 1985), pp. 182-83.

[41]*Kain*, 4 (1911), p. 57; Hennings, *Gefängnis*, p. 32.

[42]This section was suggested by Elissa Gelfand's essay 'Imprisoned women. Towards a socio-literary feminist analysis', *Yale French Studies*, 62 (1981), pp. 185-203. Gelfand's theoretical criteria are not, however, rigorous enough to be applied in this particular case.

[43]Weigel, op. cit., p. 75.

[44]See Horst and Ingrid Daemmrich, *Themen und Motive in der Literatur. Ein Handbuch* (Tübingen: UTB, 1987), pp. 60-64. Its entry under the heading 'Begrenzung – Freiheit' refers only to Marie Luise Fleißer.

[45] *Die Aktion* 11 (1921), col. 347.

[46] See Hiltrud Gnüg and Renate Möhrmann, *Frauen-Literatur-Geschichte. Schreibende Frauen vom Mittelalter bis zur Gegenwart* (Stuttgart: Metzler, 1985).

Emmy (Ball-) Hennings: Publications in Book Form

Blume und Flamme. Geschichte einer Jugend (Einsiedeln and Cologne: Benzinger, 1938, repr. Frankfurt/M.: Suhrkamp, 1987)

Das Brandmal. Ein Tagebuch (Berlin: Erich Reiß, 1920; Frankfurt/M.: Suhrkamp (forthcoming))

Briefe an Hermann Hesse (Frankfurt/M.: Suhrkamp, 1956 and 1985)

Damals in Zürich. Briefe aus den Jahren 1915-1917 (Zurich: Arche, 1978)

Das ewige Lied (Berlin: Erich Reiß, n.d. (1923))

Das flüchtige Spiel. Wege und Umwege einer Frau (Einsiedeln and Cologne: Benzinger, 1940; Frankfurt/M.: Suhrkamp, 1988)

Der Gang zur Liebe. Ein Buch von Städten, Kirchen und Heiligen (Munich: Kösel & Pustet, 1926)

Die Geburt Jesu. Für Kinder erzählt (Nuremberg: Glock, 1932)

Gefängnis (Berlin: Erich Reiß, 1919; Wetzlar: Büchse der Pandora, 1980; Berlin, Wien: Ullstein, 1985 (foreword by Heinz Ohff); Frankfurt/M.: Suhrkamp (1992)

Geliebtes Tessin (Zurich: Arche, 1976)

Helle Nacht (Berlin: Erich Reiß, 1922)

Hugo Ball. Sein Leben in Briefen und Gedichten (Berlin: Fischer, 1930)

Hugo Balls Weg zu Gott. Ein Buch der Erinnerung (Munich: Kösel & Pustet, 1931)

Das irdische Paradies und andere Legenden (Luzern: Josef Stocker, 1945)

Der Kranz (Einsiedeln and Cologne: Benzinger, 1939)

Die letzte Freude (Leipzig: Kurt Wolff, 1913 [= *Der jüngste Tag* 5])

Märchen am Kamin (Einsiedeln and Cologne: Benzinger, 1943; Frankfurt/M.: Insel, 1986)

Ruf und Echo. Mein Leben mit Hugo Ball (Einsiedeln, Zurich, Cologne: Benzinger, 1953; Frankfurt/M.: Suhrkamp, 1990)

Weihnachtsfreude (Zurich: Arche, 1976)

Emmy Hennings: A Chronology of her Life

17.1.1885	Born Emma Maria Cordsen in Flensburg
	Mother: Anna Dorothea Cordsen, née Zielfeld (17.8.1842–21.2.1916)
	Father: Ernst Friedrich Matthias Cordsen (23.4.1838–13.11.1901)
	No brothers or sisters
2.4.1900	'Frühlingsgedicht' – her first poem still extant
13.2.1904	Marriage to the typesetter Joseph Hennings
1904	Birth of a son
1905–c.1919	Actress, raconteuse, singer in travelling theatrical group; appearances in variety and cabaret, e.g. Apollo-Theater in Kattowitz, Olympia-Theater and Lindenkabaret in Berlin, Simplizissimus in Munich, and in many other towns. From 1915 in Switzerland, e.g. in the Bonbonnière in Zurich, and with the Marcelli-Damenensemble and the Maxim-Ensemble in Zurich, Basle, Baden (Argun) and in other places
Turn of the year 1905-1906	Death of her son. Separation from Joseph Hennings
18.8.1906	Birth of her daughter Annemarie Hennings in Penzig near Görlitz. She is brought up until age 10 by her maternal grandmother in Flensburg.
13.6.1907	Divorce from Joseph Hennings
1908	Recital artist in the Romanisches Café in Berlin. Becomes acquainted with Jakob van Hoddis, John Höxter, Ferdinand Hardekopf and many other literary figures.
1912–1915	Munich: Appears in Simplizissimus. Works as an artist's model, e.g. for Reinhold Rudolf Junghans. Regular customer of the Bohemian Café Stefanie also frequented by Else Lasker-Schüler.

1913	First publication: Emmy Hennings – *Die letzte Freude*, in *Der jüngste Tag*, ed. by Franz Werfel, No. 5 (Leipzig, 1913)
Autumn 1913	Meets Hugo Ball in Simplizissimus in Munich
Early 1915	Arrest in Munich, reason unknown
7.3.1915	Release from prison
12.5.1915	Takes part in an expressionist evening in Berlin. Among those present: Hugo Ball, Richard Huelsenbeck, Johannes R. Becher and Resi Langer
End of May 1915	Emigrates to Switzerland with Hugo Ball. First address: Schoffelgasse 7, Zurich
June 1915	Meets the socialist Fritz Brupbacher. Takes part in discussion sessions in the Schwänli in Zurich. Also present: Hugo Ball, Leonhard Frank, Max Oppenheimer, Richard Huelsenbeck.
17.12.1915	Participation in the Modern Authors' Evening in the Zunfthaus Zimmerleuten in Zurich. Also present: Hugo Ball, Käthe Brodnitz.
Spring 1916	Cabaret Voltaire in the Holländische Meierei, Spiegelgasse 1, Zurich. Appearances by Emmy Hennings on 5, 6, and 12 February and on 30 March. Also present on the first night: Hugo Ball, Richard Huelsenbeck, Tristan Tzara, Hans Arp and Marcel Janco.
21.3.1916	Death of mother. Annemarie comes to live with Emmy Hennings in Zurich.
Second half of 1916	Vira Magadino near Ascona
29.3.1917 to end of May	Galerie Dada in Zurich. Events by Emmy Hennings on 14 April and 12 May
1.7.–2.8.1917	With Annemarie, Hugo Ball and Friedrich Glauser on the Alp Brussada above the Valle Maggia, Ticino
Aug.–Nov. 1917	Ascona
Turn of the year 1917/1918	Moves with Annemarie to the Ticino

July 1919	Moves to Berne. Extradition order issued to her and Hugo Ball for involvement in anarchist propaganda
21.2.1920	Marries Hugo Ball
Sept. 1920	Moves with Hugo Ball and Annemarie to Agnuzzo near Lugano. Meets Hermann Hesse. Their friendship continues until her death in 1948.
October 1921	Munich
October 1922	Returns to Agnuzzo
October 1923	With Annemarie in Florence
October 1924	With Annemarie and Hugo Ball in Italy, first in Rome, then near Salerno
May 1926	Returns to the Ticino: Sorengo near Lugano
14.9.1927	Death of Hugo Ball
1927-1948	Lives in the Ticino in great poverty. Short journeys to Positano, Paris, Berlin. Arranges Hugo Ball's posthumous papers, continues to write, does casual factory work, lets out rooms etc. to make ends meet.
10.8.1948	Death of Emmy Hennings in Sorengo near Lugano

Berta Lask

9

A Voice out of Darkness:
Berta Lask's Early Poetry

Agnès Cardinal

When, in 1974, the Mitteldeutscher Verlag in Halle brought out a new edition of Berta Lask's autobiographical novel *Stille und Sturm*, few young readers in the German Democratic Republic had ever heard of her, had read her poetry, seen any of her plays or even remembered what, exactly, Lask's contribution to the socialist cause had been. In West Germany the publication passed virtually unnoticed.[1] Yet there had been a time in the 1920s when Berta Lask was at least as controversial a playwright as Bertolt Brecht or Ernst Toller. Whereas they had enjoyed some degree of official tolerance, Lask almost invariably fell foul of the Weimar censors. Some of her most important plays, such as *Thomas Münzer*, *Leuna 1921* and *Giftgasnebel über Sowjetrußland*, could only be performed privately.[2] Irrespective of government disapproval, they drew large and rapturous audiences from amongst the socialist working class.[3]

Like most nineteenth-century women of vision and achievement, Berta Lask came from a wealthy middle-class family. She was born in 1878 in Galicia, the daughter of a Jewish paper manufacturer. She died in East Berlin at the age of almost ninety, after an eventful and often tragic life dedicated to pacifism, feminism and the international workers' movement. She left Germany in 1933 after a spell in prison accused of treason and following the murder of her son by National Socialists. Twenty years later she returned to the young GDR, bringing with her the three volumes of a fictionalized account of her life. *Stille und Sturm* traces the development of a heroine from idealistic girl with an as yet unfocused passion for social and political justice to clear-sighted and purposeful socialist woman. The book is the kind of *Bildungsroman* in which the 'inner' destiny of the heroine becomes the touch-stone for a wider, 'outward' history of the German people from the Wilhelminian epoch to the First World War, to revolution, and the rise of Fascism.

Lask's earliest writings date back to the beginning of this century when she was the young wife of a welfare doctor in Berlin bringing up their four children. Through her husband's work she had come face to face with the starkness and misery of urban working-class life, and it was at this time that she began to take an active interest in the Marxist-Leninist argument and became fascinated by the revolutionary developments in Russia. In 1906 she wrote her first play, *Die Päpstin*, a historical drama set in medieval times about a woman seeking to implement her humanist ideals by pretending to be a man and letting herself be enthroned as pope. Six years later there followed a second play, *Auf dem Hinterhof, vier Treppen links* (Berlin, 1912). As the title of the new play suggests, Lask had by now radically changed her idiom. A social drama conceived in the naturalist mode, it is set in contemporary Berlin and tells the story of the wife of an unemployed alcoholic whose hopeless situation inexorably leads her to the murder of her children and to suicide. Though these plays differ fundamentally in terms of cultural reference and artistic medium, they nevertheless both revolve around the plight of the dispossessed, around social injustice and the corruptive aspect of power. These are concerns which remain constant throughout Lask's work. What does change, however, is the artistic perspective of her message. Reminiscing about her early career, Berta Lask recalls how in the 1910s she came to under-stand her own traditional humanism, her romantic feelings and the cult of individual achievement, as being politically suspect: 'Die Romantik habe ich überwunden. Die Darstellung der Wirklichkeit ist wichtiger.'[4] This new concern with the portrayal of reality was, however, soon to be politicized and to modulate towards an ideologically determined, conceptualized vision:

Und doch hatte ich die Wirklichkeit noch nicht
genügend erkannt; erst das große Morden [the war]
öffnete mir allmählich die Augen für eine von mir bisher
zu wenig beachtete Seite des Lebens: die politische.

(p. 324)

War and defeat, Germany's failed revolution of 1919 and especially the
murders of Rosa Luxemburg and Karl Liebknecht galvanized Lask into the
kind of political awareness which was to determine her entire subsequent life
and work. Indeed, the 1920s were to become her most active period, both in
terms of social engagement and artistic production. Her many articles, choral
poems and dramatic works of that period revolve around two major concerns:
the unmasking of the corrupt capitalist system as it expresses itself in the class
structure, in nationalism and in militarism,[5] and, secondly, the messianic
gesture towards a utopian socialist future, a project for which she understood
the role of women to be essential.[6] She had joined the Communist Party in
1923, and in the same year published two dramatic poems with a strong
socialist message: *Die Toten rufen*, a kind of requiem for Liebknecht and
Luxemburg, and *Mitternacht*, which depicts a group of workers in the grip of
the kind of despair that, as yet, knows nothing of the approaching socialist
dawn.[7] In 1925 the Communists asked Lask to write a play for the 'Roter
Münzertag', an important socialist rally which was to take place in Eisleben in
memory of Thomas Münzer, leader of the sixteenth-century peasant revolt.
The resulting play, *Thomas Münzer*, was, in essence, a study of revolutionary
thought, past and present, in which history and contemporary events intermingle inextricably and clear parallels are drawn between the revolt of the
peasant of Luther's time and the modern Spartakus movement. Four hours
long, the play was performed to an audience of three thousand workers whose
enthusiasm was such that the police, which was under orders to close the
assembly, did not dare move in.

Lask's most remarkable dramatic achievement came in 1927 with the
play *Leuna 1921 — Drama der Tatsachen*, which is about the failed workers'
revolt of March 1921 at the Leuna factory. It was written at the request of the
Leuna workers themselves and, to this day, it is considered one of the earliest
and purest examples of German socialist-realist drama. It survived barely two
weeks before the censors confiscated the text, and any attempt at performing
it had to be abandoned in the face of fierce police repression. Lask wrote the

play in 1926, in the same year in which Ernst Toller produced *Hoppla, wir leben*. In both plays a young revolutionary of 1921 is freed after five years of incarceration only to find that political corruption and the abuse of power are as rampant as ever. Toller's play centres on the fate of a single hero, Karl Thomas, whose life ends in absurdity and despair. Lask's *Leuna 1921*, on the other hand, is conceived in terms of a complex dramatic structure which suggests a reality reaching beyond individual destiny. Prologue and epilogue act as a frame to the contemporary situation of 1926, which is explored by means of flashbacks offering a carefully documented historical investigation of the failure of the revolt of 1921. The hero is subsumed within the revolutionary group, whose failures the audience is encouraged to understand in terms of the wider historical context of generalized socialist advance.[8]

Thomas Münzer and *Leuna 1921* were seen as important contributions to the socialist cause by a relatively small and circumscribed audience, but Lask attracted a much wider, and also much younger, readership with such lively narratives about socialist history as *Auf dem Flügelpferde durch die Zeiten. Bilder vom Klassenkampf der Jahrtausende. Erzählungen für junge Proletarier* (Berlin, 1925) and especially *Wie Franz und Grete nach Rußland kamen. Erzählungen für die Arbeiterjugend und Arbeitereltern* (Berlin, 1926) which for the first time offered the ordinary reader an easily accessible illustration of the difference between the capitalist and socialist ways of life.[9] Today Berta Lask's reputation as a poet and writer rests primarily on her contribution in the 1920s to workers' theatre and to early socialist youth literature.

By the end of the 1920s Lask had reached the height of her creative powers. From now on the single-mindedness of her political commitment was to lead her into a creative impasse from which she could never again quite extricate herself. Exiled in Russia during the 1930s, she continued to write, but of her stories the Marxist critic Andor Gábor rightly voiced this complaint:

> Da Deine Menschen, ohne Ausnahme, nicht seinsmäßig,
> sondern bewußtseinsmäßig dargestellt werden, d.h. nur
> und ausschließlich, in jeder Situation *nur* politisch sind,
> sind sie eben keine Menschen mehr, sondern nur Träger
> von draufgemalten, ideologischen Farben.[10]

What had begun as a creative vision of socialist universality sadly ended in the overdetermined plots and stereotypical heroes which characterize Lask's later narratives.

My purpose thus far has been to trace Lask's creative development as a prelude to a discussion of the poems she wrote from 1910 to 1920. Such an introduction is primarily intended to sketch the career and the role of a writer who is in danger of being forgotten, but it is essential that Lask's early poems be understood in the particular context of that career. She wrote them when she was already well into her thirties. At a time of life when other artists settle into established creative patterns, Lask was embarking on a radical artistic reorientation, and the poems she wrote during this period carry within them the tensions, ambivalences and incongruities of a sensibility at the crossroads. Thus they might well be considered, with critical hindsight, as the most interesting and revealing products of her entire literary career.

The poems written in this crucial decade were collected in two volumes: *Stimmen* (1919), and *Rufe aus dem Dunkel* (1921). *Stimmen* contains Lask's earliest poems, most of them still conceived in *fin-de-siècle* neo-romantic idiom. They are, in essence, statements about a woman's itinerary as she moves from girlhood towards exploring her role as lover, wife and mother. In calm modes of contemplation the young woman's experience is linked to a greater, impersonal and universal existence which is in turn determined by a divine order. For example, in the poem 'Das Weib' the female poetic voice speaks of itself in semi-pantheistic terms:

Ich bin das Land, durch das alle fremden Wünsche gehen,
Mann, Tier und Baum fühl' ich rauschend in mir stehen...[11]

Woman's experience here assumes universal, indeed allegorical dimensions. Other early poems such as 'Mädchen abends am Fenster', 'Das Weib spricht zum Mann' or 'Mutterlied' also speak in measured terms of the functional stations in a woman's life in a language of unspecified universality.

The tendency to move from the particular to the general, to transmute individual experience into grand existential gestures and into allegory was of course a salient and characteristic aspect of both the neo-romantic and the expressionist idiom of the time. For Berta Lask it became a mode which was to remain dominant throughout her work, from the early poems to the didactic dramas of the late 1920s. A marked exception to this kind of poetic writing occurs in an untitled poem (towards the end of the first volume) written in the second year of the war, which begins with this starkly realistic scene:

> Mit dem Gesicht gegen die Mauer
>   Liegt die kleine Channe in Krampf und Schauer.
> Mitten in der Stube auf dem Boden sitzt Esther.
>
> (*Stimmen*, p. 26)

The poem refers to an actual, and at the time widely reported, incident in Poland, in which a group of Jewish girls committed suicide after being raped by Russian soldiers. Lask, as we have seen, favours the universal rather than the specific, and she did not write many poems such as this. Rather, it seems that this particular poem was the result of a sudden emotional jolt, a kind of rude awakening which disturbed her detached and meditative stance. Her increasing awareness of the reality of such atrocities, together with her earlier encounter with urban low life in Berlin and, in particular, 'das große Morden' at the front, gradually caused her hitherto melodious poetic voice to crack, and to seek expression in new and more discordant registers. In marked contrast to the first poems in *Stimmen*, her final poem in the collection, 'Die erwachenden Frauen', takes the form of an angry expressionist shriek calling women to battle. Their awakening is envisaged in terms of a violent, convulsive explosion out of darkness into light:

> Bäumt euch empor Ihr Leiber,
> Beschwert von Millionen Toten!
> Durch die schwarze
> Blutdurchronnene Masse
> Brecht durch!
>
> (p. 31)

The sombre colours of black and red which dominate the beginning of the poem soon yield to 'weißglänzende Säulen' representing the bodies of the resurrected which, once aroused, become engulfed in the fire of revolutionary ardour:

> Schon entfacht er
> Verschüttete Flammen.
> Leuchtende Flut
> Bricht heraus
> Mit goldnen zackigen Zungen.

Were it not for its title, the poem could easily be read as one of the many expressionist visions of a vengeful resurrection of fallen soldiers. Lask's title 'Die erwachenden Frauen' makes it absolutely clear that here the poet is addressing women exclusively. Women may not have died in the trenches, yet they are 'Beschwert von Millionen Toten', as surely as if they were dead themselves. The poem is a call to rouse them so that they may, at last, begin their campaign. The emblem for their project is a great golden bird, symbol of release and power, which will sink its golden claws 'siegreich würgend' deep into the heart of a somewhat unspecified demon fiend.

Lask's poetic itinerary from gentle neo-romantic dream to violent apocalyptic vision gathers momentum in the second collection of her poems, *Rufe aus dem Dunkel*. An indicative illustration of the shift in Lask's sensibility is provided by two poems, one from each collection, which deal with the poet's closeness to nature and her love of trees. The first, 'Die Buche', is a pantheistic prayer to a beech tree which speaks of a dreamy, almost unconscious yearning for personal abnegation:

> Keines Menschen Stimme klang mir je so vertraut
> Wie deines Rauschens tiefseliger Laut.
> Keines Menschen Auge strahlte mir so heimatnah
> Wie dein goldschimmerndes Grün, in das mein träumendes Auge sah.
> (*Stimmen*, p. 14)

The celebration of this feeling of vague and barely conscious oneness with a tree stands in abrupt contrast to 'Der Befreite', from the second collection, which now speaks of human consciousness as entombed and imprisoned in a tree:

> Wie lag ich
> Eng gefesselt, gebannt.
> Eingewurzelt mein Leid
> Wuchs durch mich hindurch,
> Mitten in mir der Stamm
> Über mich breitend schattende Äste.
> (*Rufe*, p. 28)

The poem goes on to describe the moment of painful liberation when a storm uproots the tree and the spirit is set free. It is as though these two contrasting poems bear witness to Lask's own rude and painful awakening out of a nineteenth-century neo-romantic trance to a twentieth-century political awareness. In theme and style they owe much to Expressionism and as such they would make an interesting addition to the celebrated set of 'tree poems' by other Expressionists such as Theodor Däubler, Wilhelm Klemm, Paul Zech and Georg Heym which was collated by Kurt Pinthus in *Menschheits-dämmerung*.[12]

As in much expressionist poetry, themes of entombment and resurrection are a major aspect of Lask's poetry. In *Rufe aus dem Dunkel* the very title suggests that the poet understands her writings in terms of gestures reaching out of darkness, an idea reinforced by the dedication on the second page:

> Euch Toten in's [sic] Grab gesungen
> Euch Lebenden zum Aufstieg.

The notion is further developed in the prologue 'Der Dichter an seine zukünftigen Gedichte', in which Lask demands of her poems:

> Ihr sollt aus ehernen Schalen
> Als Flammen nach oben streben.
> ....
> Was aus schlafender Tiefe gewonnen
> Sollt Ihr wach dem Lichte einen.

She now begins to see her poetry in terms of messianic flares leading the way towards the Promised Land:

> Wenn Nacht und Qual und Verzweiflung
> Sich über die Erde breiten
> Dann sollt Ihr *Feuersäulen*
> Vor dem Volk durch die Wüste schreiten.

(title page)

Lask's understanding of her poetry as a redemptive religious project was, again, much in keeping with the vision of early Expressionism. The playwright Georg Kaiser, her contemporary, and other, often much younger, revolutionary writers such as Reinhard Sorge, Walter Hasenclever and especially Ernst Toller, wrote poetry with a similarly urgent sense of their messianic mission.[13] What makes Lask's creative and ideological development particularly remarkable is the fact that it took place in isolation, in her family home, away from the inspirational Berlin cafés where the poets of the new age, such as Georg Heym, Alfred Lichtenstein or Gottfried Benn and the extraordinary Else Lasker-Schüler would meet and compare their poems. Furthermore, as Walter Pollatschek has pointed out, in the crucial year of the October revolution of 1917, Lask was already thirty-nine years old; Anna Seghers, for example, was but seventeen, Brecht was nineteen, Ernst Toller was twenty-four and Claire Goll was twenty-six.[14] Indeed most of the revolutionary writers who were to make a name for themselves in the 1920s belonged to a completely new generation. Their formative years had fallen into the period of the German cultural collapse. In contrast, Lask's poetic endeavour of this period must not be understood simply in terms of a minor expressionist poet suddenly turned revolutionary. Hers was an enterprise of remarkable temerity and sweep during which she transformed herself from self-absorbed bourgeois woman poet of the nineteenth century to politically alert feminist of a new age.

Rufe aus dem Dunkel contains poems which bear direct witness to Lask's turbulent intellectual and artistic development in that period. They comprise, first of all, early poems written in the first years of war: 'Vieltausend Tode' (1914), 'Abschied' (1915) and 'Lied eines Überlebenden' (1916) deal explicitly with themes of war and death. Later poems written in 1918 and 1919 suggest that by then Lask's concern with suffering had been transformed into searching, uneasy explorations of human inadequacy, guilt and the nature of hope: as we shall see, the angry 'Lied des Ahasver' of 1920, for example, shows Lask at the flashpoint of emotional and artistic reorientation. By 1921 the process had been accomplished. From now on Lask was to understand her artistic persona in terms of guide and teacher of the working class, and would write such clearly aligned, didactic socialist verse as 'Volkserwachen I', 'Volkserwachen II', and 'Die Waage der Gerechtigkeit'.

The early war poems contained in *Rufe aus dem Dunkel* deserve attention, not least because they form part of a very small and neglected body of German expressionist war poetry written by women. Often women poets who wrote about the war, such as Ina Seidel or Ricarda Huch, were apt to adopt the non-gender-specific stance of detached omniscience when writing about soldiers marching to war, the heroic deaths of young warriors,[15] or, on rare occasions, about women's suffering.[16] In contrast, Lask writes predominantly about the inner states of women as they helplessly witness the events of war. Her poem 'Das Mädchen beim Ausmarsch der Soldaten', for example, homes in on the thoughts of a girl who watches young men march into battle and reflects: 'Es war, als marschierten sie aus der Zeit' (*Rufe*, p. 15); another poem, 'Die Mutter der gefallenen Söhne', evokes the trance-like state of a bereaved mother:

> Sie sitzt und denkt und weiß nicht, an was.
> Ihre Gedanken sind wie überwachsen mit Gras.
>
> (*Rufe*, p. 12)

In her search for a universal vision, Lask increasingly found inspiration in biblical and Christian material. One of the most interesting and striking early examples of this is 'Christus bei den Kanonen' of 1916 (*Rufe*, p. 6). In this poem, Christ, standing amongst the cannons, concedes that the old gods have triumphed and his message has had no impact on the nations of the West. As he retreats eastwards he gestures towards distant times and other places where his spirit might live on. The poem was written in the early years of war, at a time of generalized war euphoria. Lask must surely have been the first woman poet to use the emotive power of the Christ figure in a political argument on the conflict between Christian faith and the ideology of war.[17] It was an idea which, two years later, was to find a much intensified echo in a poem by another woman Expressionist: Claire Goll's 'Totendialog' of 1918 records an exchange in a cathedral between the statue of Christ and the statue of a king.[18] Christ hopes that the people, being Christian, will do everything to bring war to an end, whereas the king is confident that his subjects will fight on for king and country. In the end Christ himself is blown apart by a hand-grenade as soldiers storm the church. Ten years later the notion of the Christ-figure abused in a contemporary German political context was to find its most memorable and haunting expression in George Grosz's famous drawing of 1928, 'Maul halten und weiterdienen!', which depicts a tortured and crucified Christ wearing a gas-mask.[19] It is now impossible to ascertain to what extent Lask's work was known to the younger writers who in the 1920s elaborated on themes which Lask had been experimenting with ten years earlier. What is undeniable is the often striking similarity between her little-known early poems and the writings of the more successful rebels of the 1920s. In Lask's poem 'Der Streit der Tode' of 1916, for example, the allegorical figure of 'Der Kriegstod' argues his case against 'Der tägliche Tod' and 'Der geweihte Tod'. Such an encounter is clearly echoed in the Prologue to Ernst Toller's *Die Wandlung*, first performed in 1919.

Whatever the nature of such creative cross-fertilizations, there can be no doubt that, as far as woman's vision of war and revolution is concerned, Berta Lask's poetry was breaking new ground. From the early years of the war, and even in her neo-romantic phase, she dealt with the subject of war and women in ways more radical than any other woman pacifist writer. It is true that Hedwig Dohm, the veteran feminist, published a passionate tract entitled 'Der Mißbrauch des Todes' in 1915, in which she fiercely denounced the war mentality as a kind of collective European madness, a view echoed at the many German women's peace rallies of that year and reiterated by writers such as Annette Kolb and, of course, most eloquently of all by Käthe Kollwitz.[20] On the whole, these early women radicals saw militarism, social injustice and the war very much as the fault of those wielding power. In such a stance they did not really differ as much as they themselves believed from traditional patriotic writers, who were apt to see the war in terms of an event brought about by hostile forces. Furthermore, there were those, such as Ricarda Huch, whose poems invariably refer to the war as some kind of impersonal, apocalyptic event visited upon the magnificently innocent, be they soldiers or suffering women.[21] In marked contrast, Lask addresses herself, from the outset, to the question of responsibility. As we have already seen, her hymn to 'Die erwachenden Frauen' of 1916 takes the form of a call to women to take up responsibility, to assume their role in the conduct of human affairs. In the same year she also wrote the poem 'Selbstgericht', which contains a radical reassessment of woman's accountability. It is the first war poem in which a poet no longer points the finger at others but accepts her own personal responsibility for the disaster. The poem begins with the lines:

> Ich habe mit getötet
> Jeden, der draußen fällt.

She accuses herself of tacit complicity with a cultural consensus:

> Ich habe mich müd' und träge
> Dem Willen der Menge geneigt.

She further identifies the pernicious cowardice of women in the face of the power of men:

> Ich habe des Weibes Wissen
> Aus Scheu vor der Mannmacht erstickt.

She understands that it was her own lethargy and lack of moral fibre which must be seen as the ultimate, underlying cause of this monstrous war:

> So hab' ich aus Leib und Seele
> Den Moloch Vernichtung gezeugt.
> (*Rufe*, p. 17)

Even to this day, the question of the responsibility women share for the conduct of public affairs is not an issue frequently discussed, either by traditionalists or feminists. Lask's argument was certainly unique at the time, although, two years later, it found a powerful endorsement in Claire Goll's 'Die Frauen erwachen'.[22] In this story Goll relates in terse, unemotive words the tale of Ines, the young wife of a returning soldier, who commits suicide when she realizes that in her unthinking feminine acquiescence to the glamour of war she and thousands of women like her have been instrumental in turning their husbands into murderers, braggarts, cripples and corpses.

Women's awakening from an irresponsible lethargy is a dominant theme of all Lask's writing. Already in *Stimmen* we find poems which explore the nature of that state of trance in which women are traditionally apt to spend their lives. 'Die gemalte Madonna spricht', for example, is the lament of a woman-turned-icon who has lost all real purchase on life. Lask identifies the problem as gender-specific and speaks of the torpor which seems to engulf the feminine mind in the face of masculine forcefulness:

> Was tat er mir? Ich weiß nicht mehr, wer ich bin.
> Ein dichter Nebel umlagerte meinen Sinn.

Resentful and angry, the Madonna complains that

> Er hat mich begraben in seines Traumes Gruft.
> (*Stimmen*, p. 15)

It is an entombment from which she can find no escape. In structure and idiom 'Die gemalte Madonna spricht' is essentially an old-fashioned poem which relies on regular rhyming patterns and traditional neo-romantic images in order to reiterate the poet's yearning for liberation. On the other hand, it is also a very early and successful statement about a woman who feels herself trapped and disempowered as an object of man's dreams and desires, a notion which was to become such a touchstone in the feminist debate fifty years later.

The awakening of women to a tentative self-awareness, prefigured in 'Die gemalte Madonna spricht', was soon to modulate into an as yet unfocused expressionist rebellion in Lask's hymn-like poem 'Die erwachenden Frauen' (*Stimmen*, p. 31). Here the struggle is visualized in terms of a powerful, if unidentified golden bird of prey which will soar above the forces of darkness:

> Goldvogel, fliege voran,
> Stoßend mit leuchtender Wucht!
> Vor dir mit donnernden stampfenden Füßen
> Schreitet, behangen mit Leibern und Ländern,
> Göttlichen Geist siegreich würgend
> Der Dämon.

The poem was written during the war, a calamity which Lask here refers to in universal terms, using the image of the triumphant demon. The allegory is extended in the figure of the golden bird, emblem of a female consciousness as yet 'geschmiedet an den Felsen des Schweigens!'. This bird must be made to give up its silence and vanquish the enemy:

> Stoße ins Herz des Dämons!
> Deine goldnen Pranken
> Schlag tief hinein!

In common with many of her contemporaries, Lask was apt, in the early years of war, to perceive political events in somewhat vague allegorical terms. Towards the end of the war, however, her writings began to modulate towards forms which she perceived to be more appropriate to the urgency of her concerns. Indeed, her artistic trajectory from poetry to drama to prose was indicative of her seeing her progress in terms of a personal awakening to her own social responsibility. This was a transformation which took a decade to complete, so that by 1929 she had reached an unquestioning ideological certainty and could speak of war, women and rebellion in a totally new idiom. An example of this new mode of writing is her story 'Frauen im Kampf. Eine Erzählung aus dem Weltkrieg' of 1929.[23] Couched in the terse matter-of-fact language of realistic reportage, it tells of a group of heroic women workers, who, in an attempt to support a dock-workers' strike in 1917, are viciously mown down by armed police. It is a subject rooted in historical fact and evoked for the express purpose of making socialist women workers aware of their cultural lineage, a concern which was to become characteristic of much of Lask's later writings. In the decade or so which separates 'Die gemalte Madonna spricht' from 'Frauen im Kampf', Lask's preoccupation with the issues of social injustice and women's potential for rebellion had clearly remained unchanged. What had altered fundamentally was her attitude to her own art and, hence, her mode of expression. Within ten years she had moved from searching to knowing, and from an exploratory poetic vision to a sharply-focused socialist-realist certainty.

It is my contention that, long before this reorientation had been accomplished, indeed at the very moment when her creative and ideological endeavours were 'on the turn', so to speak, Berta Lask produced some of her best poetic writing. 'Lied des Ahasver' of 1920 (*Rufe*, p. 31), for example, must rank amongst the best expressionist poems by a German woman. The poem is, in essence, the rebellious cry of a human soul fettered in guilt and abject impotence. As such it embodies a central expressionist theme. Its irregular rhythms, its lack of consistent patterns of rhyme, its stylistic impulsiveness, and above all its highly charged emotional content, make this one of the most powerful statements of Lask's entire poetic career.

Ahasuerus is the angry, confused and ineffective king of Persia in the *Book of Esther* who, being rejected by his first wife, falls in love with and marries the beautiful Jewess Esther just at a time when, in his empire, Jews are being persecuted. His attempts at bringing justice to his land all fail as he falls prey to the intrigues of manipulative officials and his own paranoia. Yet, as if by a miracle, justice triumphs in the end. In Lask's poem Ahasuerus takes issue with an aloof God who seems to hold the king responsible without giving him the means to see and to understand. Ahasuerus thus considers the burden of his crown, the symbol of his responsibilities, to be a curse:

> Fluch liegt auf mir,
> Weltschwer geballt,
> Auf mein Haupt getürmt,
> In mein Hirn gebrannt,
> Niedertraufend auf meine Schultern
> In goldnen Klumpen.

The absurd weight of his royal power presses him abjectly to the ground, where he writhes in an agony coded in typical expressionist colours:

> Mit zerrissenen Eingeweiden
> Lieg' ich am Boden.
> Rot schreit mein Herz.
> Schwarz flutet mein Auge.

Tortured and torn as if on a battlefield by the sense of his own inadequacy, he
flounders in an impotent rage. And although he knows of a promised
redemptive dawn, he rejects all notions of hope:

> Fern träumt
> Hinter schwarzen Mauern noch
> Neuer Segentag.
> Ich ruf ihn nicht.

He denies himself this solace because he cannot even be certain whether, in
the eyes of God, he will be redeemed or cursed. Assuming that he is
simultaneously 'verworfen', 'erwählt', 'gesegnet' and 'verflucht', he makes the
final break with this cruel and teasing God. In an ultimate defiant gesture he
throws his curse, his crown, back at God:

> Und scheudre deinen Fluch
> Schwarz, schwergeballt
> Dir ins Firmament.

And now Ahasuerus can embark on the truly human quest. His final laconic
'Ich wandre' implies both resignation and the recognition that there is no
other way than to simply carry on, aimless, alone and in darkness.

Berta Lask herself ultimately rejected the stance of her Ahasuerus in
favour of a more optimistic understanding of man's destiny. Yet there can be
no doubt that, during her own 'Ahasuerus period', just before the dawning of
her socialist certainties, she briefly ranked amongst the most impressive of the
expressionist rebel poets.

NOTES

[1]Berta Lask, *Stille und Sturm* (Halle: Mitteldeutscher Verlag, 1955); reprint ed. by Myra Lask (Halle: Mitteldeutscher Verlag, 1974).

[2]*Thomas Münzer: Dramatisches Gemälde des deutschen Bauernkrieges von 1525* (Berlin, 1925); *Leuna 1921 – Drama der Tatsachen* (Berlin, 1927). These plays were published by the Vereinigung Internationaler Veranstalter. *Giftgasnebel über Sowjetrußland* was written in 1927 and performed once, on 8 July in Kassel by a *Proletkulturtheater*.

[3]See Lask's own account 'Frühes Suchen, Kampf und Verfolgung. Ein Rückblick' in *Hammer und Feder: Deutsche Schriftsteller aus ihrem Leben und Schaffen* (Berlin, 1955), p. 322, and Karl Grünberg, 'Berta Lask: fünfundsiebzig Jahre alt', *Neue Deutsche Literatur*, 2, No. 1 (1954), 167-69.

[4]*Hammer und Feder*, p. 324.

[5]See Lask, 'Vom Wesen der Gewalt' and 'Antimilitaristische Maifeier in Utrecht', in *Unsere Aufgabe an der Menschheit: Aufsätze* (Berlin, 1923).

[6]See Lask, *Der Obermenschenfresser Weltkapitalismus und die Internationale Arbeiterhilfe: ein Spiel* (Berlin, 1924) and 'Die Mission der Frauen'; 'Die Frau in der Zeitenwende'; 'Wie kann unsere Zeit Richtlinien für die Erziehung der weiblichen Jugend finden?'; and 'Mutter und Kind', in *Unsere Aufgabe an der Menschheit* (Berlin, 1923).

[7]Lask, *Die Toten rufen, Sprechchor zum Gedenken an Karl Liebknecht und Rosa Luxemburg* (Berlin, 1923) and *Mitternacht. Ein Spiel von Menschen, Marionetten und Geistern in fünf Akten* (Sannerz-Leipzig: Gemeinschafts-Verlag Eberhard Arnold, 1923).

[8]See Friedrich Rothe, 'Lask, Fuchs und Gotsche – drei literarische Vorlagen für "Märzstürme 1921"', *Sozialistische Zeitschrift für Kunst und Gesellschaft*. Politik und Theater-Märzstimme 1921. Von Wolfgang Schwiedrzik 15/16/17 (Berlin, 1972), 110-15.

[9]Five years later another socialist woman, Grete Weiskopf (1905-66), writing under the pseudonym Alex Wedding, was to publish her hugely popular socialist children's story *Ede und Unku: ein Roman für Jungen und Mädchen* (Berlin: Malik, 1931).

[10]'Ein "schrecklicher" Lehrer: Andor Gábor im Briefwechsel mit Hans Marchwitza, Karl Grünberg, Berta Lask', *Neue Deutsche Literatur*, 36, no. 10 (1988), 63-88.

[11]Lask, 'Das Weib', in *Stimmen*, p. 9 (not to be confused with the poem 'Das Weib' in *Rufe*, p. 11, which is couched in a fundamentally different mode).

[12]Cf. Theodor Däubler, 'Die Buche' und 'Der Baum'; Wilhelm Klemm, 'Der Baum'; Georg Heym, 'Der Baum': all in *Menschheitsdämmerung: ein Dokument des Expressionismus*, ed. by Kurt Pinthus (Hamburg: Rowohlt, 1959), pp. 160-61.

[13]Examples include Reinhard Sorge, *Der Bettler* (1912); Georg Hasenclever, *Die Menschen* (1918); Ernst Toller, *Die Wandlung* (1919).

[14]See Walther Pollatschek, 'Berta Lask', postscript to the reprint of *Stille und Sturm*, p. 359.

[15]See for example, Ina Seidel, *Neben der Trommel her, Gedichte* (Berlin, 1915); Ricarda Huch, 'Einem Helden' and 'Totenfeier', in *Herbstfeuer – Alte und neue Gedichte* (1920).

[16]E.g. Huch, 'Frauen', ibid.

[17]The Christ motif is, of course, already current in expressionist writing of the time. In Georg Kaiser's *Von morgens bis mitternachts* of 1916 the protagonist perishes at the end of the play, transfixed as Ecce Homo. Here ordinary contemporary man has assumed the shape of the suffering Christ.

[18]Claire Goll, 'Totendialog', in *Frauen gegen den Krieg*, ed. by Gisela Brinker-Gabler (Frankfurt/M.: Fischer, 1980), p. 135.

[19]See George Grosz, 'Maul halten und weiterdienen!', in Martin Kane, *Weimar Germany and the Limits of Political Art: a Study of the Work of George Grosz and Ernst Toller* (Tayport: Hutton Press, 1987), p. 226, fig. 23.

[20]Hedwig Dohm, 'Der Mißbrauch des Todes', in *Frauen gegen den Krieg*, p. 55. On 18 March 1915 women organised a demonstration against the war in front of the Reichstag building in Berlin. At meetings such as the Internationale Frauenkonferenz of March 1915 in Berne, the Frauenweltbund zur Förderung internationaler Eintracht of 1915 and during the Internationaler Frauenkongress in The Hague in April 1915, German women were given a chance to express their pacifist views. See Käthe Kollwitz's evocative poster 'Nie wieder Krieg!' and her polemical publication 'Keiner darf mehr fallen!' in *Frauen gegen den Krieg*, pp. 233-34, and Annette Kolb, *Dreizehn Briefe einer Deutschfranzösin* (Berlin: Reiser, 1916).

[21]Huch, 'Kriegswinter', 'Der fliegende Tod', 'An unsere Märtyrer', and 'Den jungen Gefallenen' in *Herbstfeuer – Alte und neue Gedichte* (1920).

[22]Claire Goll, 'Die Frauen erwachen', in *Frauen gegen den Krieg*, pp. 58-63.

[23]Lask, 'Frauen im Kampf. Eine Erzählung aus dem Weltkrieg', in *Frauen gegen den Krieg*, pp. 230-32.

Berta Lask: A List of Major Works

Die Päpstin (written in 1906, never published, but first performed in 1911).

Auf dem Hinterhof, vier Treppen links (written in 1912 but remains unpublished).

Stimmen. Gedichte, 'Die Silbergäule' (Hanover: Paul Steegemann, 1919).

Rufe aus dem Dunkel. Auswahl 1915-1921 (Berlin: Buchverlag der Arbeiter-Kunst-Ausstellung, 1921).

Senta. Eine Lebenslinie in acht Szenen, 'Die Silbergäule' (Hanover: Paul Steegemann, 1921).

Weihe der Jugend. Ein Chorwerk (Berlin: Kommune E. Friedrich, 1922).

Die Toten rufen. Sprechchor zum Gedenken an Karl Liebknecht und Rosa Luxemburg (This was (probably) read out aloud in meetings organized by Ernst Friedrich but never published).

Mitternacht. Ein Spiel von Menschen, Marionetten und Geistern in fünf Akten (Sannerz-Leipzig: Gemeinschafts-Verlag Eberhard Arnold, 1923).

Der Weg in die Zukunft. Dichtung für Sprechchor (Sannerz-Leipzig: Gemeinschafts-Verlag Eberhard Arnold, 1923).

Unsere Aufgabe an die Menschheit. Aufsätze (Berlin: 'Der Syndikalist' Fritz Kater, 1923).

Der Obermenschenfresser Weltkapitalismus und die Internationale Arbeiterhilfe. Ein Spiel für Menschen oder Marionetten (Berlin: Neuer Deutscher Verlag, 1924).

Thomas Münzer: Dramatisches Gemälde des Deutschen Bauernkrieges von 1525 (Berlin: Vereinigung Internationaler Verlagsanstalten, 1925).

Auf dem Flügelpferde durch die Zeiten. Bilder vom Klassenkampf der Jahrtausende. Erzählungen für junge Proletarier (Berlin: Vereinigung Internationale Verlagsanstalten, 1925).

Die Befreiung. 16 Bilder aus dem Leben der deutschen und russischen Frauen 1914-1920 (Berlin: Internationaler Arbeiter-Verlag, 1926).

Wie Franz und Grete nach Rußland kamen. Erzählungen für die Arbeiterjugend und Arbeitereltern (Berlin: Verlag der Jugendinternationale, 1926).

Leuna 1921 – Drama der Tatsachen (Berlin: Internationaler Arbeiter-Verlag, 1927).

Giftgasnebel über Sowjetrußland (written in Berlin in 1927, was performed once, on 8 July 1927, in Kassel).

Spartakus (Moscow: Gosudarstvennoe Izdatelsvo, 1928).

Kollektivdorf und Sowjetgut. Reisetagebuch (Berlin: Internationaler Arbeiter-Verlag, 1932).

Junge Helden. Erzählung aus den österreichischen Februarkämpfen (Engels: Deutscher Staatsverlag, 1934).

Ein Dorf steht auf. Erzählungen (Kiev: Staatsverlag der nationalen Minderheiten, 1935).

Januar 1933 in Berlin. Erzählung (Kiev: Staatsverlag der nationalen Minderheiten, 1935).

Die schwarze Fahne von Kolbenau. Wolgadeutsche Erzählung aus den Jahren 1930/31 (Moscow: Meshdunarodnaja Kniga, 1939).

Stille und Sturm. Roman (Halle: Mitteldeutscher Verlag, 1955; 'Neudruck' ed. Mira Lask, Mitteldeutscher Verlag, 1974).

Otto und Else. Vier Erzählungen vom Kampf der deutschen Arbeiterjugend (Berlin: Neues Leben, 1956).

Aus ganzem Herzen, ed. Mira Lask (Berlin: Deutscher Militärverlag, 1961).

Further Bibliography

Geschichte der Deutschen Literatur, Vol. 10, ed. by Hans-Günther Thalheim *et al.* (Berlin: Volk und Wissen, 1978), pp. 270-71 and 319-20.

Klaus Kändler, *Drama und Klassenkampf* (Berlin: Aufbau, 1970), pp. 130-37.

Franz Norbert Mennemeier, 'Drama der Tatsachen und proletarisches Volksstück (Berta Lask)', in *Modernes Deutsches Drama* (Munich: Fink, 1973), Vol. 1, 212-15.

Gertrud Meyer-Hepner, 'Ein Epos unserer Zeit' (a study of Berta Lask's *Stille und Sturm*), *Neue Deutsche Literatur*, 4-6 (1956), 131-37.

Ursula Münchow, 'Berta Lask, Hermynia Zur Mühlen und Maria Leitner', in *Deutsche Literatur von Frauen*, ed. by Gisela Brinker-Gabler (Munich: Beck, 1988), Vol. 2, 262-68.

Richard Sheppard, 'Straightening Long-Playing Records: The Early Politics of
    Berta Lask and Friedrich Wolf', in *German Life and Letters*, 45 (1992),
    279-87.
Ruth   Wolf,   'Wandlungen   und   Verwandlungen: Lyrikerinnen   des
    20. Jahrhunderts', in *Deutsche Literatur von Frauen*, Vol. 2, 340-41.

Frida Bettingen and her daughter

10

Frida Bettingen and Bess Brenck-Kalischer

Brian Keith-Smith

Frida Bettingen

Frida Bettingen was one of several German women writers whose works have been forgotten for at least thirty years, yet at their best reflect some of the most effective writing in German literature of their day and express emotions whose intensity and humanity reach out far beyond their witness to personal suffering. Walter Falk, whose dissertation on her as a 'Dichterin des Schmerzes' is almost the sole major item of secondary literature, counts her late poems as expressionist, some of them among the greatest written in German, but dismisses others 'die nicht allein wenig kräftig, sondern bisweilen zur Peinlichkeit schlecht erscheinen'.[1] The patchy quality of her work is doubtless the main reason why it has been forgotten; it is at times not easy to read and often appears derivative, even hesitant as a means of expression. Yet the restraint found particularly in the poems referring to classical Greek myths, attains a formal control over a range of human pain worthy of the noblest stoicism. She drew on a wide range of literary tradition, which suggests she had a more complex poetic personality than a quick reading of her works might lead one to believe. In particular, the development of her use of metaphor and of contemporary themes and poetic devices points to a talent whose potential was never stretched to the full, and this is confirmed by her unpublished works held in the Deutsches Literatur-archiv in Marbach since 1960.[2]

Her longest and most important poem appeared in 1919 edited by Wilhelm Schäfer and entitled *Eva und Abel: Dichtung* (Düsseldorf: August Bagel). Three years later he edited most of her work in *Gedichte* (Munich: Georg Müller) in an edition of 620 copies. *Himmelsbürde: Gedichte* was published in 1937 in Hamburg (Heinrich Ellermann). Walter Falk planned a complete edition to be entitled 'Die goldene Seele' to appear 1953 in Munich (Georg Müller) and 1960 in Hamburg (Heinrich Ellermann), each time without success. At a time when a series of far more individualistic expressionist writers were reappearing in major new editions, the muted and varied tones of Frida Bettingen were perhaps bound to attract little attention. In 1922 Wilhelm Schäfer was already complaining about the demands of the book market as a determining factor on the publication of a writer's works. Furthermore, Schäfer claims that Frida Bettingen's works were not easy to publish because they did not fall into one of the then sharply contrasting modes of Naturalism or Expressionism. Schäfer ranks her together with Annette von Droste-Hülshoff and Marie von Ebner-Eschenbach as an exceptional woman writer.

Frida Bettingen's works owe their inspiration to her sufferings primarily as a mother. Born in 1865, the daughter of an accountant in Ronneburg (Sachsen-Altenburg), she married a grammar-school teacher when she was nineteen and moved to Krefeld, where she lived for twenty-four years until he died and she moved with her three children to Jena. Her father died in despair during the winter of 1885-86, her twin brother died two years later, and the son of a friend was killed in the mountains in 1912. The most shattering event of all was the death of her son after he became a teacher in Düsseldorf; he was killed in the war in October 1914 at Verdun. The effects on her are recorded in *Eva und Abel*, dedicated to all mothers, but she bore the wounds of this death in particular to the end of her life. She suffered mental attacks for several years and was to spend many months in mental clinics.

Although her earliest poems were written in 1897, when she was already expressing a wish to be old, her main works belong to the years 1918 to 1921 (after her first stay in a sanatorium 1917 up to her last entry into a psychiatric clinic in 1923) during which time she was able to lead an almost normal life. The poems were thus more than usually the therapeutic products of a woman in her fifties who had undergone shattering personal experiences (including isolation from her two daughters and the devaluation of her house and property leading to poverty). She was also fully aware of the destructive significance of modern warfare on humanity in general. Her poetry is one of lament, a form of tragic resignation in the face of an apparently absurd life that ended in 1924. It is self-expression without anger but with a self-correcting sense of proportion in its gentle search for harmony and meaning beyond the ravages of the modern world. Her poetry expresses an alternative, spiritual life and the achievement of personal freedom despite or perhaps because of her suffering. Nearly every poem describes a movement of the soul, a progress towards a better, more peaceful existence. It thus contains an element of tension, at times dramatic, usually resolved in a cry of hope or resignation. Her texts often imply dialogues that appear to bridge the gulf between an existence characterized by wayward human struggles and a realm of spiritual harmony. Many of them celebrate a theocentric awareness of her fate and thus reduce its pain by entering poetically into a world apart. Yet these poems are by no means escapist, for the new dimension sought in them is always consciously defined with relation to the torment of her role as mother and as woman. Only in and through the negative aspects of such suffering and its expression can an alternative be apprehended and given voice. That voice rises above her personal grief to one of a universal motherhood in the poem 'Priesterin ewig unnennbarer Liebe':

> Ich bin durch ein zartes Herz hindurchgeglitten
> in das erhabene Herz der Erde.

> Ich bin in aller Dinge Wesen, Wanderschaft,
> Abendziel, Geburt und Sterbegebärde.

> Ich bin Sättigung aller Meere, und Durst.
> Oh, meine Freunde, dürstet!
> Heiliger Durst beseelt...

> Ich bin mit Acker und Menschengebeten
> und dem All-Odem der heiligen Sterne vermählt:

> Priesterin ewig unnennbarer Liebe.[3]

The force of such religious expressionist visionary language may be dismissed as over-subjective posturing, a form of spiritual charade. However, her subjective images of self-aggrandisement were to be counterbalanced by musical ecstatic self-sacrifice in a poem from her unpublished papers:

> In die Orgel meiner Seele
> greifen gewaltige Hände.
>
> Wachst ein, brausend Stimmen!
> Wachst ein in die letzten
> stillredenden Pfeiler und Pfeifen.

At both extremes, Frida Bettingen's poetry is governed by an almost daemonic capacity for losing herself either in an expanding gesture or in inward-turned intensity. Not for nothing did she write poems on three major sufferers in German literature: Grabbe, Heinrich von Kleist and Hölderlin.

In her choice of Grabbe as an *alter ego* the suffering is Faustian in definition and effects. Paradoxically she realizes how much responsibility she bears as a mother for the fate of her 'Kinderland' — an obvious reply to the 'Hurrahpatriotismus' of the fatherland image. The suffering here is existential but through its poetic expression issues an implied challenge.

> Grabbe
>
> "Unstern"
> taufte mich die Natur.
>
> Aber sie küßte meine Stirn.
> Und erhob sie zum Tempel.
>
> Ich bin gebaut aus Trotz, Scheu,
> Glut, Urgefühl, faustischem Drang.
>
> Die ich liebe, verwunde ich.
>
> Am meisten mich selbst.
> Das ist der Seele härtester Befehl.
>
> In meiner Brust verschmelzen sich
> Götterhimmel
> und zügellose, verrannte Triebe.
>
> Schlaf kenne ich kaum.
>
> Durch meine Nächte
> poltern Unholde.
>
> Mein Herz baut sich starre Rinde
> um weiche Ackerschollen.
>
> Es blüht und welkt viel gutes Korn.
> In Ohnmacht brüllte ich auf:

Paradiessterne sollten es werden!
Aber meiner Mutter Hand
hat sie zerdrückt.

Wenn ich an mein Kinderland denke,
überwächst mich Finsternis.
        O Mutter! (pp. 100-101)

In 'Kleist' the suffering is that of the mother who realizes, too late, what Kleist himself understood as the arch-enemy, the 'Drache Stolz'. It is a poem of deepest sympathy and empathy in response to Kleist's loneliness. Here, however, the mother-figure is seen more positively albeit in passive votive-images. The cyclical repetition in the final stanza of the first with the significant omission of 'Du Köstlicher' implies a reduction to silence:

Kleist

Wenn ich an Dich denke, Du Köstlicher,
hüllt sich meine Seele in Samt
und weint.

Oh, daß ich gelebt hätte
Dein zerpflücktes Herz
in weichste Mutterhände zu betten!

Ich hätte der Sommerlinde seidengrünes Dach entliehn,
wo die goldnen Sonnenlichter wohnen.
Ich hätte es leise um Deine stürzenden Lauben gebaut.

Du,
der es kannte, wie keiner.

Der Du dem verschwiegensten Märchenbronnen
der Weibesseele lauschtest.
Wo der reine, frische Odem der Quellblumen steigt.

Triebhaft. Unbewußt. Hinschmelzend. Voll Süße.

Und vor der Grotte der Anbetung
Der hütende Drache Stolz.

Oh, wie kanntest Du uns!
Ureinsam.
Im Dornenmantel Deiner entgötterten Welt.

Mütter sind Gnadenbilder am Wege.
Oh, daß ich es Dir hätte sein dürfen!

Wenn ich an Dich denke,
hüllt sich meine Seele in Samt
und weint. (pp. 98-99)

The 'Hölderlin' text, one of several that show both in subject and form that poet's considerable influence on Frida Bettingen's own poetry, is more

objective in its tone firstly as a prayer, then as a narrative, finally as a vision.
The angel's lament is meant presumably as one of disappointment – perhaps
at the spiritual reality of the visionary poet doomed to madness, perhaps on
his death and at first indifferent reception. The poem was written in fact at a
time when Hölderlin's poetry was becoming better known to German readers
and influencing expressionist writers.

Hölderlin

Gott öffnete die letzte Bucht seiner Hände.
Eilend, von seligen Klarheiten überschwemmt!

Seele hinab! hinab!

Da hub ein leiser, keimender Daseinswille
die zarten Fittiche.
Licht schwebte.

Am Himmelsrande trotzten die braunen Waldbäume Zeit.

Und die von ihm berührten
sprangen aus dem Kreis ihrer Stunden.
Und wuchsen zu kristallenen Säulen.
Und leuchteten weit.

Aber ein Engel senkte die Fackel,
und weinte. (p. 79)

These three poems typify a general progression in Frida Bettingen's
works from close self-identification through awareness of personal incapacity
in her role to a more detached perspective. The focus of suffering thus
develops, sometimes in its intensity, often in its educative purpose. Even the
earliest poem, 'Meine Seele leidet Gewalt', reflects this:

Meine Seele leidet Gewalt.
Sie kann es nicht verstehn,
sie weiß nur mit blendender Helle:
Ihr ist ein Leid geschehn.

Hätt ich nur Einen zum sagen.
Muß alles alleine tragen.
Die Wolken wandern so grau, so kalt.

Oh, wäre ich alt! (p. 1)

Frida Bettingen's longing to be old is not an attempt to deny the value
of her existence; it is a longing for a state where the conflicting forces within
her soul will be transfigured in what amounts to a mystic vision. Ernst
Bacmeister emphasizes the 'mystische Metapher' as a new and higher stage in
the use of metaphor in lyric poetry and points out how she develops this by

using for instance even parts of her body: 'Meine Hände sind Marienkinder' (p. 95), or 'Immer war meine Seele ein drängender Zugvogel' (p. 95). Sometimes she creates situations in which her lyrical self can express its worship, or where Mary and Sappho-figures emphasize discipline over natural impulses (pp. 84-89). These reveal her need for self-expression and self-expansion that spring from her awareness of the distance and contrast between life on earth and heaven. Frida Bettingen, however, also links body and soul in the expression of their suffering, and Bacmeister contends that this is above all a sign of her womanhood:

> Aber als Dichterin des ewigen Zwiespalts bleibt sie ungefesselt von dieser frommen Einfalt, und die über Seele und Geist schwebende Einigungsmacht, die ihr zum gestalterischen Ausdruck ihres Innern verhilft, ist eben doch immer nur der Gott in ihrer eigenen Brust, der Seelengeist, mit dem sie als Weib über alle Möglichkeiten des Mannes hinaus begnadet ist.[4]

An early awareness of the closeness of her inner life to nature around her comes in 'Ich weiß eine Bank' (1901) recording her intense listening almost à la Droste-Hülshoff, where a bitter-sweet perception of the quiet remoteness of a bench in the noonday suggests plenitude and peace punctuated only by her own heartbeat:

> Ich weiß eine Bank,
>   nicht weit − nicht weit −
> Komm mit, −
>   ich finde sie wieder.
> Von Goldgehänge überdacht.
> Und duftendem blauen Flieder.
>
> Der Garten träumt seinen Mittagsschlaf.
> Wir schleichen auf seidenen Sohlen.
> Wir schleichen durch den heißen Sand
> verstohlen − komm mit − verstohlen.
>
> Die Sonnenuhr blinzelt,
>   − vorbei − vorbei −
> Goldbienelein tränken sich träge.
> Stumm! Stumm!
>
> Nur ein einziger zitternder Laut:
> Meines Herzens hellsingende Schläge. (p. 4)

Unfolding awareness of her frustration at her own timidity of expression, of a tug of war between desire and restraint, informs 'Ich möchte

so gern' (1901). Something inhibits her from total self-surrender in a gesture
that would betray her inner feelings — the result is a hesitant poem:

> Ich möchte so gern
> mein Gesicht in Deine Hand legen
> ein kleiner Flaumvogel sein
> im schützenden Nestwall,
>
> und dann wag ich es nicht.
>
> Ich möchte so gern
> Deine süßen Augen küssen,
> daß sie schliefen einen Augenblick bei mir,
>
> und dann wag ich es nicht.
>
> Ich möchte so gern
> Deinen Herzschlag hören.
> Dein Herz hat so viel stolze Wände.
>
> Ob es wohl Holdes von mir spricht?
> Alles möchte ich!
> Alles!
>
> Aber es wird nur ein zages, kleines Gedicht. (p. 5)

The death of her friend's son in the mountains in 1912 became the first
turning-point in her poetry. Most of 'Abgestürzt' is the imagined inner
monologue of the dying mountaineer trapped in the glacier. For the first time
the poet effectively distances herself from the text which ends like a ballad:

> Sie brachten ihn dann. So still. So still.
> Die märkische Eiche, ein Halm im April.
> Schwer schwankte die Bahre.
> Die Gäste flohn.
>
> Im Hause der Aufschrei:
>
> 'Mein Sohn! Mein Sohn!' (p. 26)

Signs of less self-centred, superficial suffering are found in poems
written in 1916, such as 'Greisinnen', 'Die Parzen' and 'Von den Müttern',
where the concept of living in a future and thereby overcoming fate is
developed:

> Ich will von den Müttern reden,
> die ihre Söhne hingaben.
>
> Von denen will ich reden,
> die ihren Schmerz hintragen
> durch graue Tage,
> und das Netzwerk vieler Sorgen.

Eingeschlossen
in die köstlichen Urnen ihres Wollens.

Sie tasten nicht in das zukünftige Land.
Sie wohnen darin.

Wenn die Nacht die Fenster des Hauses blendet,
öffnen sie die schweigenden Gemächer ihrer Seele.

Ihre Hände halten kleine, leblose Dinge.
Vergilbte Kinderbilder,
ihre Seelen liegen nackt –
hinströmend –
im Schoße des geliebten Mannes.

Sie stehen an den talwärts fließenden
Wassern des Lebens.

Ohne Bitterkeit.
Hinwachsend über die verdunkelten Sterne
ihres Geschickes.

Reif
wie ein schenkender Früchtebaum
Ruhevoll.
Vollendet. (pp. 29-30)

Existence as an act of violence is one of the keynotes of her poetry, and
it was conditioned not only by personal loss but also by some of the negative
aspects found in the works of three more recent writers than Grabbe, Kleist
and Hölderlin. She knew and admired the works of Georg Trakl and their
development from melancholy towards the torment of standing alone. Thus
she wrote a poem of deep longing for a brother-figure that brings together
personal loneliness and the plaintive call for a new community. 'Wie zu einem
Bruder' (1921) is both a poem expressing her extreme sense of personal
isolation and one of many written by Expressionists at the end of the First
World War hoping for a new brotherhood. She was aware of the younger
poet Rilke's themes of existential suffering and the need to define how far he
was removed from the everyday world of politics and war. She can be linked
also to the world of Kafka through her sense of guilt and of her incapacity to
cope with life even through the medium of writing. Yet her poems have been
summed up fittingly as 'Metamorphosen des Leidens'.[5]

Evil becomes an important theme in her poetry from *Eva und Abel*
(1918) onwards (pp. 35-49). It is understood here in terms of original sin by
Eve, who has wanted her son's death. Her destiny is to will and to experience
the death of Abel, which thus becomes the formative expression of her

existence. This act of willing brings an extra meaning – albeit a negative one – to her existence: she now suffers personally but also for mankind as a whole. The poem, by far the longest Frida Bettingen wrote, is in the present tense and much of it in the first person. Its division into seven parts marks it as the first of her cyclical poems, of which five ('Sappho', 'Noah', 'Deianira' and 'Ahasver' were the others) were planned for the volume 'Die goldene Seele'. 'Evas Ahnen' pictures a landscape of the total destruction of nature into which Eve awakes – a landscape full of foreboding, but apparently a dream. She curses Abel now he is dead – 'einst schlug ich Dich im Paradies,/jetzt brech ich Dir das Herz entzwei' (p. 36), and – having realized that this new day in which she suffers has been willed by God – she feels the death of a hundred knives in her heart, their name is Cain. In 'Eva am Opfer-stein', faced with her son's corpse, she understands guilt for the first time. Natural threats (the purple trees in the wood, the young brood of otters, the blue lightning in the mountains) she interpreted as warnings, but: 'Vor jedem giftigen Insekt warnte ich Dich/vor Deinem Bruder warnte ich Dich nicht' (p. 39). Her suffering now becomes self-accusatory, and in 'Evas Heimkehr' she feels the intense loneliness of her position, all her men having left. Full of memories, she is like a stranger on the threshold of an empty home where life drips out of her heart. In 'Evas Weissagung und Gebet' the contemporary allusions to war are made clearer with the equation between murderous brothers and peoples, for:

> Das Böse wird das helle Angesicht
> der Erde decken – – weh,
> meine himmelschöne Heimat rückt
> mir fern und immer ferner. (p. 42)

Future generations will continue the fratricide engendered by her and carry on the curse. So she implored God to create someone to bring peace, the paradise she has lost as Eve. 'Evas Ruf zur Totenwacht' is a call to plants and animals to watch over Abel the shepherd boy asleep. 'Des Rufes Heimfolge' describes, with a touch of sentimentality, nature's response to Eve's call. In the final section 'Abels Grablegung' Eve's remorse is focused on her replacement of the paradise image of Abel's young life by the hideousness of his death. The way of his death causes her anxiety for her own, which she hopes will come like a dream, or – using the old classical motif – like a butterfly 'der in der frühen Kühle einer Nacht/in jungen Rosenblättern fröstelt und dabei/die zarte Seele süß beglückt, verliert' (p. 49). She calls for an angel to lead her back to a lost paradise to her own eternal sleep. The diction of this poem harks back to the Anacreontics, to some of the piety and use of classical and biblical sources found in Friedrich Hagedorn's poems. Yet, because of its date, the autobiographical background and the references to war between peoples, it is unmistakably a form of therapeutic contrition on both a personal and general level. The mother-figure, who has been an Eve to man as Adam, has to suffer because of the sins of omission in not being able to restrain the warrior element in her male offspring.

After such nightmarish visions there follows in *Gedichte* a poem that seems just the reverse. 'Blühende Bäume', at first reading apparently an evocation of spring resulting in an outburst of piety, reveals a more complex message on further analysis. For, far from being a paean to the exuberance of new life often associated with spring, each of the few images here is sparsely described, producing a sense of almost banal expression. It is only when we see the draft versions for this poem, and consider its five-year gestation, that the deliberate foreshortening and concentration of poetic expression shows that this became something intensely personal − a poem more about its creator than about nature's renewal. In 1913 the sketch 'Schimmernde Tage' included the following image:

Schimmernd reckt sich der Baum, Blumen in Arm und Glanz

with a continuation:

Von der Sonne erwärmt, blauet das Veilchenbeet.
Ruhig atmet der Wind. Aber sein Atem sinkt
Wie aus fernen, geahnten
Ländern,
Träumeschwer, und voll Duft.

Another version 'Vorfrühling' had the following final line: 'Ruhevoll steigen die Türme der ewigen Stadt'. Another attempt included the following:

jedes göttlichen Sonnenstaubes Widerspiel
jeder seufzenden Nachtgebärde.
Meine Augen sind weitgereiste Wanderer.
Alle Wurzeln und Wunder grünen zärtlich hervor.

But, over a period of five years, the sense of wonder is toned down, and the final version reads:

Blühende Bäume,
Gewölk aus Glanz und Duft.

Eine Schwarzamsel baut,
hüpfend im Zauberwald
bei den goldenen Bienen
schon ihr heimliches Nest,
    und singt!

Ruhevoll atmet der Wind.
Wie von fernen, geahnten Ländern kommend,
    atmet der Wind.

Meine Augen sind Pilgrime,
windgereist. Und durchsonnt:
Schön ist Deiner Hände Werk!

    Meister,
mein Meister! (p. 50)

The opening lines celebrate the interface of heavenly and earthly categories –
light and fragrance – in the mysterious 'Gewölk' in which the categories
intermingle. Trees too, especially 'blühende Bäume' can be interpreted to
represent the encounter between the sustenance of the earth and reaction to
the light pouring down from above. Similarly, clouds too are a meeting-place
– here identified with the trees themselves as both include light and
fragrance. This interaction of categories provides a magic home for creatures,
a place where they expand to their fullest potential. Significantly, bees are
golden thanks to their reaction to light, to their gathering of light's bounty.
However, they are accompanied by the blackbird (emphasized by the word
'Schwarzamsel' where 'Amsel' would have registered the object but not its
quality) secretly building its nest, yet eager to sing of its happy position. It is
happy, because it has been accepted, and its expression in song extends into
the world, doubtless carried forth by the breath of the wind. The interface of
the categories is used to point out how much of creation grows or expands into
an intermediary state. The blossoming trees act as a declaration of this and
trigger off a series of related observations. They are a 'cloud' because they
express themselves in gleam and fragrance. The second stanza records a
transformation into a 'Zauberwald'. This magic wood is characterized by
golden bees, golden because of the light which has reacted on the flowers and
through their pollen to produce sustenance for the winter to come. The
apparently serene bees and furtive blackbird are linked in their preparatory
work. The magic of the blossoming trees is nothing static but an ever-

changing set of relationships focused next in the peaceful breathing of the wind with its hint of distant sources. As in Hofmannsthal's poem 'Vorfrühling', the wind makes us aware of transience, of mutability and of the shifting forms of life. The instinctive work of the bees and the blackbird contrasts with the peaceful breathing of the wind as if coming from distant imagined lands. Instinctive work gives way to peaceful anticipation. The poet's eyes, called pilgrim eyes as they are affected by the wind and the sunlight, have now been opened to the beauty of the present situation, in particular to the fullness of creation within it. The poem becomes a psalm of praise to the creator for the unity now appearing between earth and heaven, and it completes that act of creation through selected images, in particular those that highlight the interaction of categories. God is finally seen as the master, not just of creation in general, but of the poet's inspiration: 'mein Meister'.

This poem can be seen as a further stage in Frida Bettingen's development, for with it came the realization not only of what she owed to her faith, but also of what she owed to her poetic gift. The former is expressly stated in a not particularly remarkable unpublished poem among her posthumous papers entitled 'Dieses ist mein Glaube' written in July 1921, the latter is explained in another unpublished poem of the same date 'Meinen Liedern':

> Hätt ich Euch nicht gehabt, stünd ich in wolkiger Not
> noch vor genieteten Toren.
>
> Hätt ich Euch nicht gehabt, wäre mein krankes Herz
> im Goldmantel seiner Liebe erfroren.
>
> Hätt ich Euch nicht gehabt, trüge mein ehernes Schicksal nicht
> die stolzflammende Gebärde seiner Stunden,
>
> Hätt ich Euch nicht gehabt, hätt ich mich nie so beseelt
> in die erhabenen Hörsäale meines lebendigen Gottes gefunden.

Yet despite this positive statement, echoed by many others in her later poetry, of a paradise regained in faith and through the agency of her writing, the fundamental wounds in her existence remain. Thus we read at the end of her poem 'Mein Sohn und ich. II': 'Als sie draußen seine Schläfe durch-bohrten,/starb mein Paradies' (p. 81). In this same year 1921 she records her resurgence of faith using the example of Mary Magdalene in the poem 'Maria Magdalena', the first part of which ends:

> Aber, als Er, der Wundersame
> Dir begegnete,
> standest Du reglos.
> Reglos.
> Eingehüllt in seinen Blick.
>
> Über die dunklen Gewässer
> wehten die Rufe
> der ewigen Meere.
>
> Da erkanntest Du
> den zertretenen Burggarten
> Deiner Seele.
>
> Und weintest laut. (p. 91)

Mary Magdalene becomes the image of the poet whose heart has been shattered and whose response to the presence of the creator is stasis and lament. This first response of awe and regret for her own spent life is modified by the 'Himmelsbürde' of creation experienced in the poem 'Der Zaubergarten' where the poet is given a new chance by the life around her: 'Tausendfarbig sprüht der wolkige Morgen auf./Alle Goldaugen spiegeln sich ein in mein Herz' (p. 102). The summing-up of the two aspects of her late poetry comes in the final poem in the collection 'Einem Freunde' where she claims

> Ich bin Paradieserde
> und Abendschatten

and

> Ich gehe leicht über
> die smaradgene Brücke.
>
> Da stehe ich in einem sanften
> Himmelreich. (p. 124)

In the last resort Frida Bettingen's poetry became for her both a therapy and a challenge, for she became aware of the potential given to her that needed to be awoken by the interface of suffering and endurance. The writing of poetry would demand pain, as we read in a poem entitled 'Aber neidet uns nicht' published in the *Rheinisch-Westfälische Zeitung* in 1934:

> Wir sind Heimruf.
> Und Angebinde ferner Welten.
>
> Aber neidet uns nicht.

Ungegürtet den Himmeln
Entfiel unser Herz.

Immer am brausenden Strome wohnt
das purpurgesättigte Gestern.

Über den unbedeckten Häuptern
der Königskinder
schweifen Nachtmare.

Bess Brenck-Kalischer

Bess Brenck-Kalischer

> Sie hat merkwürdig starre Augen, ist häßlich fett. Kurze
> graue Haare. Schreibt Gedichte und Romane und ist
> dadurch bekannt, daß alle Berliner Literaten schon
> einmal um ihre Liebe warben.[6]

Emil Szittya's summing-up of Bess Brenck-Kalischer is one of the few
hints we have of this remarkable personality whose slender work belongs to
the category of forgotten contributions to Expressionism. 'Alle Berliner
Literaten' may seem exaggerated, but this probably refers primarily to her
membership of the 'expressionistische Arbeitsgemeinschaft Dresden' from
which developed the Dresdner Verlag 1917 with its two series 'Dichtung der
Jüngsten' (1917-1919) and 'Das neuste Gedicht' (1918-1920). Some fifteen
soirées were organized to arouse interest in new art in Dresden and to further
the beliefs of young artists who aspired to change the world. A group of the
more active members presented a series of lectures on new art and recitals of
works from *Die Aktion* and *Der Sturm* and from the newly formed Felix
Stiemer Verlag. Perhaps the most significant outcome was the periodical
Menschen (1918-1922) which set out above all to oppose materialism and all
that had led to war by a new idealism inspired by works and actions from all
ages under the generic term 'Expressionism'. Bess Brenck-Kalischer's work
appeared in this context, although she was already active as a writer in 1905.
Her importance for this periodical can be seen by her presentation of its aims
on the first page of its first number alongside Conrad Felixmüller's often
reproduced woodcut of a human figure climbing towards the title:

> Wundern Sie sich Ausrufungszeichen Es gibt Menschen
> Punkt Wundern Sie sich, daß es Menschen gibt
> Fragezeichen Ja, es gibt Menschen Punkt Punkt Punkt —
> es gibt Menschen.
>   Der Blitz dieser Entscheidung treffe Sie, das Feuer
> dieser Erkenntnis zerschlage Sie so tief — bis... Wie, Sie
> sitzen noch immer regungslos vor mir, Sie beten noch
> immer die lange steife Linie an, statt einmal, ein einziges
> Mal den Sprung ins Chaos zu wagen, den Sturz, dessen
> Wirbel allein die Flamme, die heilige Flamme der
> Menschlichkeit aufschließt bis in die tiefste Höhe der
> absoluten Bewußtheit. Aber — träg und schwer liegt die
> Erde, der Rest von Glut-Geist in den Händen der
> Erniedrigten und Beleidigten, die ihren Herzkörper
> zuckend aufrissen, Mensch um Mensch zu rühren, bereit

> den w a h r e n Blutbund der Menschen zu formen. O,
> um dieser neuen Form willen − Menschen auf Erden −
> wurden Milliarden anderer verschwendet, das wache
> Leben zu töten. Aber − und verpufften sie alles für den
> Tod des Geistes, − das absolute Bewußtsein wäre
> stärker, schüfe sich einen letzten Träger. Ihr Menschen
> vor mir, gedankt sei dem Leben, noch ist diese letzte
> Zeit nicht da, aber − Minuten zählen − sie kommt,
> wenn Ihr Euch nicht schleunigst besinnt und jubelnd −
> denn es muß jubelnd geschehen − den Sprung ins
> Erleben wagt. Sekunde zählt! Wagt den Sprung in das
> Leben, das heilig tiefe Leben; erst, wenn Ihr Euch in
> Menschlichkeit aufgelöst, werden gerührt und überinnig
> aus Eurer Mitte erstehen der Zeit Not, der
> Unendlichkeit Träger,
>   Menschen!

The spelling out of punctuation in the first short paragraph tries to catch the eye. The fervour and abstract generalities of the main section typify much of her writing and set the tone for the periodical.

Details about her life are hard to find. She was born 21 November 1878 in Rostock, went to a teacher training college for women and studied philosophy for a few semesters. In 1906 she married Dr Siegmund Kalischer (1880-1911) after having trained as a reciter of literary works. She lived after 1920 in Hellerau near Dresden and later in Berlin, suffering illness for many years. She was supported by the Deutsche Schillerstiftung and died in Berlin on 2 June 1933. She published her earliest poems in *Charon* in 1905. These include a cycle of three entitled 'Grenzen' under one by S. Kalischer. They are poems of self-sacrifice and lament after the end of a love-affair. Already we see the sense of a broken world in which even perhaps longing and knowledge have refracted the light of truth:

> Ob auch die Sehnsucht das Gefäß zertrümmert...
> Und wissend ward mir wunde Wahrheit:
> In jenen Scherben such ich die Klarheit
> Des Glases, das im Glanz geschimmert.[7]

'Die Marquise von Marcuse' and 'Nun naht die Nacht' are short suggestive visions, the first a sonnet of unfulfilled longing, the second in less strict form striving for effect with playful rhymes.

Dichtung, her only published collection, contained sixty-nine short poems, and appeared in the Dresdner Verlag in 1917; some of them were also included in the periodicals *Die schöne Rarität* 1 (1917), *Menschen* 1 (1918) and

Der Einzige 1 (1919). The motto of the first section of *Dichtung*: 'Ich zwang die Platten, das Bild zu tragen./Traum faßten sie nicht'[8] underlines the essential concern underlying her work — how to reconcile the richness of her vision with the inherent restrictions of artistic and literary expression. Religious poems led her to a fuller understanding of the meaning of the Cross, the Lucifer poems that form the second cycle celebrating the carrier of light as a prototype expressionist figure: 'Er schrie das Licht' (p. 19). Mostly written in 1914, they are an attempt to apply the Lucifer myth to the devastation of war and to the burgeoning of desire in her own self. Individual poems bear witness to her clinging to the mystery of a *deus absconditus* despite the passion of life around her. The visions are constructed with sometimes unusual synaesthesia close to that in some of Georg Trakl's poems; thus in 'Das Auge flog voran': 'Um jede Wassermühle/blutet Licht' (p. 27). However, the comparison with Trakl serves to underline the difference in quality between the richly imaginative scope of his metaphor and her more limited, mainly self-centred expressions of struggle. Her descriptions of collapsing landscapes form part of the 'O-Mensch Pathos' of early First World War Expressionism with conflagrations, exploding shells, ragged flags, resounding atmospheres and 'festering' bridges. There is, too, an experimental playing with language where sometimes the meaning gives way to an attempted expression of visionary message, and in 'Gepanzert ward mein Blut' the reduction of language precedes, or is at least contemporaneous with similar attempts in *Der Sturm*:

> Gepanzert ward mein Blut.
> Voll Auge.
> Nächte
> Sehnen
> Goß ich zu Stahl.
> Klarster Blick blendet Tag.
> Traum
> Ward Bild. (No. 42)

Thematically the poems become more insistent descriptions of the intense suffering of personal existence as it attempts to create order out of chaos, whether in the role of a mother, wise man, miller or lover. The sensitivity of such poems reaches an almost oriental concision, thus:

> O Freund, Du spinnst mich in Asche,
> Ich rinne, ein grauer Tag

Um die Blüte des Chaos,
Die uns frühlingswirr küßte.
O mein Freund. (No. 55)

or:

Die beiden Wände tragen ein Gesicht.
Ihr Hang ist unbeschreiblich
Starr.
Nur manchmal, wenn in jenen kleinen Tempeln
Die Lampen sich entzünden
Zittern sie sehr leise. (No. 57)

or:

Wie fühlte ich mich tief.
Neige du deinen Kelch
Dringe.
Die sieben zitternden Hüllen
Litt ich um dich.
Du. (No. 59)

There is also a barely veiled eroticism in for instance 'Anemonen':

So drohen Anemonen in starren Nächten.
Aufgespreizt kriechen sie Gift.
Ich winde mich vor deiner Schwäche Weib,
Stoß hart in Deine Kelche
Grab ab
Zücke neue Ströme
Weib, Spinne Anemone. (No. 63)

Life, however, with its insistent need for growth, impedes true relationship:

Im Urgrund wuchsen wir.
Blaue Blüten
Immer nur Du.
Verschlungen, verweht
rankt unser Blut an fremden Hüften empor.
Wildes Gesproß.
O
Nur im Traum
Rühren wir uns noch
Du und Du. (No. 64)

In giving herself, she has become unapproachable:

Gab mein Herz Irgendwem,
Der verlors,
Irgendwo
Irgendwann.
In mir
Getier
Alle Kriege der Andern.

> Jede Sekunde Torpedoschuß.
> Aber mein Herz kann nie mehr getroffen werden.
> Welle, die sich verspielt. (No. 65)

In the final poem she dedicates herself to continuous struggle and to confrontation with life.

The frame of mind in which Bess Brenck-Kalischer wrote her main work, the novel *Die Mühle*, is perhaps best illustrated by the poem 'Nach dem Alten' which was published in the periodical *Der Einzige* 1 (1919) on 25 July 1919:

> Wer in der Schau ist sieht sich nicht mehr.
> Wer sich nicht mehr sieht ist ohne Spiegel.
> Ohne Spiegel sein heißt wesenlos sein.
> Also:
> Der Nichtsehende ist ohne Gegenüber.
> Wer ohne Gegenüber ist ist hauslos.
> Hauslos sein heißt ohne Gebrechen sein.
> Darum:
> Wirf den Sinn ab.
> Wer den Sinn abwirft ist im Wesen.
> Wer im Wesen ist ist inmitten.
> Über die Mitte hinaus geht nichts.
> Einhalt ist keimender Tod. (p. 222)

The anarchic, freely associative attitudes suggested here find their fuller expression in the at first sight chaotic structure and shifting perspectives of her novel. Its title might well suggest a metaphor of the windmill with sails ready to move at the slightest breath of wind from any direction. This is supported by one of Richard Janthur's three illustrations showing a windmill with an apocalyptic landscape including images of war, an anonymous city, an eye surveying a hill with a cross and souls falling into chaos. It might also suggest the creative potential of a watermill driven by the stream of life. This is supported by an early reference in the text to an image showing the kneading of dough from cereal into life on earth. The subtitle *Eine Kosmee* is both a clue to and a hindrance towards precise interpretation. On first reading this can be taken to mean a cosmic adventure, a form of space odyssey allowing for the suspension of normal categories of place and time. Further reflection on its meaning as a large sub-species of plants suggests the perhaps playful intention of the writer to present another significance. This would then sum up the variety in forms and perspectives of the various episodes in the text, as a garland rich in profusion and colour. The link with the original Greek *kosmos*, meaning both order and decoration, thus becomes relevant.

Die Mühle, a high-point in Brenck-Kalischer's work, was published in an edition of one hundred copies in 1922 by Leon Hirsch Verlag in Berlin. It is under fifty pages long, and with its at times breathtaking changes and daring images is reminiscent of the much more effective and famous work *Bebuquin oder die Dilettanten des Wunders* by Carl Einstein. The more extreme effect-seeking phrases of the section 'Das Vorspiel' are replaced by an overall style that is made up of short sentences often with a single statement. The effect of these is breathless, the intention visionary. Rhythmic and rhyming patterns, sometimes printed as lines of poetry, produce an emphatic pathos where at times the verbal meaning is sacrificed for overall effect. An onslaught on the imagination takes place whose aim is implicit in the Swedish saying used as a motto: 'Es wächst viel Brot in einer Winternacht'. The metaphor of yeast proving is taken up in the first one-line paragraph: 'Es drängte, zuckte, schrie. Schwang. Kruste zersprang.' The crust is that of the earth, from whose centre arises a crystal mill, a challenge to the current generation to participate in a cataclysmic rebirth out of chaos into light and day. The shock techniques used in the introductory section prepare the reader for a text divided into twenty-six individual sections, usually with an enigmatic title. Each of these is best understood as an individual story or episode, self-contained, yet having a formal function within the whole work, although several are linked together syntactically and thematically later in the novel.

The first section 'Die Steinzeit' records the pressure of a primordial age on the narrator. As a metaphor for expressionist disillusion in the closing stages of the First World War the direct equation of fossilization and a dead society is taken a step further in the phrase: 'Wäre es die Eiszeit, so könnte man noch auf einen Sommer hoffen.' The visions that follow are close to the world of Paul Scheerbart's *Lesabendio* or Alfred Kubin's *Die andere Seite*. Each is punctuated by sudden explosions — often rockets that herald a series of weird transformations in the manner of the surrealist artist A. Paul Weber, and these become physical pointers to a new stage in the narrator's awareness. Thus we read:

> Mein Erstaunen wuchs, aber ks ks platzten gleich vier
> Raketen auf einmal. Und dabei merkte ich erst ein

> neues Wunder; ich hatte auch außen an der Haut
> Millionen Augen bekommen. So konnte ich also
> bequem mehrere Geschichten auf einmal lesen. (p. 6)

In the nightmare that follows there are direct attacks on rival groups and at times individuals. In particular Activists become the butt in ribald, barely veiled comments on contemporary figures of the literary and publishing world:

> Unter den Kleinsten, uns unsichtbaren Sternen brach die
> Aktivistenseuche aus. Sie rissen sich von ihren Sicher-
> heitsnadeln los, und beschlossen in gemeinsamen
> Bünden die Zentralsonne abzusetzen. Doch schon auf
> dem Wege zum Ziel zerfielen sie alle zu Sternstaub. Ein
> himmlischer, intelligenter Verleger ließ den Vorgang
> photographieren, und gab eine schön gebundene Mappe
> heraus mit dem Titel: Los von der Sicherheitsnadel.
> (p. 6)

Animal allegories follow with snails founding a league against individualism, suffering monkeys changing colour in some hideous illness and a Hegelian interpretation of history quoted from a contemporary writer. Later in the novel some contemporaries are named, notably Salomo Friedlaender (Mynona), student and writer on speculative philosophy, friend of Alfred Kubin and joint editor of *Der Einzige. Organ des Individualistenbundes*, on the need to be sceptical about the Christian and Muslim faiths. Both his major work *Schöpferische Indifferenz* (Munich: Georg Müller, 1918) and his utopian visions and grotesque prose clearly influenced the writing of *Die Mühle*.

The novel can be interpreted as a search for a hidden self — the true, pristine self of the narrator free from all cultural influences. It thus bears witness to an attempt to break free from the legacy of war, of materialism, of history, of all identifying traits such as institutional, family or genetic factors. A vision is described of a world populated with featureless creatures with no signs of recognition or communication: 'Da sprach mich mein geheimnisvolles Wesen so an. Hier sieht eben ein Dichter die Verheerung des Schierling-bechers' (p. 9). Socrates is praised for the nobility of his suicide, but significantly criticized for glossing over a personal act as a general ethical statement. Each such action, each personal decision — as for the artists in the Dresden group — has its own independent value free from any universal application. Thus the author can claim: 'Das Welken der Welt begann in Athen' (p. 10). Subjectivism and a denunciation of material gain to the detriment of spirituality become the thematic basis of a novel rich in extravagant and playful uses of language and form. At times this reaches a poetic quality reminiscent of the imagery and visionary quality of Else Lasker-Schüler:

> Kennst du Nächte, in denen die Sterne weinen, weil der Mond sie nicht küssen will. Er befruchtet die Meere der Erde, damit Aphrodite geboren werde. Einer wird immer dran glauben müssen. Vielleicht ist es ein himmlisches Schicksal, daß Sterne weinen.
> Auch Immortellen haben goldenen Glanz. Einmal saß ich am Nil, als die Barke der toten Königin übers Delta trieb. So hatte sie es selbst bestimmt. Weißt du, daß ihre letzten Worte an Cäsar waren: Wer seinen Namen vorausschickt, trifft keine Königin. (p. 11)

This poetic quality sometimes turns to poetic prose, especially at the beginnings of sections where short-line prose poems are followed by less rhythmic commentary. The search is on for 'Urbilder', for ways of reactivating the downtrodden, often forgotten longing for the exclusive self. The narrative becomes a struggle to release the secret self from the 'Klettenartige', the burdock-like tendency of people to cling to others and, by mimicry, form themselves. However, the self needs to be on guard, for:

> Seit ich aus mir herausgetreten bin, sagte da mein geheimnisvolles Wesen, sehe ich alles viel klarer. Nichts verbindet Gestirne so sehr wie Scheidungen. Im Moment der reinen Trennung sind beide wieder auf die große gemeinsame Bahn angewiesen. Das Klettenartige der Menschen aber. (p. 12)

Nature — flowers and birdsong with their sun-worship — offers more than dreams and longing based on memories. It offers faith in something that cannot be lost, faith in chance, in reawakening, for: 'Im Grunde ist nur unsere eigene Vergeßlichkeit der rote Faden für die Perle des Zufalls' (p. 16). Culture, represented by the violin from Cremona, has been overused, hence will eventually split into pieces. Artificial, closed-form harmonies will give way to the open-form song of larks mimicked by the harp.

The wall of tradition and habit has to be broken, and several forms such as parables, legends, romances and oriental tales are used to illustrate this. In the section 'Die Insel der Verhängnisse' the narrator becomes a pillar in the mausoleum:

> Und plötzlich starrte ich selber Säule die Toten an. In
> meine Strenge ritzten sich die heiligen Zeichen. Ich
> klang stumm.
> In mir sprachen die Tiere von tausend Jahren.
> Ich klang. Klang starr.
> Da bäumte sich ein Sturm gegen mich auf, und rüttelte
> mich, rüttelte solange, daß ich fast erlag.
> Im letzten Augenblick aber riß sich der Vogel der Isis
> heraus, und zerhackte mit seinem langen Schnabel den
> Sturm. Ich wollte schon atmen; das Tier aber fand nicht
> mehr zurück; ich aber ohne Halt wollte zusammenfallen.
> Da sprach eine Stimme neben mir: Siehst du nun, was es
> heißt, sich zu tief in Vergangenes einzulassen. (p. 24)

The metamorphoses implied – into stone and back – are metaphors for a narrative consciousness that shifts between intense enclosed suffering and ecstatic visionary freedom. The normal restrictions of place and time are broken, ideas and phrases are released to form their own contexts whose boundaries shift at will. Each time a recognizable narrative form is adopted, it is soon shattered – not to bring formlessness but to emphasize the basic expressionist experiences of collective imprisonment and of fractured self. The sheer weight of tradition and interpretation is lamented – hence for example the section 'Des 4. Amenophes Tochter weint' where the very fact of being the daughter of a great king imprisons her not just in her lifetime, but for eternity: 'O König, deine Tochter weint. Zwiefach bin ich. Deiner Seele Unendlichkeit und meines Tempels Grenze' (p. 25). Trying not to be accepted as the daughter of a king, as the relative of someone else, as a member of an organization, or as any other limiting description may demand a metamorphosis – the example is suggested of a camel that bought the stomach of an old ass in the hope of becoming different by eating thistles. When this failed, the camel went to Europe, where it was last seen in the Stirner Society.

With this allusion to Max Stirner, the core of the novel is reached. For his ideas (admired by among others Alfred Kubin, Paul Scheerbart, Carl Sternheim and Frank Wedekind) inspired the underlying aims of this work. Aphorisms such as the following are relevant:

> Die Wahrheit selbst besteht in nichts Anderem, als in
> dem Offenbaren seiner selbst, und dazu gehört das
> Auffinden seiner selbst, die Befreiung von allem
> Fremden, die äußerste Abstraktion oder Entledigung
> von aller Autorität, die wiedergewonnene Naivetät.

or:

> Mein Eigentum aber ist kein Ding, da dieses eine von
> Mir abhängige Existenz hat; mein eigen ist nur meine
> Gewalt. Nicht dieser Baum, sondern meine Gewalt oder
> Verfügung über ihn ist die meinige.

or:

> Nicht als Mensch und nicht den Menschen entwickle Ich,
> sondern als Ich entwickle ich — Mich.[9]

The acme of any creature is the sensitivity that allows it to respond creatively to its environment to produce something new. Hence the wonder expressed in the novel for the bloom of the cosmos:

> Wie wunderbar ist die Blüte der Kosmee, sagte ich leise
> als Antwort zu meiner Begleiterin. Schmal und schlank,
> jeder Strahl himmlische Flamme. Die grenzenlose
> Empfindungsmöglichkeit der Materie in die vollendetste
> Ordnung gebracht. (p. 29)

Doubtless Brenck-Kalischer was aware of German traditions memorably expressed by Philipp Otto Runge on the meaning of flowers as a key to the better understanding of the self:

> Alles Lebendige hat in unserer Seele seinen Spiegel, und
> unser Gemüt nimmt alles *recht* auf, wenn wir es mit
> Liebe ansehen. Dann erweitert sich der Raum in
> unserm Innern, und wir werden zuletzt selbst zu einer
> großen Blume, wo sich alle Gestalten und Gedanken wie
> Blätter in einem großen Stern um das Tiefste unsrer
> Seele, um den Kelch, wie um einen tiefen Brunnen
> drängen, aus welchem bloß die Staubfäden als die Eimer
> und die tiefen Leidenschaften unsrer lebendigen Seele
> herauskommen, und wir uns selbst immer verständlicher
> werden.[10]

The 'Märchen' that follows, 'Auf dem Sirius', is told to the narrator by an old inhabitant of the cosmos and is seen as necessary for the world to come to its senses. It is an account removed from any purposeful action, an imaginary flight to glory in a realm of eternal love. The narrator of the novel experiences a further metamorphosis:

> Ich gehe wie ein Mond durch mein Sehnen. Ich mag die
> starre Kunst des Tages nicht mehr.
> Ich will die weiche, weiche graue Nacht.
> Und plötzlich, das Harte fiel ja schon von mir ab, bin ich
> eine kleine Maus. (p. 33)

Her encounter as a mouse with a poet leads her eventually to an empty barrel
which brings back memories of an earlier existence in which she is lying in
hospital. The long episode recounts her delirium in a style that moves away
from the novel's earlier direction, but which illustrates how easily the narrative
can slip from one perspective into another:

> Die Doppeltüren kommen ganz leise an mein Bett.
> Schwere weiche Nacht öffnet sich. Aus Ebenholz
> springen weiße Rosen. Und ich bin Schneewittchen.
> Alle die Rosen küssen mich, alle. Ich habe gar keine
> böse Stiefmutter mehr. Mein Sarg ist aus Mordstrahlen
> [sic] (Mondstrahlen), und mein Brautkleid aus Schnee-
> ballen. Der Prinz bringt mir den großen Orion. Ich
> pflanze den Stern in mein Herz, lauter Granaten
> springen auf. (p. 35)

The Snow-White perspective becomes an extension of consciousness of a
brain-injured patient, registering sketches of ideas, visions, fears and hopes
drifting in no apparent order. A sequence develops where the hallucinations
are far less controlled than for instance in Kasimir Edschmid's parallel story
'Der tödliche Mai' (1915). Brenck-Kalischer does not give an explanation of
the style, summed up by Edschmid's narrator in a moment of self-aware
lucidity:

> Aber ich empfand alles im Gleichnis, und oft ist
> Gleichnis uns die nächste und verwirrend deutlichste
> Realität. Ich sehe vieles im Bilde, weil ich in einer über-
> steigerten Sekunde über das Leben und gewöhnte Maß
> hinaus *erkannt* habe.[11]

The section 'Aus einem Brief' narrates the emptiness of inner and
outer landscapes of a woman who is recovering from a nervous breakdown.
This is written out of personal experience and as a general phenomenon, for:
'Sag doch selbst, welche sensible Frau kann das Leben, wie es heute ist,
ertragen ohne seelisch krank zu werden' (*Die Mühle*, p. 41). The evocative
description of a moonlit snowscape parallels her consciousness culminating in
a complex lurid image that plays for expressionistic effect:

> Ich bin allein. Der Schnee fällt, aber unter der Decke
> des Verbindungsweges setzen die feinen, feinen Wurzeln
> schon das Grün des ersten Lindenblattes an. Ich sinke,
> sinke. Bis der Urwald klingt. Aus meinem Wurzelrot
> keimt eine weiße Blüte. Millionen toter Affen hüten sie.
> Aus grünen Hirnen rinnt Saft. (p. 42)

Gradually, despite relapses and frightening glimpses of herself in a mirror and of the others in the ward, Lea recovers – the first time we are given her name is when she leaves the hospital. The novel ends with a narrative coda in which images of childhood and of the setting sun splintering into thousands of hearts form a backdrop as she goes with her lover, the doctor, first towards the town and then hand in hand to the sanatorium.

In a 'Sprechender Anhang' Brenck-Kalischer asks the reader to decide whether the novel has been serious or comic, and she specifically distances herself from one of her literary mentors, Jean Paul. Her task has been to break through layers of tradition, and to explain this she uses the story of Baron Münchhausen left with his horse at the top of a church spire. She asks if anyone has found a corpse at the bottom of such a church tower and ends: 'Ich, ich suche nach einem Kadaver vor Kirchentüren' (*Die Mühle*, p. 48).

Brenck-Kalischer alludes also to Don Quixote, and it is perhaps with him in mind that the title takes on a third possible meaning. For, as with Frida Bettingen, the world is found to be an exciting delusion, only useful as a mirror to the self and as a challenge to create new meanings. Both writers indulged in suffering because they at first believed that all events must have some meaning as an extension of the past. Each of them was to find that the self had to struggle through the tortures of life and could only find its own authenticity by creating its meaning.[12]

NOTES

[1]Walter Falk, 'Schmerz und Wort — Eine Studie über Frida Bettingen als Dichterin des Schmerzes' (unpublished doctoral thesis, University of Freiburg im Breisgau, 1957), p. 1.

[2]The unpublished works put in order by Walter Falk include some sixty poems, a plan for 'Die goldene Seele', aphorisms, sections from her letters, a list of over sixty letters concerning her work and these papers compiled by her daughter Lise Bettingen, twelve notebooks with notes, variants, first drafts etc, school essays, material on her life and on her work and an interpretation of 'Blühende Bäume' by Werner Falk.

[3]In: Frida Bettingen, *Gedichte*, p. 72.   All references in the section on Frida Bettingen are to page numbers in *Gedichte*.

[4]Ernst Bacmeister, 'Frida Bettingen', *Das innere Reich* (1935), Heft 11, 1417-1427, quotation on p. 1417.

[5]Werner Falk, 'Schmerz und Wort...', p. 79.

[6]Emil Szittya, in *Das Kuriositäten-Kabinett* (Constance: See Verlag, 1923), p. 160.

[7]In: *Charon* 2 (1905), 45.

[8]In: Bess Brenck-Kalischer, *Dichtung*, p. 7.   All references in the section on Bess Brenck-Kalischer are to page numbers in *Dichtung*, later to *Die Mühle*.

[9]In: Max Stirner, *Der Einzige und sein Eigentum und andere Schriften*, ed. by Hans G. Helms (Munich: Hanser, 1970^3), 17, 174, 220.

[10]Letter to his mother of 15 June 1803 in: Philipp Otto Runge, *Briefe und Schriften*, ed. by Peter Betthausen (Munich: Beck, 1982), 148-49.

[11]Quoted from *Prosa des Expressionismus*, ed. by Fritz Martini (Stuttgart: Philipp Reclam jun., 1970), p. 228.

[12]Two works by Bess Brenck-Kalischer not examined in this essay are 'Das Vorspiel' in *Die schöne Realität* 1 (1917), Heft 3, 45-49 and her interesting review of an early performance of Else Lasker-Schüler's drama *Die Wupper* in *Der Einzige* 1 (1919), 177-78.

Anna Seghers

11

Beyond Ideology: The Early Works of Anna Seghers

Martin Kane

When Anna Seghers died in 1983, the shadow which would be cast upon her reputation with the appearance of Walter Janka's *Schwierigkeiten mit der Wahrheit*[1] and its revelations about her failure to intervene in the shameful trial in July 1957 of the publisher of her masterpiece *Das siebte Kreuz* still lay in the future.[2] In East Germany she was a legend and, despite the ideological battering she and her work had received at the hands of commentators such as Marcel Reich-Ranicki and Peter Jokostra,[3] was also a well-respected literary figure in the West.

The tributes which marked her death and the many honours she received during her lifetime invariably stressed her championing of the oppressed and underprivileged. Henryk Kreisch's comment that the young Anna Seghers had become '...weltanschaulich und politisch zur Gefährtin der Arbeiterklasse' is here typical.[4] This much-vaunted identification with the proletariat was not, however, something to which Netty Reiling (Anna Seghers's real name) was born on 19 November 1900. Her father was a prosperous art dealer who, according to Kurt Batt (although he does not corroborate this), was custodian of the fine art collection in Mainz cathedral.[5] He was also Jewish, and a well-integrated member of the community. Whether this was, as one contemporary of Netty Reiling puts it, because his political views were 'deutsch-national', or because he enjoyed the patronage of Grand Duke Ernst Ludwig, the ruler of Hessen-Darmstadt from 1892 to 1918 and a man inimical to the 'wilhelminischer Ungeist' emanating from Berlin, is unclear.[6] She studied History, History of Art and Sinology at the University of Heidelberg, and spent two semesters at the 'Museum für ostasiatische Kunst' in Cologne. In 1924, the year in which she published her first story,[7] she returned to Heidelberg to complete a PhD thesis on 'Jude und Judentum im Werke Rembrandts'.[8]

Virtually nothing of these family and personal circumstances finds its way in immediately identifiable form into Anna Seghers's subsequent fiction. Conspicuously unforthcoming in matters autobiographical in her essays, speeches and interviews, she is somewhat more expansive on the geographical and historical dimension of her origins. The celebrated passages at the beginning of Das siebte Kreuz are eloquent testament to her affection – magnified by the circumstances of exile – for the landscape of the region where she was born and grew up, as is the haunting evocation of time and place in 'Der Ausflug der toten Mädchen', the only one of Seghers's works which acknowledges any direct point of contact with her own life.

Despite this abiding reticence about personal matters – she told Christa Wolf that 'die Erlebnisse und die Anschauungen eines Schriftstellers [...] werden am allerklarsten aus seinem Werk, auch ohne spezielle Biographie'[9] – Seghers's early writings may nonetheless be read in the light of her biographical development. They may be interpreted as an act of transformation, of liberation from her privileged origins to the point where she dedicates her work (as Wieland Herzfelde has noted[10]) to what is described in the final line of 'Der Ausflug der toten Mädchen' as 'die befohlene Aufgabe'. It is from the sense of a world in massive revolutionary flux and change and the dramatization of that 'unermeßlicher Strom von Zeit',[11] that the narrator of this story draws her inspiration.

And yet close scrutiny of her early work and the way it was received – particularly by Seghers's political and ideological allies – shows that this transformation was far from smooth. One may speculate that in the piece 'Bücher und Verwandlungen' which she wrote in 1969 she may well have been more than usually revealing about her own life and work and the difficulties she had encountered: 'Im Grunde genommen, stellen meine Romane, stellt das meiste, was ich geschrieben habe, eine Art von Verwandlung dar... Die Verwandlung kann langsam, entsetzlich langsam, unter Leiden und Widerspruch vor sich gehen.'[12]

Anna Seghers was not always a legend. The figure beyond all literary and ideological reproach which she was to become in the GDR was a world away from that of the young aspiring communist writer and the reputation she enjoyed in left-wing circles in the late 1920s. What becomes clear from examination of her work of this period, in conjunction with the sparse biographical detail available to us, is that Anna Seghers – fully aware of the nature and origins of the problems of poverty, oppression and exploitation she saw in the world all around her, and fully conscious of the implications the revolution in Russia would have for the solution of these problems – was quite able to make the intellectual leap which the embracing of Communism would involve. She was less capable, however, – subconsciously reluctant even at first – to make the artistic leap which Communism would demand of its artists and writers at this time.

It is important to preface any discussion of Anna Seghers's work in the period up to 1933 with some brief comment on the literary and intellectual climate in which she and other communist writers of bourgeois origins had to make their way. In 1929, the year after she had won the 'Kleist-Preis' for *Aufstand der Fischer von St. Barbara* and had also become a member of the KPD, she joined the BPRS, the 'Bund proletarisch-revolutionärer Schriftsteller'. Under the chairmanship of Johannes R. Becher, this organization of communist writers had been formed to turn literature away from the purely esoteric and aesthetic and to make of it a weapon with which to intervene in and influence the political and social process. This was not a straightforward matter. The organization was constantly beset, as Helga Gallas has described,[13] with questions about ways and means, of precisely what mode of writing might best further the cause of revolutionary socialism.

In general, a hard line was taken. Amidst the plethora of theoretical discussion for instance at the second 'Weltkongreß der revolutionären Literatur' held at Charkow in the Soviet Union at the beginning of October 1930, the contribution of Otto Biha may stand as an example of BPRS authoritarianism at its most vigorous. What Communism and the revolutionary struggle expected from its writers is made palpably clear at the outset of his address:

> Unter proletarisch revolutionärer Literatur verstehen wir die Literatur, die die Welt vom Standpunkt des revolutionären Proletariats erkennt und die Lesermassen den Aufgaben der Klasse entsprechend zum Kampf gegen den Kapitalismus erzieht. Der proletarische Schriftsteller kann nur auf Grund einer konsequenten marxistischen Weltanschauung die gesellschaftliche Wirklichkeit erkennen und den Aufgaben der kämpfenden Arbeiterklasse dienen.[14]

These highly prescriptive remarks reveal Otto Biha as one of the most outspoken critics of bourgeois writers such as Anna Seghers who had thrown in their lot with the KPD and the BPRS. In his report on the activities of the BPRS in 1929 Seghers was mentioned along with Ludwig Renn as one of the recently recruited writers who 'in der Bourgeoisie einen guten Namen hatten' and who 'kamen nicht etwa als "Sympathisierende", sie nahmen unsere Literaturlosungen völlig an und stellten sich auch organisatorisch zur Verfügung'.[15] Despite this, Biha, in his discussion of her Kleist-Preis-winning *Aufstand der Fischer von St. Barbara*, is only able to give Seghers very grudging and limited approval. He does little for his credibility as critic, however, by getting the title wrong: he calls it *Der Aufruhr der Fischer von Santa Barbara*.[16] He grants the story a certain merit for having been able to move 'relativ große Schichten des Kleinbürgertums' and, despite the fact that the 'mit dem Proletariat sympathisierende Problemstellung' was a product of 'Gefühl' rather than of 'kritische<n> Vernunft', for having managed to achieve an 'immerhin revolutionisierende Wirkung'. Nevertheless, without going into specific detail, he detects in the book 'verwirrende, vernebelnde und hemmende Einflüsse' and declines to accept it as a 'Bestandteil der proletarisch revolutionären Literatur in ihrem eigentlichsten Sinn'. It is apparent, moreover, from the generally Pecksniffian drift of his argument where his priorities in the evaluation of literature lay — certainly not in the application of aesthetic criteria: 'das hohe künstlerische Niveau ihrer Gestaltung braucht nicht besonders unterstrichen zu werden'.

Otto Biha did not concern himself either with 'Die Toten auf der Insel Djal' or 'Grubetsch', the only other of Anna Seghers's works to which he might have had access at this time. It is in any case unlikely that he would have found pleasure in either of them; they are unpromising material for the 'Gegenoffensive der proletarischen Literatur gegen die Unterdrückung aller Werktätigen' (p. 122).

In an interview with Christa Wolf in 1971 Anna Seghers hinted at the existence of what we now know was the first of these stories:

> Ich schrieb und veröffentlichte doch schon kleine Geschichten vor dem 'Aufstand der Fischer'. Darunter war eine – wie sagt man: gruslige oder grausliche Geschichte von einem holländischen Kapitän. Ich schrieb sie in der Ich-Form, als ob dieser Kapitän mein Großvater war. Ich mußte ihm ja auch einen Namen geben. Auf der Suche nach einem holländischen kam ich auf Seghers, das ist ein Graphiker aus der Rembrandt-Zeit;... Nun mußte ich die Geschichte ja irgendwie zeichnen, und da dachte ich mir, als Enkelin des Alten müßte ich mich auch Seghers nennen...[17]

'Die Toten auf der Insel Djal', which owed its publication to the good offices of Alfred Kerr, gives us the origin of her pseudonym and also demonstrates that taste for elements of the fairy tale which frequently recurs, in more sober manifestation, throughout Anna Seghers's later work.[18] 'Anna mag Männermärchen,' wrote Paul Wiens in the decorative margin to a poem in celebration of Seghers's 80th birthday.[19] She herself notes, 'Ich habe ja niemand gehabt als kleines Kind, der mir Märchen erzählte, bestimmt nicht. Ich mußte sie mir selbst erzählen.'[20] Here, in her first published story, we see Anna Seghers's predilection for the 'Märchen' at its most utterly bizarre in the figure of the 'Pfarrer' who, for all his ecclesiastical trappings of office, holds demonic rather than Christian sway over the mutinous collection of shipwrecked mariners who threaten to rise by night from their island graves: 'Ein sonderbarer Kerl [...] Er hätte der Leibhaftige sein können' (p. 129). In seeing 'Die Toten auf der Insel Djal' as significant for Seghers's subsequent development, one would wish to concur with and elaborate on Christa Wolf's comment and see the character of the 'Pfarrer' as the first and strangest of a series of male figures – Grubetsch, Hull, Wallau and Heisler for instance – who stand apart, mysterious and attractive, legendary almost, and are able to impose themselves on individuals or the community, sometimes to benevolent, occasionally to sinister effect.[21]

In the case of the eponymous central figure of 'Grubetsch', the second of Seghers's stories to be published by the *Frankfurter Zeitung und Handelsblatt*, this time in serialized form in March 1927, the latter would hold true. At first sight there would appear to be little to link this with the earlier story. The milieu and setting for 'Grubetsch' are indicated in only the vaguest of terms: '"Grubetsch" spielt am Fluß (Rhein?) in einer Umgebung, die mich wahrscheinlich als junges Ding beunruhigt hat.'[22] Not precision of social and economic location but an atmosphere of psychological and material wretchedness is of the essence here. This is immediately established in the opening scene of the story, which is lit, as Christa Wolf observed in her introduction to Anna Seghers's doctoral thesis[23] with Rembrandtesque effect. The dim and guttering light of a cellar door lantern is there merely to illuminate '...die Pfütze im gerissenen Holzpflaster, einen weggeworfenen Pantoffel und einen Haufen verfaulter Äpfel';[24] its function is that of a miner's lamp to guide the rain into the pit-like 'Hof' − 'Ein böser Hof'[25] − where this grim and oppressive tale unfolds. Setting then has none of the outlandish elements which indicated in 'Die Toten' an imagination locked into a world of fairy-tale fantasy; it now indicates the maturing writer of emergent social consciousness formulating a response to conditions she had first observed and been troubled by as a child. Despite these differences, however, the two stories have links in their central characters. The 'Pfarrer' in 'Die Toten auf der Insel Djal' is a demonic creation who could have been the Devil himself. The impact which Grubetsch has on the lives of those who inhabit the 'Hof' is entirely for the bad. As an exotic figure who works the rafts on the nearby river in the summer, to then overwinter in the 'Hof', he brings with him a sense of liberating possibilities, of a mysterious and enticing wider world: 'Grubetsch, so ein Floß − ist es groß? Ist es klein? Kann man darauf schlafen, darauf tanzen? Fährt es schnell? Wohin fährt es? Warum?...' (p. 37). He exerts an irresistible fascination on men and women, young and old, exploiting the power this gives him to seduce the innocent, steal wives, betray friendships. None of those who become involved with him are left unscathed; his power is malevolent and destructive.

It is a malevolence which raises certain questions. What, we may ask, is the origin of Seghers's interest in an enigmatic and demonic figure such as

Grubetsch, and how are we to regard him in the light of the Marxist beliefs she was about to embrace? Friedrich Albrecht, in a recent article, gives us help here in detecting what he calls 'Dostojewski-Töne' in the story,[26] while Seghers herself, in the essay 'Woher sie kommen, wohin sie gehen', explains the impact which the discovery of Dostoevsky had had on her and her contemporaries. Of his creation of individual characters she writes:

> [...] der einzelne Mensch (stand) in einem grellen Licht. Er war besonders erhöht in seiner Größe und besonders erniedrigt in seiner Schlechtigkeit und Erbärmlichkeit. Solche Menschen, mit furchtbar auf die Spitze getriebenen Leidenschaften, die auf einen gewaltigen Ausbruch zutrieben [...] Wir verglichen sie mit unseren eigenen bläßlich-kleinbürgerlichen Sippen, die zu keinem starken Gefühl, zu keinem Gefühlsausbruch fähig waren.[27]

It is not difficult to see how the fascination Dostoevsky's characters exerted on Seghers might lead her to create similar figures in her own fiction. It was also inevitable that this would lead to a conflict with what would be expected from her as a member of the BPRS, since Dostoevsky's explanation for human behaviour has precious little to do with a Marxist and scientific view of the world.

   In 'Grubetsch' we find much more of Dostoevsky than we do of Marx. The misery and personal misfortune which emanate from Grubetsch do not have their roots in a particular constellation of tangible economic and social factors. They are existential in nature, the product of an irrational force for evil. Although it is not made explicit, there seems to be a further point of contact here, in explaining the character of Grubetsch, with the perpetual debate which we find in Dostoevsky — embodied particularly in the figure of Ivan in *The Brothers Karamazov*, a novel to which Seghers was especially drawn — which concludes that in a world in which God does not exist everything would be permitted. It is little wonder that Seghers's Marxist critics in the *Rote Fahne* and *Die Linkskurve* could not give this and other stories in the collection *Auf dem Wege zur amerikanischen Botschaft und andere Erzählungen* their blessing, explaining them away with the comment that they were the product of 'Dumpfe Erinnerungen aus der Vergangenheit, die sich der Autor vom Herzen geschrieben hat'.[28]

This view of 'Grubetsch' as a kind of self-imposed therapy is implausible. In the brief comments of 'Selbstanzeige' in 1931 Seghers is critical of these early stories and seems to be committing herself to a more orthodox, BPRS portrayal of human wretchedness.[29] Nevertheless, it is clear from her intensive preoccupation with Dostoevsky in the postwar period in the GDR, and from later comments on 'Grubetsch', that she does not seriously reject her presentation of the darker elements which give the story its fascination and psychological complexity. In June 1961, for instance, she wrote: 'Gewiß verstand ich damals gut den Wunsch vieler Menschen, auch wenn sie erniedrigt und verkommen waren oder gleichgültig und flott, nach etwas Hellem, das von ihrer gleichförmigen Umgebung abweicht. Mag es gut oder schlecht sein, es weicht ab.'[30] This describes perfectly the origins of the love-hate relationship which the 'Hof'-dwellers have for the exciting but destructive Grubetsch. They, the victims of their obsession with him, of the promise of escape he seems to offer, finally exact their revenge by killing him. But their lives are left duller. All that remains after his death are 'gewöhnliche Liebschaften, gewöhnliche Tode' (p. 66). An enigmatic conclusion, in its moral ambivalence unexpectedly evocative − as is the whole story − of the lines of another winner of the 'Kleist-Preis': 'Alle Laster sind zu etwas gut/Nur der Mann nicht, sagt Baal, der sie tut.'[31]

The story 'Die Ziegler', written in 1927/28 and first published in the same collection, *Auf dem Wege zur amerikanischen Botschaft*, is, to use Seghers's own words, 'eine Novelle des Zugrundegehens des Klein-bürgertums'[32] depicting the unavailing struggle of a once reasonably prosperous family to survive in the face of ill health, family misfortune and, above all, an increasingly unforgiving business climate. As in 'Grubetsch', narrow and stifling domestic confines are not only, in the process of downward spiral, both product and consequence of economic and social impoverishment, they also provide it with a darkly poeticized objective correlative. Clear psychological and atmospheric affinities with the earlier story arise as gloomy images of incarceration are spun out of a portrayal of tenements evocative of mine shafts cut off not only from the light, but also from the outside world, from all hope and aspiration.

Yearnings for wider horizons are, as in 'Grubetsch', vital to the story's meaning. Here, only the Zieglers' elder son succeeds, forsaking the family as a consequence of semi-criminal escapades. He liberates himself into a wider world by living out the promise made to the young boy in 'Grubetsch' which was never fulfilled: 'Einen wilden Teufel, einen gerissenen Lumpen will ich aus dir machen' (p. 44). In his sister Marie, whose dreary, doomed life is at the heart of the story, are awakened other, more modest possibilities by the glimpses she is given into the securer lives of benevolent customers as she delivers and collects the bits and pieces of repaired and to-be-repaired clothing which is all that is left of her father's declining business:

> Sie hatte an vier, fünf einzelne Familien Ware abzuliefern mit neuen Ärmeln und eingesetzten Rückenteilen. Einer nahm ihr alles in der Flurtür ab, andere führten sie ins Wohnzimmer. Es war heiß, es roch nach Kaffee, eine Uhr tickte. Ein Knabe mit einer Brille sah von einem Bilderalbum auf. Jemand redete ihr freundlich zu und bot ihr einen Stuhl an. Sie trat dicht an den Tisch und setzte sich nicht. Einen Augenblick gehörte sie in das helle Kreisrund der Lampe hinein. Es wurde hell in ihr, ihre Wünsche, ihr Kummer, ihre Angst.
>
> (*Die Ziegler*, p. 78)

In another important respect, however, Seghers has moved on from 'Grubetsch'. This may be seen by brief comparison with a novel such as *Kleiner Mann — was nun?* which originates in roughly the same period and deals with related problems. Fallada, with his highly detailed descriptions of a variety of work places and social institutions, of dole queue and 'Stehkragenprolet'-milieu, as well as his insights into escalating political tensions between left and right, locates the novel quite specifically, first in a small provincial town, and then in Berlin in the pre-Hitler years of growing slump and unemployment. 'Die Ziegler' cannot be pinned down so exactly, but nonetheless, the circumstances which it depicts (and this claim could not be made with anywhere near the same degree of certainty for 'Grubetsch') are clearly a product of gathering German economic depression in the late 1920s. The declining commissions for Ziegler's small textile manufacture and repair business are surely another version of Pinneberg's increasingly hopeless battle to meet his monthly sales quota; shorn of the elements of pathos exemplified in episodes such as his humiliating attempt to persuade an actor – Franz Schlüter, purveyor on celluloid of salt-of-the-earth roles – to buy a suit.[33]

Further comparisons spring to mind. Ziegler's distress at the thought of having to stand in line with others who are 'erwerbslos': 'Da mußte einer schon ganz gegerbt sein mit Schande, wenn er es ertrug, hier unter freiem Himmel für sein Geld anzustehen' (p. 88). Or his feelings of shame and disgust when the casual and amiably-meant gesture of a drunken down-and-out seem to invite collusion, to suggest a common fate: 'Ziegler drehte sein Gesicht in das andere Gesicht, das war rot und dick, winzige Äugelchen. Er riß sich los. Er lief heim' (p. 89).

In view of the psychological veracity of moments such as these, one can only regard as churlish the otherwise sympathetic Marxist critic Albrecht's view of Ziegler's behaviour and attitudes as representative of petty-bourgeois false consciousness, of the preference of his class to cling at all costs, and in the face of social and economic reality, on to misconceived notions of status, rather than seeking out, and fostering, solidarity with those similarly afflicted, regardless of class.[34]

This particular passage of events and the devastating moment of self-awareness for the dying Ziegler have their clear parallels in Fallada. They recall Pinneberg's sudden moment of realization, when, while staring at his reflection in a shop window, he is ordered by a policeman to move on: 'Und plötzlich begreift Pinneberg alles, [...] daß er draußen ist, daß er hier nicht mehr hergehört, daß man ihn zu Recht wegjagt: ausgerutscht, versunken, erledigt.'[35]   What Pinneberg, when still psychologically protected by his respectable overcoat, had half feared and suspected in contemplating the crowds of unemployed thronging aimlessly through a Berlin park, now comes home to him with shattering effect. The status conferred by a white collar is a shabby illusion; it is no consolation for being jobless and impoverished. The peremptory tone of the 'Schupo', his half-drawn truncheon, remind Pinneberg that he is just another insignificant cipher in the growing underclass of the hopeless. Fallada attempts, in the final sentimental scene of the novel, to draw the teeth of this wretched situation by having the Pinnebergs find consolation in their love for each other. Seghers, on the other hand, in lower but more authentic key, finds a psychologically persuasive end for Ziegler.

Death spares him the ultimate consequence of economic downfall. Remaining true to the end to those values which Albrecht feigns for ideological reasons to despise, but which Seghers, for all the objectivity of her account, clearly admires, he resists the slide into slovenly resignation which had overtaken others amongst his erstwhile business colleagues. To the last he maintains his dignity, managing one final, painful walk through the town, to be greeted with a respect which his commercial standing can no longer command.

This emphasis on the figure of Ziegler should not blind us to the fact that it is his daughter Marie who is at the heart of the story. The story opens with her; she it is who slumps to the pavement to bring this grim tale to an end. 'Die Ziegler' reminds us of Anna Seghers's frequent response to those in search of helpful biographical detail that anything of importance about her life was there for all to see in her work. In conversation with Wilhelm Girnus in 1967 she noted that from a very early age, and consolidated in part by the events of the Russian Revolution, she had been made very aware of class and economic differences:

> Ich hatte zum erstenmal voll und ganz verstanden, noch bevor es mir jemand erklärte, daß es ein Oben und Unten, ein Hoch und Niedrig gibt. Das, was wir heute einfach Klassen nennen, das hatte ich damals in meiner Weise als ganz junger Mensch verstanden.[36]

She does not elaborate, gives no examples of where specifically this awareness might be found reflected in her fiction. However, we need only turn to the moving but characteristically understated opening scene of 'Die Ziegler' to see immediately why Seghers steers in the direction of her work those who are curious about her life. We meet Marie Ziegler, here going door to door about her father's business, as she chances upon two of her former schoolmates:

> Vor ihr her liefen zwei Mädchen, lachten und schlenkerten. Sie erkannte von hinten ihre roten und dunkelblauen Mützen. Sie hatten letztes Jahr in der Schule vor ihr gesessen. Sie erschrak und ging langsam. Aber die Mädchen blieben stehen und sahen sie an. "Ach, Marie!" Die Mädchen standen schön und aufrecht auf hohen, hellen Beinen. "Was machst du denn jetzt?" — "Ich helf zu Hause." Die Mädchen betrachteten sie, sie preßte den Mund zu. Die Mädchen kannten auch noch ihr Kleid, ihr Halskettchen, ihren Scheitel, ihre hellen Brauen. Alles war wie vor Ostern, nur ein

bißchen verschwommen.   Sie wurden verlegen und
gaben sich die Hände.

(p. 68)

There is no authorial comment or explanation for this painful scene. None is
needed. We learn later that Marie has had to leave school to help out in her
father's workshop, but at this point the deceptively simple physical
observation that her two friends 'standen schön und aufrecht auf hohen,
hellen Beinen', contrasted with the harassed bearing of Marie we remember
from the opening paragraph – 'Ihr Herz zog sich zusammen vor Angst oder
vor Kummer' (p. 67) – is sufficient to indicate the social gulf which has
opened up between the former classmates. We do not know at this point, nor
is it necessary that we should, why Marie left school.   The air of
embarrassment in the encounter, the hint of shift in the relationship ('Alles
war wie vor Ostern, nur ein bißchen verschwommen') tell their own story. The
delicate nuances of behaviour illuminate fully and painfully the change in
economic circumstances which has sent the girls off into quite different worlds.

Seghers has been criticized for being too unspecific in her depiction of
the collapse of Ziegler's business and the ruinous effect on the family, as well
as for giving a far too unanalytical and imprecisely located portrayal of what
might befall the unsuspecting under the inexorable harshness of capitalism.
Typical of these strictures are the comments of the GDR critic Friedrich
Albrecht, who writes that the tale is 'so allgemein und andeutend gehalten,
daß unklar bleibt, in welcher historischen Phase die Handlung spielt. [...] die
Umstände lassen lediglich die Grundzüge kapitalistischer Verhältnisse
erkennen.'[37]

Reservations of this kind seem relevant now only in the context of what
appears increasingly to be a parochial debate inspired by ideological
imperatives about what a revolutionary socialist literature should and should
not be. What is of the foremost importance to Seghers at the moment of
writing 'Die Ziegler' is not, as her later BPRS colleagues would have
demanded, to disclose unambiguously the precise nature of the brutal
mechanisms of capitalism, but what they occasion in terms of human
behaviour and response. Her keen and poetic eye for the significant detail
stands her in good stead here.   In passing but telling reference to the
crumbling of orderly routine, to unwonted carelessness in matters of dress, the

collapse of a man's world, and with it the fear of the downward slide of a whole imperilled, precariously situated class, are registered: 'Elliser ging um zehn Uhr eins trinken. Er hatte ihn mal ohne Weste mit einem verrutschten Vorhemd getroffen' (p. 77).

But the harsher edge of capitalism can, as Brecht once remarked about the struggle against fascism, also mobilize what is most human and courageous in man. It would go against the understated grain in Seghers's writing for this to manifest itself as extravagant gesture. We would look more to the discrete tenderness of a scene such as that between Marie and her father at the moment when it is clear that he is dying: 'Er streichelte ihre Hände, ihr Haar. Er hatte vielleicht gerade keine Schmerzen, da wollte er ihr etwas Gutes tun; er redete leise auf sie ein, ihre Hand in der seinen, und betupfte mit dem Daumen ihre Knöchel.' (p. 102) Little enough. But in this tiny gesture is caught a rare moment of humanity in a story of otherwise unremitting gloom.

In 'Selbstanzeige' Anna Seghers had acknowledged that her earliest stories were populated with 'verzweifelte und untergehende Menschen' and that 'Wenn man schreibt, muß man so schreiben, daß man hinter der Verzweiflung die Möglichkeit und hinter dem Untergang den Ausweg spürt'. The implicit note of self-reproach levelled at what she had written up till then offers an interesting perspective from which to examine *Aufstand der Fischer von St. Barbara*, published in 1928.[38]

This, her first longer work, does not live off expectations about its outcome; all is over in the opening sentences. The fishermen's revolt and its prime movers have been crushed. Order and the old economic injustices have been restored. And yet, in a metaphor which draws its strength from the personification of an abstraction, it is clear that something crucial has changed. Awareness born of defeat has planted a tiny grain of hope for the future:

> Aber längst, nachdem die Soldaten zurückgezogen, die
> Fischer auf der See waren, saß der Aufstand noch auf
> dem leeren, weißen, sommerlich kahlen Marktplatz und
> dachte ruhig an die Seinigen, die er geboren,
> aufgezogen, gepflegt und behütet hatte für das, was für
> sie am besten war.
>
>   (p. 7)

It is difficult to conceive that Anna Seghers was not, at least subconsciously, affected by Hauptmann's *Die Weber* in creating the harrowing detail of the fishermen's revolt and its outcome. Their suffering and unequal struggle against the remote, barely identifiable and comprehensible economic and political forces which control their lives, as well as the inevitable retribution which an orgy of destruction born of sheer frustration brings, all recall the plight of Hauptmann's weavers. If, however, as Friedrich Spielhagen said of *Die Weber*, the collective deprivation of the community may be said to be the 'hero' of this tale, unlike in the earlier work it is possible in *Aufstand der Fischer von St. Barbara* to identify dominant individual figures.

Hull and Andreas, who had been singled out in the opening paragraph, are at the philosophical heart of the tale. In Hull, Seghers has created an agitator of unspecified political provenance who sits uneasily in the tradition of such characters in socialist literature. He is a figure of contradictions to which the reader, but not the inhabitants of St. Barbara, are privy. With a reputation built in previous struggles, Hull is perceived by the fishing community as a mysterious and messianic figure: his voice 'versetzte [...] jeden, der sie anhörte, in Erregung, erweckte in jedem etwas wie Hoffnung' (p. 35). He himself, however, is fraught with self-doubt, his will and energy on the verge of exhaustion. At points he is overcome with that mixture of melancholy and despair verging on the existential which we shall next encounter in *Transit*: 'Plötzlich, als ob sie in einem Winkel der Kammer gehockt und nur gewartet hätte, bis er ganz wach war, fiel solche Traurigkeit an ihn, fest an die Kehle' (p. 15).

As the revolt gathers momentum, his influence on events slackens and his significance declines. But what is in process of being extinguished in Hull is rekindled in Andreas. He is another of those early Seghers creations who are oppressed by, but struggle against, the narrowness of their circumstances. Twice, in refusing to knuckle under, he tastes the euphoria of rebellion. As he tips a basket of fish at the feet of a truculent foreman, as he brandishes a bread knife at the neck of a captain who has been hounding him, he briefly experiences what self-assertion and the restoration of pride in the face of unreasonable power may bring: 'einen Augenblick war alles anders gewesen' (p. 12).

This momentary insight is vital to the meaning of the novel as a whole. *Aufstand der Fischer von St. Barbara* yields no easy lessons for the struggles of revolutionary socialism. Its harsh depiction of the manifest injustices inflicted on the fishing community declines to sentimentalize or heroicize their helplessness. As the fishermen abandon their strike and put out to sea again, they have gained nothing in material terms. And yet nothing can ever be quite the same again. As Andreas is shot while fleeing his pursuers, his body falls to the ground but his spirit runs on: 'aber etwas in ihm rannte noch immer weiter, rannte und rannte und zerstob schließlich nach allen Richtungen in die Luft in unbeschreiblicher Freude und Leichtigkeit' (p. 64).

In Andreas's gestures of rebellion and, paradoxically, in his death, is articulated a muted but unmistakable note of hope. In his dying vision we are meant to sense, as we are in the story's opening metaphor and in the eyes of the defeated fishermen (their wives detect there 'etwas Neues, Festes, Dunkles', p. 58), that this is not the last word, that a silent solidarity has arisen which leaves the way open for future struggles. How plausible this is, on the other hand, is debatable. While not expressed with the unambivalence the BPRS would have expected of her, and without the vast draught of confidence we find in the concluding lines of *Das siebte Kreuz*, the optimism which Anna Seghers brings to bear here in these isolated observations seems to be at odds with the grim picture she draws of the realities of economic and political power attendant upon the fishermen's struggle and its outcome. One is left with the impression that the refusal to abandon hope for the human spirit contradicts the facts as depicted.

Die Gefährten was the last work Anna Seghers was to publish in Germany until after the war. She hoped it would take her writing a step forward by not merely depicting suffering and despair but also offering an 'Ausweg' to them. In giving the work an exact historical and political location she moves away from the tightly circumscribed but deliberately imprecise setting of *Aufstand*.[39] The novel fails, however, to live up to the challenge it sets itself. Seghers attempts to do justice to the plight of those political refugees who had flooded into Germany in the 1920s ('Wir horchten erregt ihren Berichten, die damals vielen in Deutschland wie Greuelmärchen erschienen'[40]) by creating a plethora of players and settings (the by no means exhaustive 'Personenverzeichnis' lists some twenty-three characters from Hungary, Poland, Italy, Bulgaria and China) with frequent and rapid switches between them. This panoptic view inhibits proper fleshing out of figure and situation. In too many characters the personal and psychological complexities involved in engagement with a political ideology as ruthlessly demanding as Communism are either ignored or cut down to formulistic simplicities. The single biggest problem for any communist of conviction who has not eliminated all human response – the expendability of the individual which the doctrine of ends and means might actually entail – never hoves even remotely into view.

While it may well be much easier to write about the God who failed than the God of whom fervent expectations are made, one cannot help comparing *Die Gefährten* and its waxworks selection of valiant and battered socialist heroes with the anguished, ingenuous and betrayed characters of a novel such as *Darkness at Noon*. Quite apart from the fascination which Rubashov exerts, Koestler's minor characters – little Loewy, or Arlova with her torpid sensuality – lodge themselves in the soul of the reader, their image permanently vibrant. Who on the other hand will remember Pali or Liau Han-tschi, the ready-made Communists devoid of all doubts and uncertainties? Only the raw-boned peasant revolutionary Dudoff or the bourgeois intellectual Steiner racked by indecision and vacillation which may, intermittently (one thinks of *Transit*) have been Anna Seghers's own, rise briefly above the two-dimensional to make some more lasting impact.

It would be a mistake, however, to regard *Die Gefährten* as being entirely without redeeming features. As in all her attempts to depict the struggle of the exploited to assert themselves, Seghers never flies in the face of the historical and political realities of the time. She is unsparing in her presentation of the systematic, ubiquitous triumph of the forces of reaction, the crushing of the aspirations of the oppressed.

But where, on the other hand, is there in *Die Gefährten* the 'Ausweg' she had promised in 'Selbstanzeige'? She had clearly intended that the appeal of the communist ideal which she attempts to articulate explicitly in her work for the first time might, despite the setbacks to which it is subject, carry the day in terms of the promise it holds out. It does not. Seghers fails to breathe life into the bearers and incorporators of that ideal. Nor does she, unlike in her most accomplished works — one thinks especially of *Das siebte Kreuz* and the quiet, summarizing affirmation of its final lines — succeed in compensating for this failing by drawing on her greatest strength as a novelist: the ability to enact and explore those deeper indomitable qualities of the human spirit which lie beyond ideology.

But there is, nonetheless, in *Die Gefährten* and, indeed, in all of her work at this time which depicts the struggle against fascism, a certain honesty about its rampant ascendancy. Only rarely does she permit the victims a victory. There is the Chinese driver Wu Pei-li in the story 'Der Führerschein' who rebels by driving both himself and the Japanese officers he has been forced to chauffeur into the river.[41] Or Woytschuk in 'Bauern von Hruschowo' who, we are told, in an act of simple-minded communist heroics takes his scythe in his hand and 'ermähte [...] seinen Weg nach Rußland, wo er hinkam',[42] although there is also something of a lapse here in narrative taste and credibility which the less generous critic might see as pointing ahead to the wood-cut simplicities of the 'Friedensgeschichten' of 1950.

What one may deduce from this discussion is that, apart from *Die Gefährten* where the common ideal of communist solidarity proves an entirely unpersuasive link for the novel's fragmented, episodic structure, Anna Seghers, in what she wrote in the late 1920s and early 1930s, seldom sported ideological allegiances on her sleeve; she would never be tempted to express outright sentiments such as those of Johannes R. Becher in 1930: 'Ich legte ab meinen Namen. / Ich heiße: Genosse. / Ich trat unter die rote Fahne der Komintern.'[43] 'Auf dem Wege zur amerikanischen Botschaft', for instance, a story at first glance about a protest march in support of Sacco and Vanzetti, Italian immigrants and anarchists executed in 1927 for their alleged involvement in murdering a paymaster and his guard, is memorable not because of its political statement, but because of an adventurous narrative technique deployed to catch the shift and flow of conflicting concern and emotion in four of the figures caught up in the demonstration. The Sacco and Vanzetti case was an important rallying point for the left. But here, in Seghers's story, potential for political capital is pushed into the background. In the interior monologue of characters described simply as 'der Fremde', 'der

Mann', 'die Frau', 'der Kleine', dimly articulated concern for the fate of Sacco and Vanzetti takes second place to private anxieties and preoccupations. As is the case with the narrator of Nicholas Born's *Die erdabgewandte Seite der Geschichte* (1976) and his distanced participation – fed by a confusion of response – in the protest against the visit of the Shah to Berlin in June 1967, apparent political motivation and involvement are not quite what they seem on the surface of things.[44]

This examination of Anna Seghers's early work has attempted to argue that while the commitment to revolutionary socialism she demonstrated by joining the KPD in 1928 was total, she declined to follow wholeheartedly in her writing the prescriptions laid down about content and form by the BPRS and succeeded in maintaining a strong degree of artistic independence. This raises a key question with regard to not only Seghers's work up until 1933, but to all she wrote. It is a question which does not have a straightforward answer, nor is it one which can be answered in terms of linear, chronological development. One can, for instance, at various points in Anna Seghers's life single out works which richly deserve the faintly derogatory title 'Die kommunistische Erzählerin Anna Seghers' conferred by Marcel Reich-Ranicki. The early work *Die Gefährten*, and the later novels *Das Vertrauen* and *Die Entscheidung*, as well as a story such as 'Der Traktorist', would fit this bill. It is clear that *Die Gefährten* was too much in thrall to a desire to erect a monument to the unsung heroes of a failed revolution, and that much of what she wrote in the GDR was the product of how she would have liked history to have been, rather than the fruit of dispassionate observation of it. Equally, however, we must not forget that a decade after *Die Gefährten* she was to write *Das siebte Kreuz* and *Transit*, works quite uncluttered by ideological constraints and two of the finest novels written in German in the twentieth century.

In formulating considerations of this kind, one would wish strongly to take issue with Kurt Batt who suggests that her work from the end of the 1920s on was determined by 'die jeweilige Strategie der Partei'.[45] In fact, throughout her life, her work moved between the tensions of writing in a way which articulated the social concerns which had motivated her to join the Party and the desire to allow her creativity – her attraction to fantasy, fairy-tale elements, the strange and the bizarre – to have free play. Anna Seghers's work does, of course, at various points fall prey to the ideological, but it is overwhelmingly her dramatization of the eternally human, of what was 'unangreifbar' and 'unverletzbar' (we move again to the final lines of *Das siebte Kreuz*), and not least the unfathomable mystery of man which dominates. She was never guilty of the crime of which, in her correspondence with Georg Lukács in the late 1930s, she accused certain of her BPRS colleagues: 'Sie hatten es fertiggebracht, die Welt ganz zu *ent*zaubern.'[46]

Odd to reflect that this was precisely – if much more vituperatively – what Gottfried Benn, from the opposite end of the ideological and cultural spectrum, had been arguing at the beginning of the 1930s in his essay on Heinrich Mann and 'Die neue literarische Saison'.[47]

NOTES

[1]Walter Janka, *Schwierigkeiten mit der Wahrheit* (Reinbek: Rowohlt, 1989).

[2]*Das siebte Kreuz* was first published in 1942 by 'El Libro Libre', the publishing house founded by Walter Janka in Mexico.

[3]See Marcel Reich-Ranicki, 'Die kommunistische Erzählerin Anna Seghers', in *Deutsche Literatur in West und Ost* (Munich: Piper, 1963), pp. 354-85 and Peter Jokostra, 'Offener Brief an einen Verleger', *Die Welt*, 1. August 1962, reprinted in *Anna Seghers. Materialienbuch*, ed. by Peter Roos and Friderike J. Hassauer-Roos, (Darmstadt and Neuwied: Luchterhand, 1977), pp. 11-14.

[4]Henryk Kreisch, 'Für Anna Seghers', *Neue Deutsche Literatur*, 28, no. 11 (1980), 34.

[5]Kurt Batt, *Anna Seghers, Versuch über Entwicklung und Werke* (Leipzig: Reclam, 1980), p. 14.

[6]The most thoroughly researched account of Anna Seghers's early years and family circumstances is to be found in Jörg B. Bilke's article 'Auf der Suche nach Netty Reiling'. *Blätter der Carl-Zuckmayer-Gesellschaft*, 6, no. 4 (Nov. 1980), 186-201.

[7]*Die Toten auf der Insel Djal. Sage aus dem Holländischen. Nacherzählt von Anna Seghers* was published in the feuilleton of the Christmas 1924 number of the *Frankfurter Zeitung*. The story was thought to be lost until discovered, simultaneously, by Jörg Bernhard Bilke and Sigrid Bock. It was first republished in *die horen*, 23, no. 3 (1978), 128-31. Also in *Blätter der Carl-Zuckmayer-Gesellschaft*, 6, no. 4 (Nov. 1980), 223-26.

[8]Netty Reiling (Anna Seghers), *Jude und Judentum im Werke Rembrandts* (Leipzig: Reclam, 1983).

[9]In an interview with Christa Wolf 1965, in *Anna Seghers, Aufsätze, Ansprachen, Essays 1954-1979, Gesammelte Werke in Einzelausgaben* (Berlin und Weimar: Aufbau, 1980) IV, 411.

[10]Wieland Herzfelde, 'Anna Seghers zu ihrem 50. Geburtstag', in *Heute und Morgen* II (1950), 678.

[11]Seghers, 'Der Ausflug der toten Mädchen' in *Erzählungen 1926-1944, Gesammelte Werke in Einzelausgaben* (Berlin and Weimar: Aufbau, 1981), XI, p. 362.

[12]Seghers, 'Bücher und Verwandlungen', *Neues Deutschland*, 21. September 69. Reprinted in *Deutsch als Fremdsprache*, 17 (Sonderheft 1980), 1.

[13]Helga Gallas, *Marxistische Literaturtheorie, Kontroversen im Bund proletarisch-revolutionärer Schriftsteller* (Neuwied and Berlin, Luchterhand, 1971).

[14]O(tto) Biha (Oto Bihalji-Merin), 'Die proletarische Literatur in Deutschland', in *Literatur der Weltrevolution*, no. 3, August 1931, p. 106. A photocopy of this article is reproduced in *Sozialistische Zeitschrift für Kunst und Gesellschaft*, 11/12, (1972), 64-82. Page references here refer to the original article.

[15]'Bericht über Tätigkeit des Bundes proletarisch-revolutionärer Schriftsteller im Jahre 1929', in *Zur Tradition der sozialistischen Literatur in Deutschland. Eine Auswahl von Dokumenten* (Berlin and Weimar: Aufbau, 1967), pp. 166-67.

[16]Biha, p. 119. Seghers attended the Charkow Congress and presumably was present at Biha's address. See her interview with Wilhelm Girnus in 1967, in *Aufsätze, Ansprachen, Essays 1954-1979*, p. 435.

[17]'Anna Seghers', in Christa Wolf, *Die Dimension des Autors. Essays und Aufsätze, Reden und Gespräche 1959-1985* (Darmstadt and Neuwied: Luchterhand, 1987), p. 332.

[18]*Die Toten auf der Insel Djal, die horen*, 23, no. 3. See Bilke, 'Auf der Suche nach Netty Reiling', p. 62.

[19]Paul Wiens, 'Für Anna Seghers', in *Neue deutsche Literatur*, 28, no. 11 (November 1980), 25.

[20]See the interview with Christa Wolf (1965), op. cit., p. 418.

[21]She notes that the figure of the 'Pfarrer' in *Die Toten auf der Insel Djal* is the first of a series of 'furchtlose Männer' in Seghers's work who are 'gelassen, kühn, frei [...] unberührt durch die Schicksale, die sie heraufbeschwören. Unbeschwert von irdischen Bindungen. Kühl. Nüchtern. Allein. Zum Abenteuer bereit. Gebrannt von der Gier nach Leben [...]'. See 'Nachwort' to Seghers's *Ausgewählte Erzählungen* (Darmstadt and Neuwied: Luchterhand, 1983), p. 366.

[22]Seghers, *Briefe an Leser* (Berlin and Weimar: Aufbau, 1970), p. 7.

[23]   Christa Wolf, 'Foreword' to *Jude und Judentum*, pp. 10-11.

[24]In Seghers, *Erzählungen 1926-1944*, in *Gesammelte Werke in Einzelausgaben* (Berlin and Weimar: Aufbau, 1981), IX, 5. Page references are to this edition.

[25]Seghers, 'Selbstanzeige', in *Aufsätze, Ansprachen, Essays 1927-1953*, in *Gesammelte Werke in Einzelausgaben* (Berlin and Weimar: Aufbau, 1984), XIII, 7.

[26]Friedrich Albrecht, 'Woher sie kommen, wohin sie gehen. Zu Problemen der Menschengestaltung bei Anna Seghers', *Weimarer Beiträge*, 35, no. 1 (1989), 5.

[27]Anna Seghers, 'Woher sie kommen, wohin sie gehen', in *Aufsätze, Ansprachen, Essays 1954-1979*, pp. 203-04.

[28]Anonymous review of *Auf dem Wege zur amerikanischen Botschaft und andere Erzählungen* (Berlin: Kiepenheuer, 1930), in *Die rote Fahne*, no. 21 (1931).

[29]See note 25.

[30]*Briefe an Leser*, pp. 7-8.

[31]Bertolt Brecht, *Gesammelte Werke*, 8. vols. (Frankfurt/M.: Suhrkamp, 1967), I, 4.

[32]Seghers, *Briefe an Leser*, p. 8.

[33]Hans Fallada, *Kleiner Mann — was nun?* (Reinbek: Rowohlt, 1968), p. 216f.

[34]See Friedrich Albrecht, *Die Erzählerin Anna Seghers 1926-1932* (Berlin: Rütten & Loening, 1965), p. 47ff.

[35]*Kleiner Mann — was nun?*, p. 239.

[36]Seghers, *Aufsätze, Ansprachen, Essays 1954-1979*, p. 433.

[37]Albrecht, *Die Erzählerin Anna Seghers 1926-1932*, p. 55.

[38]Seghers, *Aufstand der Fischer von St. Barbara / Die Gefährten*, in *Werke*, 10 vols (Darmstadt and Neuwied: Luchterhand, 1977), p. 7. Quotations are from this edition.

[39]In a letter of 18 May 1957, in reply to a query about the location of the story, Anna Seghers wrote, 'Wie ich die Novelle "Aufstand der Fischer von St. Barbara" schrieb, tat ich das mit einer sehr starken Verbundenheit mit allem, was Meer und Fischer heißt, auch mit gewissen primitiven Kenntnissen, die ich mir seit meiner Kindheit, ziemlich unbewußt, angeeignet hatte. Ich bin vom Rhein und sah jeden Tag den Rhein mit Neid an, weil er bald in Holland ins Meer fließen wird. Später kam ich in die Bretagne. Die von Ihnen gesuchte Insel schwimmt wahrscheinlich zwischen beiden Gegenden herum.' In *Briefe an Leser*, pp. 10-11.

[40]Seghers, 'Ein Wort zur zweiten Auflage', in *Die Gefährten* (Berlin: bb Taschenbuch, 1959), p. 6.

[41]In *Erzählungen 1926-1944*, pp. 186-87.

[42]Ibid., p. 157.

[43]See the poem 'Genosse!' in Johannes R. Becher, *Gesammelte Werke*, vol. 3, *Gedichte 1926-1935* (Berlin and Weimar: Aufbau, 1966), p. 288.

[44]See Nicholas Born, *Die erdabgewandte Seite der Geschichte* (Reinbek: Rowohlt, 1979), p. 46f.

[45]Kurt Batt, *Anna Seghers. Versuch über Entwicklung und Werke*, p. 61.

[46]See letter to Georg Lukács of 28 June 1938, in *Anna Seghers. Aufsätze, Ansprachen, Essays 1927-1953* (Berlin and Weimar: Aubau, 1984), p. 75.

[47]In *Gottfried Benn. Gesammelte Werke*, ed. by Dieter Wellershoff, IV: *Reden und Aufsätze* (Wiesbaden: Limes, 1968), pp. 974-94.

Gertrud von le Fort

12

Gertrud von le Fort's *Hymnen an die Kirche*

Margaret Ives

Like Annette von Droste-Hülshoff (1797-1848), who in many respects could be regarded as her spiritual ancestor, Gertrud von le Fort (1876-1971) came originally from the north of Germany. Her family, too, was an aristocratic one: her father owned large estates in Mecklenburg and in the course of his military duties − for he was an officer in the Prussian army − was stationed at Minden, Berlin and Hildesheim. Perhaps because of these frequent changes of location, Gertrud had very little formal education before the age of fourteen, but from 1908 onwards was nevertheless allowed to attend university and read history and theology at Heidelberg, Marburg and Berlin. It was during her studies at Heidelberg that she first encountered the theologian Ernst Troeltsch (1865-1923) whose lectures on the history and philosophy of religion were to prove an important turning-point in her life. Although she had been brought up as a Protestant and although Troeltsch himself remained within this confession, under his tuition Gertrud gradually developed a deep understanding of the older Catholic tradition to which she felt increasingly drawn. She did not actually become a Catholic until 1926, but the volume of poetry she published in 1924 under the title *Hymnen an die Kirche* is, in effect, the record of her conversion. Generally well received and favourably reviewed in the Catholic press of the time, the poems have since been depreciated as esoteric in conception and scarcely intelligible to those who do not share the same religious persuasion. While it would be tedious to refute all such negative criticism in detail, an unbiased approach can, I believe, lead us to discover a writer who, despite the anagogic nature of much of her subject matter, still has significance for us today.[1]

The *Hymnen an die Kirche* consist of three main sections, prefaced by a prose introduction and a prologue. The prose introduction explains the character of the dialogue between the soul and the Church, whereby the soul, at first argumentative and recalcitrant, finally becomes a receptive listener; in the prologue the soul complains of her isolation and imprisonment within the confines of the self and wonders how she can escape into the depth, breadth and catholicity of true religious experience. 'Immer, immer bin ich nur in mir,' she cries in deep spiritual anguish and separation from God. She thus turns, in the first main section, to the Church, but the approach is difficult, since the Church demands silence and surrender, the total suspension of reason, unbelief and individuality. The demands seem impossible, but slowly the soul comes to accept the violence done to her cherished defences and is able to praise the Church in a spirit of awe and wonder. In a sub-section entitled 'Das Beten der Kirche' the prayers of the Church are said to sustain all life on this planet and are linked to the Sacred Mystery of the Incarnation. This leads directly to an avowal of the Church as the Mystical Body of Christ, after which, in a passage of great beauty, the Church takes complete charge of the soul as the latter finishes her pilgrimage. In the next section the Church then reveals her secrets as the festivals of the traditional Christian calendar are each invoked in turn, and the mood becomes more and more liturgical. Finally, in the third part, the poet speaks of the Day of Judgement when a shocked silence will descend upon the world and the meaning of everything will be revealed. In a vision similar to that of Newman's *Dream of Gerontius* everything dissolves into eternity as the Church is at last united with her God.[2]

The hymns are thus really a sequence of rhapsodic odes which chart le Fort's own progression from doubt and misgiving towards acceptance and serenity. That this is a complex and arduous process can be seen from the fact that, although in 'Das Jahr der Kirche' there are two poems written in the form of a litany, she nowhere lapses into that simplicity of style that occasionally characterizes Novalis's *Hymnen an die Nacht*.

> Hinüber wall ich,
> Und jede Pein
> Wird einst ein Stachel
> Der Wollust sein

is not the voice of the twentieth-century seeker after God. Instead, we find in the first part a series of agonized statements, questions and interjections, often straightforward enough syntactically, but shot through with inconsistency and contradiction. Then, as we move towards certainty, the language becomes ecstatic with long flowing lines, enjambement, and convoluted syntax. The close of the third poem in 'Die letzten Dinge' reads:

> Denn an dem, was du nicht siehst, sollst du mich erkennen,
> und an dem, was dir bange macht,
> *soll mich deine Seele glauben.*

> (my italics)

This passage, defiant in its difficulty and uncompromising in its meaning, immediately challenges the reader. The imagery, too, is everywhere very unusual and striking, often with rapid changes of pattern reminiscent of Hölderlin and in the same way redolent of spiritual turmoil. A passage in the fourth poem of the first section 'An die Kirche' captures very forcefully the fear and terror of the soul no longer able to avoid confrontation with the Divine:

> Du hast meine Ufer weggerissen,
> und hast Gewalt angetan der Erde zu meinen Füßen!
> Meine Schiffe treiben im Meer:
> alle meine Anker hast du gelichtet!
> Die Ketten meiner Gedanken sind zerbrochen,
> sie hängen wie Wildnis im Abgrund.

The desperate attempts to comprehend a seemingly incomprehensible Church are compared in the previous poem of this sequence to those of a climber on 'Halden von Eis', in the eighth poem the soul appears as a frightened deer in the forest of dark passions, and later on the prayers of the Church are likened to ships setting sail on a sea of fog, surely a very telling simile for the adventure of faith. It could be objected that, in many places throughout the work, le Fort is using a code, that of traditional Catholic theology, which has no validity for many readers. On the other hand, if we enter into the spirit of her quest, as she asks us to do in the introduction, we cannot help but experience with her the revelation of a spiritual dimension or, as Rilke called it, 'der andere Bereich'.

It is, however, through a close examination of lexis that we begin to discover Gertrud von le Fort at her most powerful. The outstanding feature here is paradox. The soul laments in the third poem of the opening section that the Church orders 'Blindheit, daß ich sehe' and 'Taubheit, daß ich höre'. In the sixth poem the Church replies:

> Was ich zerbreche, das ist nicht zerbrochen,
>   und was ich in den Staub beuge, das hebe ich empor!
> Ich bin dir gnadelos geworden aus Gnade
>   und erbarmungslos aus Erbarmen.

In the poems of 'Heiligkeit der Kirche' the saints are referred to as 'Wasser, die aufwärts fließen gegen die Berge' and 'Feuer, die ohne Herdstatt brennen'. By contrast, in the poem beginning 'Wer errettet meine Seele vor den Worten der Menschen?' we are told that the material blessings of this world are no guarantee of satisfaction:

> Wir sind verdurstet bei euren Quellen,
>   wir sind verhungert bei eurer Speise,
>   wir sind blind geworden bei euren Lampen!

The reader is thus constantly forced to stop and ponder what is going on in the text. The committed Christian will doubtless be reminded of the teaching at the heart of the Gospels. The words of the Magnificat ('He hath put down the mighty from their seats and exalted them of low degree', Luke 1:52), of the Sermon on the Mount ('Blessed are they that mourn, for they shall be comforted', Matthew 5:4), and of St John's Gospel ('He that loveth his life shall lose it, and he that hateth his life in this world shall keep it unto life eternal', John 12:25) spring to mind, as does also the Pauline reminder that 'the foolishness of God is wiser than men and the weakness of God is stronger than men' (I Corinthians 1:25). For, as Paul emphasizes, the religion of Christ crucified 'unto the Jews a stumbling-block and unto the Greeks foolishness' (I Corinthians 1:23) is a religion of paradox, and by speaking in these terms le Fort shows that she has penetrated its deepest secrets. At the same time she also compels the uncommitted to re-examine their position. Is it not possible that what we call illumination *can* so dazzle us with its glamour and glitter that we become blind to spiritual insight? Is it not possible that we *do* need the isolation of complete darkness to rediscover our selves again? These are uncomfortable questions, but ones which need to be asked in face of the vanity and shallowness of so many of our affluent life-styles. By drawing our attention to a supremely different set of values running as a counterpoint throughout human history, Gertrud von le Fort admonishes us for our short-sightedness and lack of perspective. Elsewhere space and time are fused together as the poet contemplates both the life of the Church and the presence of the Divine from Everlasting to Everlasting. In 'Heiligkeit der Kirche' the Church announces:

> ich habe noch Tau in meinen Haaren
> aus Tälern der Menschenfrühe

and claims to be

> ...die Straße aller ihrer Straßen:
> auf mir ziehen die Jahrtausende zu Gott!

Very occasionally the aridity of human experience bereft of God is expressed in linguistic compression and tension that points forward to Celan. Thus, in the second poem of 'Corpus Christi Mysticum' the extent of human anguish becomes a geographical dimension:

> Sie rufen sich von Schweigen zu Schweigen,
> sie küssen sich von Einsamkeit zu Einsamkeit.
> Sie lieben sich *tausend Schmerzen weit* von ihren Seelen.
>
> (my italics)

But whereas Celan, after Auschwitz, can find no way out of the abyss into which the human race seems to have fallen, le Fort in the Weimar Republic is still able to ascend to spiritual heights to which she now invites us to follow her. Having reached the mountain-tops, she begins to create her own vocabulary. In 'Advent' at the beginning of 'Das Jahr der Kirche' the soul is addressed as 'Leiderin and 'Sehnerin', in 'Litanei zum Fest des allerheiligsten Herzens' the idea of the world as a wilderness is tautened into 'Weltnis', and there are a number of equally bold compounds such as 'Rotdorn' and 'Schmerzdorn'. In 'Das Königsfest Christi' ordinary verbs no longer suffice, and instead we read:

> Er *mächtigt* in ihrer Rede,
> und er *gewaltigt* in ihrem Schweigen;
> Er *einsamt* in ihrer Verlassenheit,
> und er *herrlicht* in ihrer Ehre.
>
> (my italics)

Admittedly, the force of a compound such as 'Schmerzdorn' may be lost on someone who does not apprehend the reference to the Crown of Thorns presented to Christ in mockery, but the sheer audacity of the neologisms in the lines just quoted leaves us in no doubt that these are no mere rhetorical tricks, still less 'sounding brass' or 'tinkling cymbal' (I Corinthians 13:1), but the accents of an authentic voice speaking with authority.

If Annette von Droste-Hülshoff's collection *Das geistliche Jahr* ranks, according to one critic, among 'die bedeutendste religiöse Lyrik des 19. Jahrhunderts', then these poems of Gertrud von le Fort are surely a significant achievement of twentieth-century spirituality.[3] At the same time, a comparison is illuminating. As is well known, Droste-Hülshoff's work by her own testimony is not for the pious; it is riddled with doubt, scepticism and guilt over her inability to believe.[4] The opening lines of 'Am Pfingstmontage' with their reference to the Gospel appointed for the day ('He that believeth not is condemned already', John 3:18) form a famous passage:

> Ist es der Glaube nur, dem du verheißen,
> Dann bin ich tot.
> O Glaube, wie lebend'gen Blutes Kreisen,
> Er tut mir not
> Ich hab ihn nicht.

The staccato statements here speak of hopelessness and despair. Unable to bring the basic tenets of Christianity concerning Incarnation and Resurrection into line with the findings of nineteenth-century science and scholarship, Droste-Hülshoff can ultimately only throw herself on the mercy of God in a heartfelt plea for forgiveness:

> Was durch Verstandes Irren ich verbrochen,
> Ich hab es ja
> Gebüßt so manchen Tag und manche Wochen;
> So sei mir nah!

It is a position le Fort has known, but has soon transcended. In 'Heimweg zur Kirche' she is able to make an unconditional surrender:

> Du sprichst zu den Zweifelnden: "Schweiget!"
> und zu den Fragenden: "Kniet nieder!"

Her poem 'Pfingsten' is thus one of proclamation as the Church rejoices:

> Jubel ist mein Name, und Frohlocken ist mein Antlitz:
> ich bin wie eine junge Flur in Kränzen der Morgenröte!

In place of the tears and cold stone of the Droste-Hülshoff poem with its emphasis on judgement, sin and fear, there is a welter of natural springtime imagery as the world and the Church experience new life:

> Er ist über mich gekommen,
>   wie das Knospen über den Strauch kommt
> ....
> Ich blühe mit feurigen Zungen,
>   ich blühe mit flammendem Vollbringen:
>   ich blühe aus dem heil'gen Geist des Herrn!

It would be a mistake to dismiss this as facile evangelism. Le Fort, too, writes out of the depths of a spiritual crisis, albeit one of a very different nature from that of her nineteenth-century counterpart. The well-regulated world of the Prussian military aristocracy had crashed resoundingly about her ears in 1918; the family estates had been confiscated after her brother was implicated in the Kapp putsch of 1920. The collapse of the old order thus seemed to her, as to many, to herald the collapse of all civilized standards and behaviour, and the chaos, confusion and intermittent anarchy of the Weimar Republic did little to alleviate her despondency. There was, furthermore, in many intellectual and theological circles a sense of doom and foreboding. Spengler's *Untergang des Abendlandes* had appeared during the years 1918-1922 prophesying the decline of the Western world and the subsequent rise of Asiatic and African powers. In this situation Karl Barth, appointed as extraordinary professor at Göttingen in 1921, had already begun a radical questioning of received theology which he believed to be essentially erroneous, especially since the Enlightenment, in its attempts to emulate science, reason and logic in its exposition of the workings of the Divine. Instead, Barth held that the supremacy and transcendence of God rendered all aspirations of human reason worthless. God's sole revelation is in Jesus Christ, and the Word of God, which it is the duty of all Christians to proclaim, is His one and only means of communication with Man.[5] Similarly Tillich, at this stage of his development, declared Western civilization to be under the judgement of God, perhaps even approaching Apocalypse. The comfortable 'private' religion, which had come to be endorsed by Christian churches of all denominations, was no longer adequate; fear and trembling were the only fitting responses to the possibility of a new Revelation. Moreover, apologetics were outdated; 'Nicht Verteidigung, sondern Verkündigung' was now the most urgent necessity, for without a genuine religious content cultures and civilizations, according to Tillich, lose their vitality and perish.[6] However, while Barth preached a return to the Prophetic teaching of the Bible, of which he considered the sixteenth-century Protestant reformers to be the most vigorous exponents, Tillich – for a time at least – and le Fort's mentor Troeltsch strove to establish a new cultural synthesis held together by a new spirituality. Troeltsch's sympathy with the Catholic tradition, which he saw as a great repository of spiritual values and thus an instrument of cultural unity, strengthened le Fort at a time when, in her own search for stability, she became increasingly interested in contemporary movements of Catholic revival. An encounter with the Catholic publication *Hochland* which she had bought by chance to read on a train journey seems to have been another decisive influence.

> Ich befand mich... im geistigen Raum einer Katholischen Zeitschrift, aber gleichzeitig in meiner eigensten Heimat... weil die ganze Haltung dieser Zeitschrift meine teuersten Besitztümer, das Erbe meines frommen, protestantischen Elternhauses, gleichsam einzuschließen schien... ich erlebte die geistige Haltung einer Katholischen Zeitschrift als universale, christliche Geistes- und Liebeshaltung, ich erlebte die umfangende, die mütterliche Gebärde des Katholischen – ich erlebte also damals das Wesen des wahrhaft Katholischen überhaupt.[7]

Like Newman before her, whose studies of Church history during his leadership of the Oxford Movement in nineteenth-century Britain convinced him of the need to leave the Church of England and return to Rome not as a rejection of Anglican values but as their fulfilment, le Fort felt that by converting she was not abandoning the Lutheranism of her youth but uniting it once again with the mainstream from which it had deviated. This is graphically expressed in the first poem of 'Heimweg zur Kirche' where she refers to herself as 'ein Reis aus entwurzeltem Stamm' on whom the shadow of the Catholic forest nevertheless lies, and 'eine Schwalbe, die im Herbste nicht heimfand' who hears in the voice of the Catholic Church the wing-beats of the flock to which she belongs.

Seen against this background, the Church becomes for le Fort a bulwark against catastrophe, and again and again she finds images which testify to permanence in an all too unstable world. In 'Heiligkeit der Kirche', the Church is 'ein Fels, der gegen die Ewigkeit abstürzt', the prayers of the Church are like 'tausendjährige Eichen', and her doctrine is 'eine Feste auf uneinnehmbaren Bergen'. While the poet can thus rejoice that she has found her way home and has been welcomed back into the fold, it is vital that she communicate to others what she believes to be their only hope of redemption. To this extent the *Hymnen* are rooted in the 'proclamation theology' of the Weimar Republic. Le Fort here stands alongside such giants as Barth, Troeltsch and Tillich and, like Novalis and Hölderlin during an earlier period of European upheaval, strives to remind her compatriots of their true mission and purpose. As several poems of her next collection *Hymnen an Deutschland* (1926) show, if the confessional divide could be overcome, Germany could once again, she contends, be the seedbed of spiritual salvation, a specially chosen nation tried and tested by years of calamity and suffering. It is easy enough in the light of our knowledge of the deteriorating situation within the late Weimar Republic to view this as either dangerous conservative nonsense or incredible political naïvety. But this is to judge with hindsight... When Hitler and his ideology finally gained supremacy in 1933, le Fort was in no doubt whatsoever as to the magnitude of the disaster. In one of the most moving poems of her *Lyrisches Tagebuch aus den Jahren 1933 bis 1945* she laments that her people have drunk 'vom Wein des Verderbens' and that the Nazi evil has destroyed all that was sacred:

> Es fielen Flügel zur Erde herab, doch niemand fragte:
> Was tat man den heiligen Engeln?
> Tot sind sie, tot! Man hat die Engel ermordet:
> Die Krippe des Heilands ist leer,
> Und wo der Friedensgesang der Himmlischen schwebte,
> Da jagen die Geschwader der wildernden Hölle!

As is well known, le Fort herself retreated in 1939 to Oberstdorf in the Bavarian mountains to practise a form of 'innere Emigration' and remain loyal to her country without compromising her integrity. Again, it is easy enough to criticize. We can understand her sense of deliverance:

> O daß ich gerettet bin in die lichte Wahrheit der Gipfel!
> Hocheinsame Einsamkeit, die du den Menschen
> Majestätisch verschweigst, wie gibst du dem Menschen
>   seine Herrlichkeit wieder!
>   (*Gesang aus den Bergen*)[8]

Yet we remember that for some, such as the Jewish poet Gertrud Kolmar who perished in the extermination camps, such an option was not open, and that others, such as Pastor Kolbe, refused to take it. Who shall say, however, that Gertrud von le Fort's response lacks validity? She reminds us in *Hymnen an die Kirche* that earthly hatreds and enmities look different in the eyes of God:

> Siehe, ihre Grenzen sind wie Mauern aus Schatten vor deinem Antlitz
>   und das Brausen ihres Hasses ist wie ein Gelächter,
> Ihre Waffen sind wie ein Klirren aus Glas,
>   und ihre Siege sind wie Lichter in kleinen Kämmern!

This is not to deny the existence of wars and conflicts, but rather to offer solace to those caught up in them as a prayer that they will be given strength to survive and sow fresh seeds of hope for future generations.

In any case an identification with human suffering lies at the heart of the Christian experience, and in le Fort's work the Church several times speaks of this. In the second poem of 'Die letzten Dinge' the Church describes her anguish and pleads to God to have compassion:

> Meine Ohren werden nicht mehr still von ihrem Jammern,
>   und mein Angesicht ist bleich von ihren Ängsten.

All victims of human sin and folly are her children − 'ich sterbe tausendfach mit meinen Kindern' − and by the same token she is Mother Church, making intercession for us through Mary, Mother of Our Lord. In the long poem 'Litanei zur Regina Pacis' another contrast between Gertrud von le Fort and Annette von Droste-Hülshoff becomes apparent. The earlier poet, beset by her own shortcomings, can only regard Mary with awe approaching fear:

> O Maria, Mutter Christi!
> Nicht zu dir will ich mich wagen,
> Denn du bist mir viel zu helle,
> Meine Seel ergraut vor dir;
>
> Bist mir fast wie zum Entsetzen
> In der fleckenlosen Reine,
> Die du siegreich hast bewahret,
> Da du wandeltest gleich mir.
>   ('Am Feste Mariä Lichtmess')

Gertrud von le Fort, however, sees her as the omnipresent medium of God's mercy and protection:

> Die du bei den Sterbenden warst,
>   als ihr Blut das Schlachtfeld tränkte,

> Erbarme dich des Friedens –
> Die du zu uns in die Keller stiegest,
>   als die grausen Bomben fielen,
> Erbarme dich des Friedens –
>
> Die du dich der armen Frauen annahmst,
>   die geschändet wurden,
> Erbarme, o erbarme dich des Friedens –

Moreover, what le Fort calls 'die mütterliche Gebärde des Katholischen' takes on even greater significance when we consider her views on womanhood *per se*. In her essay *Die ewige Frau* (1934) she sees in the Mystery of the Incarnation, by which God becomes Man through the obedience of a woman, the supreme example of the specifically female virtues of humility, devotion, piety, and self-sacrificial love. That some latter-day feminists find this difficult to accept and consider it yet another variant of the 'Kinder, Küche, Kirche' ideology should not blind us to the fact that le Fort is here adopting a very radical stance. Conflict, war, desecration and destruction all arise in her view from masculine pride, aggression, greed and selfishness; only the previously mentioned maternal values, which are in effect the true Christian values, can provide healing, and in a secular materialist society which has all but forgotten God it is the sacred task of women to point up the alternative. Practically all of le Fort's later fictional narratives in some way exemplify this viewpoint. Veronika in *Das Schweißtuch der Veronika* (1928) rescues her lover from the evil forces at work in Germany; Blanche in *Die Letzte am Schafott* (1931), who is humble and honest enough to confess her terror, is given grace to achieve martyrdom in the midst of revolutionary violence; Claudia in *Die Frau des Pilatus* (1955) recognizes that only by identifying with the persecuted Christians and sharing their fate can she atone for her husband's guilt and complacency. Taken as a whole, le Fort's *oeuvre* forms a very eloquent plea for what we now call the feminization of our value systems, and the Church becomes the all-embracing Mother who is to be our teacher and our guide. Those who see the Roman Catholic Church as a bastion of patriarchy will find this bizarre, but le Fort is not, of course, speaking about an institutionalized hierarchy but about a living religious tradition handed down from generation to generation.

The *Hymnen an die Kirche* must thus be seen as the wellspring of all Gertrud von le Fort's later creativity. With their Psalm-like cadences and ecstatic visions the poems also place her firmly in the line of Christian women mystics writing in German from Hildegard von Bingen (1098-1179) and Mechthild von Magdeburg (1212-1282) onwards. It has rightly been said that, in the grandeur of her conception, 'the church she hymns is no mere organization, dusty and a little soiled with earthly polity; it is the Mystical Body of Christ seen as no poet has seen it for centuries, with all its mystery and magnificence and terror'.[9] Yet even as she proclaimed this Church and fashioned a blueprint for a radical re-appraisal of cultural values, Gertrud von le Fort was well aware that the world was quite capable of rejecting the offer of deliverance and hastening its own destruction. A poem like 'An die Natur' from one of her later collections is spine-chillingly prophetic:

> Diese Kräfte, die man dir entrissen
> Diese scheuen, die man dir entwand –
> Furchtbar werden sie durch unser Wissen,
> Grausam werden sie in unsrer Hand.
>
> Aufgeschreckt zu rasendem Verlangen
> Bieten sie den Tod der Erde feil –[10]

In the last analysis her Muse is a tragic one. In 'Tragische Dichtung' she views it as the greatest task of the poet to keep alive in memory all the good and brave things that have vanished from the world, including the unsullied natural landscape:

> Und in der Ferne die hohen Wälder alle, die doch ermordet waren,
> Umruhen wieder die Landschaft mit Rauschen und Schweigen
> Ganz unversehrt
> Heut und für immer,
> Denn was da liedeinging, das hat den Tod überwunden.[11]

She sees this as a Christian task – 'christverwandt ist der Dichter' – since Christ Himself taught compassion for the weak and helpless, and without such compassion we forfeit our humanity. And not only that. Once compassion has gone, could it not be that Christ too died in vain? This poem ends with the harrowing words:

> Dann, dann, ja dann ist es aus...
> Es fließt keine Träne mehr, es bebt kein heiliges Erschauern
> Um das entgöttlichte Wort – die Musen verhüllen ihr Haupt –
> Kahl wie der Baum des Gesanges, unendlich einsam
> Ragt das vergebliche Kreuz.

The poet here reveals a vista in which the cruel masculine world of mass technocracy has finally triumphed and the feminine has gone to the wall. It has often been said that the Weimar Republic produced many portents of things to come, many symptoms of a sickness to which we may all yet succumb. As we contemplate our dying forests and hear every day fresh rumours of ecological disaster, we may well begin to feel that in her constant emphasis on the need to search for a spiritual dimension, in her plea for the re-incorporation of the maternal element into a caring Christianity, Gertrud von le Fort, who first began to write during those turbulent years, stands as a signpost back to sanity, a poet of stature, and an apostle of salvation.

NOTES

[1]For a recent discussion of the reception of Gertrud von le Fort's work in Germany and elsewhere, see Margaret Klopfle Devinney, *The Legends of Gertrud von le Fort: Text and Audience*, Studies in Modern German Literature, vol. 27 (New York: Peter Lang, 1989), which also contains a comprehensive bibliography of the most important primary sources and secondary literature to date.

[2]All quotations from *Hymnen an die Kirche* are from Gertrud von le Fort, *Hymnen an die Kirche*, 22nd edition (Munich: Ehrenwirth, 1990), the most easily obtainable edition. Since the numeration of the individual poems is slightly confusing, I have tried to indicate in the text where exactly in the sequence the quotations will be found.

[3]See Clemens Heselhaus, 'Nachwort', in Annette von Droste-Hülshoff, *Sämtliche Werke*, ed. by Clemens Heselhaus (Munich: Carl Hanser Verlag, 1966), pp. 1105-1128 (p. 1114). All quotations from *Das geistliche Jahr* are taken from this edition.

[4]See the letter to her mother of 9 October 1820, quoted as a preface to *Das geistliche Jahr* in *Sämtliche Werke*, pp. 469-71.

[5]*The Oxford Dictionary of the Christian Church*, ed. by F. L. Cross (London: OUP, 1958), p. 135.

[6]John Clayton, 'Paul Tillich — ein "verjüngter Troeltsch" oder noch "ein Apfel vom Baume Kierkegaards"?', *Troeltsch-Studien*, vol. 4 (Gütersloh: Gütersloher Verlagshaus, 1987), pp. 259-83 (p. 269).

[7]Gertrud von le Fort, *Aufzeichnungen und Erinnerungen* (Cologne: Benzinger, 1951), p. 78.

[8]Quotations from the *Lyrisches Tagebuch aus den Jahren 1933 bis 1945* and from *Gesang aus den Bergen* are taken from Gertrud von le Fort, *Gedichte und Aphorismen* (Munich: Ehrenwirth, 1984).

[9]Dust cover preface to Gertrud von le Fort, *Hymns to the Church*, trans. Margaret Chanter (New York: Steed and Ward, 1953).

[10]*Gedichte und Aphorismen*, p. 24

[11]*Ibid.*, pp. 10-12.